The Performance of
Open Source Applications

The Performance of Open Source Applications
Speed, Precision, and a Bit of Serendipity

Edited by Tavish Armstrong

The Performance of Open Source Applications
Edited by Tavish Armstrong

This work is licensed under the Creative Commons Attribution 3.0 Unported license (CC BY 3.0). You are free:

- to Share—to copy, distribute and transmit the work
- to Remix—to adapt the work

under the following conditions:

- Attribution—you must attribute the work in the manner specified by the author or licensor (but not in any way that suggests that they endorse you or your use of the work).

with the understanding that:

- Waiver—Any of the above conditions can be waived if you get permission from the copyright holder.
- Public Domain—Where the work or any of its elements is in the public domain under applicable law, that status is in no way affected by the license.
- Other Rights—In no way are any of the following rights affected by the license:
  - Your fair dealing or fair use rights, or other applicable copyright exceptions and limitations;
  - The author's moral rights;
  - Rights other persons may have either in the work itself or in how the work is used, such as publicity or privacy rights.
- Notice—For any reuse or distribution, you must make clear to others the license terms of this work. The best way to do this is with a link to http://creativecommons.org/licenses/by/3.0/.

To view a copy of this license, visit http://creativecommons.org/licenses/by/3.0/ or send a letter to Creative Commons, 444 Castro Street, Suite 900, Mountain View, California, 94041, USA.

The full text of this book is available online at http://www.aosabook.org/.
All royalties from its sale will be donated to Amnesty International.

Product and company names mentioned herein may be the trademarks of their respective owners.

While every precaution has been taken in the preparation of this book, the editors and authors assume no responsibility for errors or omissions, or for damages resulting from the use of the information contained herein.

Front cover photo ©Michelle Enemark
Cover design by Amy Brown

Revision Date: October 7, 2013

ISBN: 978-1-304-48878-7

Contents

	Introduction by Tavish Armstrong	vii
1	High Performance Networking in Chrome by Ilya Grigorik	1
2	From SocialCalc to EtherCalc by Audrey Tang	21
3	Ninja by Evan Martin	33
4	Parsing XML at the Speed of Light by Arseny Kapoulkine	43
5	MemShrink by Kyle Huey	59
6	Applying Optimization Principle Patterns to Component Deployment and Configuration Tools by Doug C. Schmidt, William R. Otte, and Aniruddha Gokhale	69
7	Infinispan by Manik Surtani	87
8	Talos by Clint Talbert and Joel Maher	97
9	Zotonic by Arjan Scherpenisse and Marc Worrell	103
10	Secrets of Mobile Network Performance by Bryce Howard	119
11	Warp by Kazu Yamamoto, Michael Snoyman, and Andreas Voellmy	133
12	Working with Big Data in Bioinformatics by Eric McDonald and C. Titus Brown	151

Introduction
Tavish Armstrong

It's commonplace to say that computer hardware is now so fast that most developers don't have to worry about performance. In fact, Douglas Crockford declined to write a chapter for this book for that reason:

> If I were to write a chapter, it would be about anti-performance: most effort spent in pursuit of performance is wasted. I don't think that is what you are looking for.

Donald Knuth made the same point thirty years ago:

> We should forget about small efficiencies, say about 97% of the time: premature optimization is the root of all evil.

but between mobile devices with limited power and memory, and data analysis projects that need to process terabytes, a growing number of developers *do* need to make their code faster, their data structures smaller, and their response times shorter. However, while hundreds of textbooks explain the basics of operating systems, networks, computer graphics, and databases, few (if any) explain how to find and fix things in real applications that are simply too damn slow.

This collection of case studies is our attempt to fill that gap. Each chapter is written by real developers who have had to make an existing system faster or who had to design something to be fast in the first place. They cover many different kinds of software and performance goals; what they have in common is a detailed understanding of what actually happens when, and how the different parts of large applications fit together. Our hope is that this book will—like its predecessor *The Architecture of Open Source Applications*—help you become a better developer by letting you look over these experts' shoulders.

— Tavish Armstrong

Contributors

Tavish Armstrong (editorial): Tavish studies software engineering at Concordia University and hopes to graduate in the spring of 2014. His online home is http://tavisharmstrong.com.

Michael Snoyman (Warp): Michael is the lead software engineer at FP Complete. He is the founder and lead developer of the Yesod Web Framework, which provides a means of creating robust, high-performance web applications. His formal studies include actuarial science, and he has previously worked in the US auto and homeowner insurance industry analyzing large data sets.

Kazu Yamamoto (Warp): Kazu is a senior researcher of IIJ Innovation Institute. He has been working for open source software around 20 years. His products include Mew, KAME, Firemacs and mighty.

Andreas Voellmy (Warp): Andreas is a PhD candidate in Computer Science at Yale University. Andreas uses Haskell in his research on software-defined networks and has published open source Haskell packages, such as nettle-openflow, for controlling routers using Haskell programs. Andreas also contributes to the GHC project and is a maintainer of GHC's IO manager.

Ilya Grigorik (Chrome): Ilya is a web performance engineer and developer advocate on the Make The Web Fast team at Google, where he spends his days and nights on making the web fast and driving adoption of performance best practices. You can find Ilya online on his blog at `igvita.com` and under `@igrigorik` on Twitter.

Evan Martin (Ninja): Evan has been a programmer at Google for nine years. His background before that includes degrees in computer science and linguistics. He has hacked on many minor free software projects and a few major ones, including LiveJournal. His website is `http://neugierig.org`.

Bryce Howard (Mobile Performance): Bryce is a software architect who obsesses about making things go fast. He has 15+ years in the industry, and has worked for a number of startups you've never heard of. He is currently taking a stab at this whole "writing" thing and authoring an introductory Amazon Web Services book for O'Reilly Associates.

Kyle Huey (Memshrink): Kyle works at the Mozilla Corporation on the Gecko rendering engine that powers the Firefox web browser. He earned a Bachelor's degree in mathematics from the University of Florida before moving to San Francisco. He blogs at `blog.kylehuey.com`.

Clint Talbert (Talos): Clint has been involved in the Mozilla project for almost a decade, first as a volunteer and then as an employee. He currently leads the Automation and Tools team with a mandate to automate everything that can be automated, and a personal vendetta to eliminate idle cycles on any automation machine. You can follow his adventures in open source and writing at `clinttalbert.com`.

Joel Maher (Talos): Joel has over 15 years of experience automating software. In the last 5 years at Mozilla, Joel has hacked the automation and tools at Mozilla to extend to mobile phones as well as taken ownership of Talos to expand tests, reliability and improve regression detection. While his automation is running, Joel likes to get outdoors and tackle new challenges in life. For more automation adventures, follow along at `elvis314.wordpress.com`.

Audrey Tang (Ethercalc): A self-educated programmer and translator based in Taiwan, Audrey currently works at Socialtext with the job title "Untitled Page", as well as at Apple on localization and release engineering. Audrey has previously designed and led the Pugs project, the first working Perl 6 implementation, and served in language design committees for Haskell, Perl 5, and Perl 6, with numerous contributions to CPAN and Hackage. Follow Audrey on Twitter at `@audreyt`.

C. Titus Brown (Khmer): Titus has worked in evolutionary modeling, physical meteorology, developmental biology, genomics, and bioinformatics. He is now an Assistant Professor at Michigan State University, where he has expanded his interests into several new areas, including reproducibility and maintainability of scientific software. He is also a member of the Python Software Foundation, and blogs at `http://ivory.idyll.org`.

Eric McDonald (Khmer): Eric McDonald is a developer of scientific software with an emphasis on high performance computing (HPC), the area in which he has worked much of the past 13 years. Having previously worked with several varieties of physicists, he now helps bioinformaticians. He holds a bachelor's degree in Computer Science, Mathematics, and Physics. Eric has been a fan of FOSS since the mid-nineties.

Douglas C. Schmidt (DaNCE): Dr. Douglas C. Schmidt is a Professor of Computer Science, Associate Chair of the Computer Science and Engineering program, and a Senior Researcher at the Institute at Software Integrated Systems, all at Vanderbilt University. Doug has published 10 books and more than 500 technical papers covering a wide range of software-related topics, and led the development of ACE, TAO, CIAO, and CoSMIC for the past two decades.

Aniruddha Gokhale (DaNCE): Dr. Aniruddha S. Gokhale is an Associate Professor in the Department of Electrical Engineering and Computer Science, and Senior Research Scientist at the Institute for Software Integrated Systems (ISIS) both at Vanderbilt University. He has over 140 technical articles to his credit, and his current research focuses on developing novel solutions to emerging challenges in cloud computing and cyber physical systems.

William R. Otte (DaNCE): Dr. William R. Otte is a Research Scientist at the Institute for Software Integrated Systems (ISIS) at Vanderbilt University. He has nearly a decade of experience developing open source middleware and modeling tools for distributed, real-time and embedded systems, working with both government and industrial partners including DARPA, NASA, Northrup Grumman and Lockheed-Martin. He has published numerous technical articles and reports describing these advances and has participated in the development of open standards for component middleware.

Manik Surtani (Infinispan): Manik is a core R&D engineer at JBoss, Red Hat's middleware division. He is the founder of the Infinispan project, and Platform Architect of the JBoss Data Grid. He is also the spec lead of JSR 347 (Data Grids for the Java Platform), and represents Red Hat on the Expert Group of JSR 107 (Temporary caching for Java). His interests lie in cloud and distributed computing, big data and NoSQL, autonomous systems and highly available computing.

Arseny Kapoulkine (Pugixml): Arseny has spent his entire career programming graphics and low-level systems in video games, ranging from small niche titles to multi-platform AAA blockbusters such as FIFA Soccer. He enjoys making slow things fast and fast things even faster. He can be reached at mail@zeuxcg.org or on Twitter @zeuxcg.

Arjan Scherpenisse (Zotonic): Arjan is one of the main architects of Zotonic and manages to work on dozens of projects at the same time, mostly using Zotonic and Erlang. Arjan bridges the gap between back-end and front-end Erlang projects. Besides issues like scalability and performance, Arjan is often involved in creative projects. Arjan is a regular speaker at events.

Marc Worrell (Zotonic): Marc is a respected member of the Erlang community and was the initiator of the Zotonic project. Marc spends his time consulting for large Erlang projects, the development of Zotonic and is the CTO of Maximonster, the builders of MaxClass and LearnStone.

Acknowledgments

This book would not exist without the help of Amy Brown and Greg Wilson, who asked me to edit the book and convinced me that it was possible. I'm also grateful to Tony Arkles for his help in the earlier stages of editing, and to our technical reviewers:

Colin Morris
Corey Chivers
Greg Wilson
Julia Evans
Kamal Marhubi

Kim Moir
Laurie MacDougall Sookraj
Logan Smyth
Monica Dinculescu
Nikita Pchelin

Natalie Black
Pierre-Antoine Lafayette

A small army of copyeditors and helpers ensured the book got published this decade:

Adam Fletcher	Jeff Schwab	Alexandra Phillips
Amy Brown	Jessica McKellar	Peter Rood
Danielle Pham	Michael Baker	
Erik Habbinga	Natalie Black	

Amy Brown, Bruno Kinoshita, and Danielle Pham deserve special thanks for their help with the book's build process and graphics.

Editing a book is a difficult task, but it gets easier when you have encouraging friends. Natalie Black, Julia Evans, and Kamal Marhubi were patient and enthusiastic throughout.

Contributing

Dozens of volunteers worked hard to create this book, but there is still a lot to do. If you'd like to help, you can do so by reporting errors, translating the content into other languages, or describing other open source systems. Please contact us at aosa@aosabook.org if you would like to get involved.

[chapter 1]

High Performance Networking in Chrome
Ilya Grigorik

1.1 History and Guiding Principles of Google Chrome

Google Chrome was first released in the second half of 2008, as a beta version for the Windows platform. The Google-authored code powering Chrome was also made available under a permissive BSD license—also known as the Chrome project. To many observers, this turn of events came as a surprise: the return of the browser wars? Could Google really do much better?

> "It was so good that it essentially forced me to change my mind…" - Eric Schmidt, on his initial reluctance[1] to the idea of developing Google Chrome.

Turns out, they could. Today Chrome is one of the most widely used browsers on the web (35%+[2] of the market share according to StatCounter) and is now available on Windows, Linux, OS X, Chrome OS, as well as Android and iOS platforms. Clearly, the features and the functionality resonated with the users, and many innovations of Chrome have also found their way into other popular browsers.

The original 38-page comic book[3] explanation of the ideas and innovations of Google Chrome offers a great overview of the thinking and design process behind the popular browser. However, this was only the beginning. The core principles that motivated the original development of the browser continue to be the guiding principles for ongoing improvements in Chrome:

Speed: Make the **fastest** browser
Security: Provide the **most secure** environment to the user
Stability: Provide a **resilient and stable** web application platform
Simplicity: Create sophisticated technology, wrapped in a **simple user experience**

As the team observed, many of the sites we use today are not just web pages, they are applications. In turn, the ever more ambitious applications require speed, security, and stability. Each of these deserves its own dedicated chapter, but since our subject is performance, our focus will be primarily on speed.

---

[1] http://blogs.wsj.com/digits/2009/07/09/sun-valley-schmidt-didnt-want-to-build-chrome-initially-he-says/
[2] http://gs.statcounter.com/?PHPSESSID=oc1i9oue7por39rmhqq2eouoh0
[3] http://www.google.com/googlebooks/chrome/

1.2 The Many Facets of Performance

A modern browser is a platform, just like your operating system, and Google Chrome is designed as such. Prior to Google Chrome, all major browsers were built as monolithic, single process applications. All open pages shared the same address space and contended for the same resources. A bug in any page, or the browser, ran the risk of compromising the entire experience.

By contrast, Chrome works on a multi-process model, which provides process and memory isolation, and a tight security sandbox[4] for each tab. In an increasingly multi-core world, the ability to isolate the processes as well as shield each open tab from other misbehaving pages alone proves that Chrome has a significant performance edge over the competition. In fact, it is important to note that most other browsers have followed suit, or are in the process of migrating to similar architecture.

With an allocated process in place, the execution of a web program primarily involves three tasks: fetching resources, page layout and rendering, and JavaScript execution. The rendering and script steps follow a single-threaded, interleaved model of execution—it is not possible to perform concurrent modifications of the resulting Document Object Model (DOM). This is in part due to the fact that JavaScript itself is a single-threaded language. Hence, optimizing how the rendering and script execution runtimes work together is of critical importance, both to the web developers building the applications as well as the developers working on the browser.

For rendering, Chrome uses Blink, which is a fast, open-source, and standards compliant layout engine. For JavaScript, Chrome ships with its own, heavily optimized V8 JavaScript runtime, which was also released as a standalone open-source project and has found its way into many other popular projects—e.g., runtime for Node.js. However, optimizing V8 JavaScript execution, or the Blink parsing and rendering pipelines will not do much good if the browser is blocked on the network, waiting for the resources to arrive.

The ability of the browser to optimize the order, priority, and latency of each network resource is one of the most critical contributors to the overall user experience. You may not be aware of it, but Chrome's network stack is, quite literally, getting smarter every day, trying to hide or decrease the latency cost of each resource: it learns likely DNS lookups, it remembers the topology of the web, it pre-connects to likely destination targets, and more. From the outside, it presents itself as a simple resource fetching mechanism, but from the inside it is an elaborate and a fascinating case study for how to optimize web performance and deliver the best experience to the user.

Let's dive in.

1.3 What is a Modern Web Application?

Before we get to the tactical details of how to optimize our interaction with the network, it helps to understand the trends and the landscape of the problem we are up against. In other words, *what does a modern web page, or application look like?*

The HTTP Archive[5] project tracks how the web is built, and it can help us answer this question. Instead of crawling the web for the content, it periodically crawls the most popular sites to record and aggregate analytics on the number of used resources, content types, headers, and other metadata for each individual destination. The stats, as of January 2013, may surprise you. An average page, amongst the top 300,000 destinations on the web is:

---

[4]http://dev.chromium.org/developers/design-documents/sandbox
[5]http://httparchive.org/

- **1280 KB** in size
- composed of **88 resources**
- connects to **15+ distinct hosts**

Let that sink in. Over 1 MB in size on average, composed of 88 resources such as images, JavaScript, and CSS, and delivered from 15 different own and third-party hosts. Further, each of these numbers has been steadily increasing[6] over the past few years, and there are no signs of stopping. We are increasingly building larger and more ambitious web applications.

Applying basic math to the HTTP Archive numbers reveals that an average resource is about 15 KB in size (1280 KB / 88 resources), which means that most network transfers in the browser are short and bursty. This presents its own set of complications because the underlying transport (TCP) is optimized for large, streaming downloads. Let's peel back the onion and inspect one of these network requests.

1.4 The Life of a Resource Request on the Wire

The W3C Navigation Timing specification[7] provides a browser API and visibility into the timing and performance data behind the life of every request in the browser. Let's inspect the components, as each is a critical piece of delivering the optimal user experience:

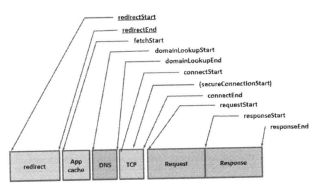

Figure 1.1: Navigation Timing

Given the URL of a resource on the web, the browser starts by checking its local and application caches. If you have previously fetched the resource and the appropriate cache headers[8] were provided (Expires, Cache-Control, etc.), then it is possible that we are allowed to use the local copy to fulfill the request—the fastest request is a request not made. Alternatively, if we have to revalidate the resource, if it expired, or if we simply have not seen it before, then a costly network request must be dispatched.

Given a hostname and resource path, Chrome first checks for existing open connections it is allowed to reuse—sockets are pooled by {scheme, host, port}. Alternatively, if you have configured a proxy, or specified a proxy auto-config[9] (PAC) script, then Chrome checks for connections through the appropriate proxy. PAC scripts allow for different proxies based on URL, or other

---

[6]http://httparchive.org/trends.php
[7]http://www.w3.org/TR/navigation-timing/
[8]https://developers.google.com/speed/docs/best-practices/caching
[9]http://en.wikipedia.org/wiki/Proxy_auto-config

specified rules, each of which can have its own socket pool. Finally, if neither of the above conditions is matched, then the request must begin by resolving the hostname to its IP address—also known as a DNS lookup.

If we are lucky, the hostname will already be cached in which case the response is usually just one quick system call away. If not, then a DNS query must be dispatched before any other work can happen. The time taken to do the DNS lookup will vary based on your internet provider, the popularity of the site and the likelihood of the hostname to be in intermediate caches, as well as the response time of the authoritative servers for that domain. In other words, there are a lot of variables at play, but it is not unusual for a DNS lookup to take up to several hundred milliseconds. Ouch.

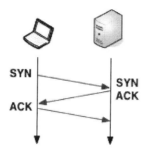

Figure 1.2: Three-way handshake

With the resolved IP address in hand, Chrome can now open a new TCP connection to the destination, which means that we must perform the "three-way handshake": SYN > SYN-ACK > ACK. This exchange adds a full round-trip of latency delay to each and every new TCP connection—no shortcuts. Depending on the distance between the client and the server, as well as the chosen routing path, this can yield from tens to hundreds, or even thousands, of milliseconds of delay. All of this work and latency is before even a single byte of application data has hit the wire.

Once the TCP handshake is complete, and if we are connecting to a secure destination (HTTPS), then the SSL handshake must take place. This can add up to two additional round-trips of latency delay between client and server. If the SSL session is cached, then we can "escape" with just one additional round-trip.

Finally, Chrome is able to dispatch the HTTP request (requestStart in Figure 1.1). Once received, the server can process the request and then stream the response data back to the client. This incurs a minimum of one network round-trip, plus the processing time on the server. Following that, we are done—unless the actual response is an HTTP redirect, in which case we may have to repeat the entire cycle once over. Have a few gratuitous redirects on your pages? You may want to revisit that decision.

Have you been counting all the delays? To illustrate the problem, let's assume the worst case scenario for a typical broadband connection: local cache miss, followed by a relatively fast DNS lookup (50 ms), TCP handshake, SSL negotiation, and a relatively fast (100 ms) server response time, with a round-trip time (RTT) of 80 ms (an average round-trip across continental USA):

- 50 ms for DNS
- 80 ms for TCP handshake (one RTT)
- 160 ms for SSL handshake (two RTTs)
- 40 ms for request to server
- 100 ms for server processing
- 40 ms for response from the server

That's 470 milliseconds for a single request, which translates to over 80% of network latency overhead as compared to the actual server processing time to fulfill the request—we have some work to do here. In fact, even 470 milliseconds may be an optimistic estimate:

- If the server response does not fit into the initial TCP congestion window (4-15 KB), then one or more additional round-trips of latency is introduced [10].
- SSL delays could get even worse if we need to fetch a missing certificate or perform an online certificate status check (OCSP), both of which will require an entirely new TCP connection, which can add hundreds and even thousands of milliseconds of additional latency.

1.5 What is "Fast Enough"?

The network overhead of DNS, handshakes, and the round-trip times is what dominates the total time in our earlier case—the server response time accounts for only 20% of the total latency. But, in the grand scheme of things, do these delays even matter? If you are reading this, then you probably already know the answer: yes, very much so.

Past user experience research[11] paints a consistent picture of what we, as users, expect in terms of responsiveness of any application, both offline and online:

Delay	User Reaction
0–100 ms	Instant
100–300 ms	Small perceptible delay
300–1000 ms	Machine is working
1 s+	Mental context switch
10 s+	I'll come back later...

Table 1.1: User Perception of Latency

Table 1.1 also explains the unofficial rule of thumb in the web performance community: render your pages, or at the very least, provide visual feedback in under 250 ms to keep the user engaged. This is not speed simply for speed's sake. Studies at Google, Amazon, Microsoft, as well as thousands of other sites show that additional latency has a direct impact on the bottom line of your site: faster sites yield more pageviews, higher engagement from the users, and see higher conversion rates.

So, there you have it, our optimal latency budget is 250 ms, and yet as we saw in the example above, the combination of a DNS lookup, the TCP and SSL handshakes, and propagation times for the request add up to 370 ms. We are 50% over budget, and we still have not factored in the server processing time!

To most users and even web developers, the DNS, TCP, and SSL delays are entirely transparent and are negotiated at network layers to which few of us descend or think about. However, each of these steps is critical to the overall user experience, since each extra network request can add tens or hundreds of milliseconds of latency. This is the reason why Chrome's network stack is much, much more than a simple socket handler.

Now that we have identified the problem, let's dive into the implementation details.

---

[10] Chapter 10 covers this issue in greater detail.
[11] http://www.useit.com/papers/responsetime.html

1.6 Chrome's Network Stack from 10,000 Feet

Multi-Process Architecture

Chrome's multi-process architecture carries important implications for how each network request is handled within the browser. Under the hood, Chrome actually supports four different execution models[12] that determine how the process allocation is performed.

By default, desktop Chrome browsers use the process-per-site model, that isolates different sites from each other, but groups all instances of the same site into the same process. However, to keep things simple, let's assume one of the simplest cases: one distinct process for each open tab. From the network performance perspective, the differences here are not substantial, but the process-per-tab model is much easier to understand.

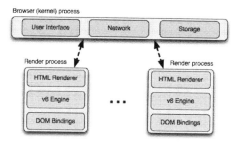

Figure 1.3: Multi-process architecture

The architecture dedicates one *render process* to each tab. Each render process contains instances of the Blink layout engine and the V8 JavaScript engine, along with glue code that bridges these (and a few other) components[13].

Each of these render processes is executed within a sandboxed environment that has limited access to the user's computer—including the network. To gain access to these resources, each render process communicates with the main browser (or *kernel*) process, which is able to impose security and access policies on each renderer.

Inter-Process Communication and Multi-Process Resource Loading

All communication between the renderer and the kernel process in Chrome is done via inter-process communication (IPC). On Linux and OS X, a `socketpair()` is used, which provides a named pipe transport for asynchronous communication. Each message from the renderer is serialized and passed to a dedicated I/O thread, which dispatches it to the main browser process. On the receiving end, the kernel process provides a filter interface, which allows Chrome to intercept resource IPC requests (see

The singleton interface allows the browser to control each renderer's access to the network, but it also enables efficient and consistent resource sharing. Some examples include:

- **Socket pool and connection limits:** the browser is able to enforce limits on the number of open sockets per profile (256), proxy (32), and {scheme, host, port} (6) groups. Note that this allows up to six HTTP and six HTTPS connections to the same {host, port}.

---

[12] http://www.chromium.org/developers/design-documents/process-models

[13] If you are curious, the Chromium wiki contains a great introduction to the plumbing here: http://www.chromium.org/developers/design-documents/multi-process-architecture.

- **Socket reuse:** persistent TCP connections are retained in the socket pool for some time after servicing the request to enable connection reuse, which avoids the extra DNS, TCP, and SSL (if required) setup overhead imposed on each new connection.
- **Socket late-binding:** requests are associated with an underlying TCP connection only once the socket is ready to dispatch the application request, allowing better request prioritization (e.g., arrival of a higher priority request while the socket was connecting), better throughput (e.g., re-use of a "warm" TCP connection in cases where an existing socket becomes available while a new connection is being opened), as well as a general-purpose mechanism for TCP pre-connect, and a number of other optimizations.
- **Consistent session state:** authentication, cookies, and cached data is shared between all render processes.
- **Global resource and network optimizations:** the browser is able to make decisions across all render processes and outstanding requests. For example, giving network priority to the requests initiated by the foreground tab.
- **Predictive optimizations:** by observing all network traffic, Chrome is able to build and refine predictive models to improve performance.

As far as the render process is concerned, it is simply sending a resource request message over IPC, which is tagged with a unique request ID to the browser process, and the browser kernel process handles the rest.

Cross-Platform Resource Fetching

One of the chief concerns in the implementation of Chrome's network stack is portability across many different platforms: Linux, Windows, OS X, Chrome OS, Android, and iOS. To address this challenge, the network stack is implemented as a mostly single-threaded (there are separate cache and proxy threads) cross-platform library, which allows Chrome to reuse the same infrastructure and provide the same performance optimizations, as well as a greater opportunity for optimization across all platforms.

Component	Contents
net/android	Bindings to the Android runtime
net/base	Common net utilities, such as host resolution, cookies, network change detection, and SSL certificate management
net/cookies	Implementation of storage, management, and retrieval of HTTP cookies
net/disk_cache	Disk and memory cache implementation for web resources
net/dns	Implementation of an asynchronous DNS resolver
net/http	HTTP protocol implementation
net/proxy	Proxy (SOCKS and HTTP) configuration, resolution, script fetching, etc.
net/socket	Cross-platform implementations of TCP sockets, SSL streams, and socket pools
net/spdy	SPDY protocol implementation
net/url_request	URLRequest, URLRequestContext, and URLRequestJob implementations
net/websockets	WebSockets protocol implementation

Table 1.2: Components of Chrome

All of the network code is, of course, open source and can be found in the src/net subdirectory. We will not examine each component in detail, but the layout of the code itself tells you a lot about its capabilities and structure. A few examples are listed in Table 1.2.

The code for each of the components makes for a great read for the curious—it is well documented, and you will find plenty of unit tests for every component.

Architecture and Performance on Mobile Platforms

Mobile browser usage is growing at an exponential rate and even by modest projections, it will eclipse desktop browsing in the not so distant future. Needless to say, delivering an optimized mobile experience has been a top priority for the Chrome team. In early 2012, Chrome for Android[14] was announced, and a few months later, Chrome for iOS[15] followed.

The first thing to note about the mobile version of Chrome, is that it is not simply a direct adaptation of the desktop browser—that would not deliver the best user experience. By its very nature, the mobile environment is both much more resource constrained, and has many fundamentally different operating parameters:

- Desktop users navigate with the mouse, may have overlapping windows, have a large screen, are mostly not power constrained, usually have a much more stable network connection, and have access to much larger pools of storage and memory.
- Mobile users use touch and gesture navigation, have a much smaller screen, are battery and power constrained, are often on metered connections, and have limited local storage and memory.

Further, there is no such thing as a "typical mobile device". Instead there is a wide range of devices with varying hardware capabilities, and to deliver the best performance, Chrome must adapt to the operating constraints of each and every device. Thankfully, the various execution models allow Chrome to do exactly that.

On Android devices, Chrome leverages the same multi-process architecture as the desktop version—there is a browser process, and one or more renderer processes. The one difference is that due to memory constraints of the mobile device, Chrome may not be able to run a dedicated renderer for each open tab. Instead, Chrome determines the optimal number of renderer processes based on available memory, and other constraints of the device, and shares the renderer process between the multiple tabs.

In cases where only minimal resources are available, or if Chrome is unable to run multiple processes, it can also switch to use a single-process, multi-threaded processing model. In fact, on iOS devices, due to sandboxing restrictions of the underlying platform, it does exactly that—it runs a single, but multi-threaded process.

What about network performance? First off, Chrome uses the same network stack on Android and iOS as it does on all other versions. This enables all of the same network optimizations across all platforms, which gives Chrome a significant performance advantage. However, what is different, and is often adjusted based on the capabilities of the device and the network in use, are variables such as priority of speculative optimization techniques, socket timeouts and management logic, cache sizes, and more.

For example, to preserve battery, mobile Chrome may opt in to use lazy closing of idle sockets—sockets are closed only when opening new ones to minimize radio use. Similarly, since prerendering

---

[14] http://www.google.com/intl/en/chrome/browser/mobile/android.html
[15] http://www.google.com/intl/en/chrome/browser/mobile/ios.html

(which we will discuss below), may require significant network and processing resources, it is often only enabled when the user is on Wi-Fi.

Optimizing the mobile browsing experience is one of the highest priority items for the Chrome development team, and we can expect to see a lot of new improvements in the months and years to come. In fact, it is a topic that deserves its own separate chapter—perhaps in the next installment of the POSA series.

Speculative Optimization with Chrome's Predictor

Chrome gets faster as you use it. This feat is accomplished with the help of a singleton `Predictor` object, which is instantiated within the browser kernel process, and whose sole responsibility is to observe network patterns and to learn and anticipate likely user actions in the future. A few example signals processed by the `Predictor` include:

- Users hovering their mouse over a link is a good indicator of a likely, upcoming navigation event, which Chrome can help accelerate by dispatching a speculative DNS lookup of the target hostname, as well as potentially starting the TCP handshake. By the time the user clicks, which takes ~200 ms on average, there is a good chance that we have already completed the DNS and TCP steps, allowing us to eliminate hundreds of milliseconds of extra latency for the navigation event.
- Typing in the Omnibox (URL) bar triggers high-likelihood suggestions, which may similarly kick off a DNS lookup, TCP pre-connect, and even prerender the page in a hidden tab.
- Each one of us has a list of favorite sites that we visit every day. Chrome can learn the subresources on these sites and speculatively pre-resolve and perhaps even prefetch them to accelerate the browsing experience.

Chrome learns the topology of the web, as well as your own browsing patterns, as you use it. If it does the job well, it can eliminate hundreds of milliseconds of latency from each navigation and get the user closer to the Holy Grail of the "instant page load". To achieve this goal, Chrome leverages four core optimization techniques listed in Table 1.3.

Name	Action
DNS pre-resolve	Resolve hostnames ahead of time, to avoid DNS latency
TCP pre-connect	Connect to destination server ahead of time, to avoid TCP handshake latency
Resource prefetching	Fetch critical resources on the page ahead of time, to accelerate rendering of the page
Page prerendering	Fetch the entire page with all of its resources ahead of time, to enable instant navigation when triggered by the user

Table 1.3: Network optimization techniques used by Chrome

Each decision to invoke one or several of these techniques is optimized against a large number of constraints. After all, each is a speculative optimization, which means that if done poorly, it might trigger unnecessary work and network traffic, or even worse, have a negative effect on the loading time for an actual navigation triggered by the user.

How does Chrome address this problem? The predictor consumes as many signals as it can, which include user generated actions, historical browsing data, as well as signals from the renderer and the network stack itself.

Not unlike the `ResourceDispatcherHost`, which is responsible for coordinating all of the network activity within Chrome, the `Predictor` object creates a number of filters on user and network generated activity within Chrome:

- IPC channel filter to monitor for signals from the render processes
- `ConnectInterceptor` object is added to each request, such that it can observe the traffic patterns and record success metrics for each request

As a hands-on example, the render process can trigger a message to the browser process with any of the following hints, which are conveniently defined in `ResolutionMotivation` (url_info.h [16]):

```
enum ResolutionMotivation {
  MOUSE_OVER_MOTIVATED,      // Mouse-over initiated by the user.
  OMNIBOX_MOTIVATED,         // Omnibox suggested resolving this.
  STARTUP_LIST_MOTIVATED,    // This resource is on the top 10 startup list.
  EARLY_LOAD_MOTIVATED,      // In some cases we use the prefetcher to warm up
                             // the connection in advance of issuing the real
                             // request.

  // The following involve predictive prefetching, triggered by a navigation.
  // The referring_url_ is also set when these are used.
  STATIC_REFERAL_MOTIVATED,  // External database suggested this resolution.
  LEARNED_REFERAL_MOTIVATED, // Prior navigation taught us this resolution.
  SELF_REFERAL_MOTIVATED,    // Guess about need for a second connection.

  // <snip> ...
};
```

Given such a signal, the goal of the predictor is to evaluate the likelihood of its success, and then to trigger the activity if resources are available. Every hint may have a likelihood of success, a priority, and an expiration timestamp, the combination of which can be used to maintain an internal priority queue of speculative optimizations. Finally, for every dispatched request from within this queue, the predictor is also able to track its success rate, which allows it to further optimize its future decisions.

Chrome Network Architecture in a Nutshell

- Chrome uses a multi-process architecture, which isolates render processes from the browser process.
- Chrome maintains a single instance of the resource dispatcher, which is shared across all render processes, and runs within the browser kernel process.
- The network stack is a cross-platform, mostly single-threaded library.
- The network stack uses non-blocking operations to manage all network operations.
- Shared network stack allows efficient resource prioritization, reuse, and provides the browser with ability to perform global optimization across all running processes.
- Each render process communicates with the resource dispatcher via IPC.
- Resource dispatcher intercepts resource requests via a custom IPC filter.
- Predictor intercepts resources request and response traffic to learn and optimize future network requests.

---

[16] http://code.google.com/searchframe#OAMlx_jo-ck/src/chrome/browser/net/url_info.h&l=35

- Predictor may speculatively schedule DNS, TCP, and even resource requests based on learned traffic patterns, saving hundreds of milliseconds when the navigation is triggered by the user.

1.7 The Lifetime of Your Browser Session

With the 10,000 foot architecture view of the Chrome network stack in mind, let's now take a closer look at the kinds of user-facing optimizations enabled within the browser. Specifically, let's imagine we have just created a new Chrome profile and are ready to start our day.

Optimizing the Cold-Boot Experience

The first time you load your browser, it knows little about your favorite sites or navigation patterns. However, many of us follow the same routine after a cold boot of the browser, where we may navigate to our email inbox, favorite news site, a social site, an internal portal, and so on. The specific sites will vary, but the similarity of these sessions allows the Chrome Predictor to accelerate your cold-boot experience.

Chrome remembers the top ten most likely hostnames accessed by the user following the browser start—note that this is not the top ten global destinations, but specifically the destinations following a fresh browser start. As the browser loads, Chrome can trigger a DNS prefetch for the likely destinations. If you are curious, you can inspect your own startup hostname list by opening a new tab and navigating to chrome://dns. At the top of the page, you will find the list of the top ten most likely startup candidates for your profile.

Future startups will prefetch DNS records for 10 hostnames

Host name	How long ago (HH:MM:SS)	Motivation
http://www.google-analytics.com/	15:31:33	n/a
https://a248.e.akamai.net/	15:31:30	n/a
https://csi.gstatic.com/	15:31:16	n/a
https://docs.google.com/	15:31:18	n/a
https://gist.github.com/	15:31:34	n/a
https://lh6.googleusercontent.com/	15:31:16	n/a
https://secure.gravatar.com/	15:31:29	n/a
https://ssl.google-analytics.com/	15:31:29	n/a
https://ssl.gstatic.com/	15:31:16	n/a
https://www.google.com/	15:31:16	n/a

Figure 1.4: Startup DNS

The screenshot in Figure 1.4 is an example from my own Chrome profile. How do I usually begin my browsing? Frequently by navigating to Google Docs if I'm working on an article such as this one. Not surprisingly, we see a lot of Google hostnames in the list.

Optimizing Interactions with the Omnibox

One of the innovations of Chrome was the introduction of the Omnibox, which unlike its predecessors handles much more than just destination URLs. Besides remembering the URLs of pages that the user visited in the past, it also offers full text search over your history, as well as a tight integration with the search engine of your choice.

As the user types, the Omnibox automatically proposes an action, which is either a URL based on your navigation history, or a search query. Under the hood, each proposed action is scored with respect to the query, as well as its past performance. In fact, Chrome allows us to inspect this data by visiting `chrome://predictors`.

User Text	URL	Hit Count	Miss Count	Confidence
g	http://gmail.com/	594	186	0.7615384615384615
gi	http://githubarchive.org/	25	55	0.3125
gi	https://gist.github.com/	16	49	0.24615384615384617
gist	https://gist.github.com/	19	1	0.95
gist	https://gist.github.com/	19	1	0.95
githuba	http://githubarchive.org/	3	0	1
gm	http://gmail.com/	411	1	0.9975728155339806

Figure 1.5: Omnibox URL prediction

Chrome maintains a history of the user-entered prefixes, the actions it has proposed, as well as the hit rate for each one. For my own profile, you can see that whenever I enter "g" in the Omnibox, there is a 76% chance that I'm heading to Gmail. Once I add an "m" (for "gm"), then the confidence rises to 99.8%—in fact, out of the 412 recorded visits, I did not end up going to Gmail after entering "gm" only once.

What does this have to do with the network stack? The yellow and green colors for the likely candidates are also important signals for the `ResourceDispatcher`. If we have a likely candidate (yellow), Chrome may trigger a DNS prefetch for the target host. If we have a high confidence candidate (green), then Chrome may also trigger a TCP pre-connect once the hostname has been resolved. Finally, if both complete while the user is still deliberating, then Chrome may even prerender the entire page in a hidden tab.

Alternatively, if there is no good match for the entered prefix based on past navigation history then Chrome may issue a DNS prefetch and TCP pre-connect to your search provider in anticipation of a likely search request.

An average user takes hundreds of milliseconds to fill in their query and to evaluate the proposed autocomplete suggestions. In the background, Chrome is able to prefetch, pre-connect, and in certain cases even prerender the page, so that by the time the user is ready to hit the "enter" key, much of the network latency has already been eliminated.

Optimizing Cache Performance

The best, and the fastest request, is a request not made. Whenever we talk about performance, we would be amiss if we did not talk about the cache—you are providing `Expires`, `ETag`, `Last-Modified`, and `Cache-Control` response headers[17] for all the resources on your web pages, right? If not, go fix it. We'll wait.

Chrome has two different implementations of the internal cache: one backed by local disk, and second which stores everything in memory. The in-memory implementation is used for the Incognito browsing mode and is wiped clean whenever you close the window. Both implement the same

---

[17] https://developers.google.com/speed/docs/best-practices/caching

internal interface (`disk_cache::Backend`, and `disk_cache::Entry`), which greatly simplifies the architecture and—if you are so inclined—allows you to easily experiment with your own experimental cache implementations.

Internally the disk cache implements its own set of data structures, all of which are stored within a single cache folder for your profile. Inside this folder there are index files, which are memory-mapped when the browser starts, and data files, which store the actual data alongside the HTTP headers and other bookkeeping information.[18] Finally, for eviction, the disk cache maintains a Least Recently Used (LRU) cache that takes into account ranking metrics such as frequency of access and resource age.

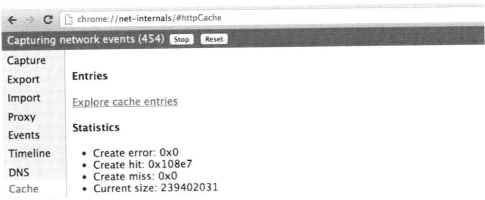

Figure 1.6: Exploring the state of the Chrome cache

If you are ever curious about the state of the Chrome cache you can open a new tab and navigate to `chrome://net-internals/#httpCache`. Alternatively, if you want to see the actual HTTP metadata and the cached response, you can also visit `chrome://cache`, which will enumerate all of the resources currently available in the cache. From that page, search for a resource you are looking for and click on the URL to see the exact, cached headers and response bytes.

Optimizing DNS with Prefetching

We have already mentioned DNS pre-resolution on several occasions, so before we dive into the implementation, let's review the cases in which it may be triggered, and why:

- The Blink document parser, which runs in the render process, may provide a list of hostnames for all the links on the current page, which Chrome may choose to resolve ahead of time.
- The render process may trigger a mouse hover or "button down" event as an early signal of a user's intent to perform a navigation.
- The Omnibox may trigger a resolve request based on a high likelihood suggestion.
- The Predictor may request hostname resolution based on past navigation and resource request data.
- The owner of the page may explicitly indicate to Chrome which hostnames it should pre-resolve.

In all cases, DNS pre-resolution is treated as a hint. Chrome does not guarantee that the pre-resolution will occur, rather it uses each signal in combination with its own predictor to assess the hint and decide on a course of action. In the "worst case", if Chrome was not able to pre-resolve

---

[18]Resources up to 16 KB in size are stored in shared data block-files, and larger files get their own dedicated files on disk.

the hostname in time, the user would have to wait for an explicit DNS resolution followed by TCP connection time, and finally the actual resource fetch. However, when this occurs, the predictor can take note and adjust its future decisions accordingly—it gets faster, and smarter, as you use it.

One of the optimizations we have not covered previously is the ability of Chrome to learn the topology of each site and then use this information to accelerate future visits. Specifically, recall that an average page consists of 88 resources, which are delivered from 15+ distinct hosts. Each time you perform a navigation, Chrome may record the hostnames for the popular resources on the page, and during a future visit, it may choose to trigger a DNS pre-resolve and even a TCP pre-connect for some or all of them.

Host for Page	Page Load Count	Subresource Navigations	Subresource PreConnects	Subresource PreResolves	Expected Connects	Subresource Spec
https://plus.google.com/	688	6	4	17	0.013	https://apis.google.com/
		2	3	8	0.065	https://csi.gstatic.com/
		152	27	33	0.194	https://lh3.googleusercontent.com/
		2	3	1	0.509	https://lh6.googleusercontent.com/
		896	296	386	1.853	https://plus.google.com/
		79	22	18	0.194	https://ssl.gstatic.com/

Figure 1.7: Subresource stats

To inspect the subresource hostnames stored by Chrome, navigate to `chrome://dns` and search for any popular destination hostname for your profile. In the example above, you can see the six subresource hostnames that Chrome remembered for Google+, as well as stats for the number of cases when a DNS pre-resolution was triggered, or a TCP pre-connect was performed, as well as an expected number of requests that will be served by each. This internal accounting is what enables the Chrome predictor to perform its optimizations.

In addition to all of the internal signals, the owner of the site is also able to embed additional markup on their pages to request the browser to pre-resolve a hostname:

```
<link rel="dns-prefetch" href="//host_name_to_prefetch.com">
```

Why not simply rely on the automated machinery in the browser? In some cases, you may want to pre-resolve a hostname which is not mentioned anywhere on the page. A redirect is the canonical example: a link may point to a host—like an analytics tracking service—which then redirects the user to the actual destination. By itself, Chrome cannot infer this pattern, but you can help it by providing a manual hint and get the browser to resolve the hostname of the actual destination ahead of time.

How is this all implemented under the hood? The answer to this question, just like all other optimizations we have covered, depends on the version of Chrome, since the team is always experimenting with new and better ways to improve performance. However, broadly speaking, the DNS infrastructure within Chrome has two major implementations. Historically, Chrome has relied on the platform-independent `getaddrinfo()` system call, and delegated the actual responsibility for the lookups to the operating system. However, this approach is in the process of being replaced with Chrome's own implementation of an asynchronous DNS resolver.

The original implementation, which relied on the operating system, has its benefits: less and simpler code, and the ability to leverage the operating system's DNS cache. However, `getaddrinfo()` is also a blocking system call, which meant that Chrome had to create and maintain a dedicated worker thread-pool to allow it to perform multiple lookups in parallel. This unjoined pool was capped at six worker threads, which is an empirical number based on lowest common denominator of hardware—turns out, higher numbers of parallel requests can overload some users' routers.

For pre-resolution with the worker-pool, Chrome simply dispatches the `getaddrinfo()` call, which blocks the worker thread until the response is ready, at which point it just discards the returned result and begins processing the next prefetch request. The result is cached by the OS DNS cache, which returns an immediate response to future, actual `getaddrinfo()` lookups. It's simple, effective, and works well enough in practice.

Well, effective, but not good enough. The `getaddrinfo()` call hides a lot of useful information from Chrome, such as the time-to-live (TTL) timestamps for each record, as well as the state of the DNS cache itself. To improve performance, the Chrome team decided to implement their own, cross-platform, asynchronous DNS resolver.

Figure 1.8: Enabling the asynchronous DNS resolver

By moving DNS resolution into Chrome, the new async resolver enables a number of new optimizations:

- better control of retransmission timers, and ability to execute multiple queries in parallel
- visibility into record TTLs, which allows Chrome to refresh popular records ahead of time
- better behavior for dual stack implementations (IPv4 and IPv6)
- failovers to different servers, based on RTT or other signals

All of the above, and more, are ideas for continuous experimentation and improvement within Chrome. Which brings us to the obvious question: how do we know and measure the impact of these ideas? Simple, Chrome tracks detailed network performance stats and histograms for each individual profile. To inspect the collected DNS metrics, open a new tab, and head to `chrome://histograms/DNS` (see Figure 1.9).

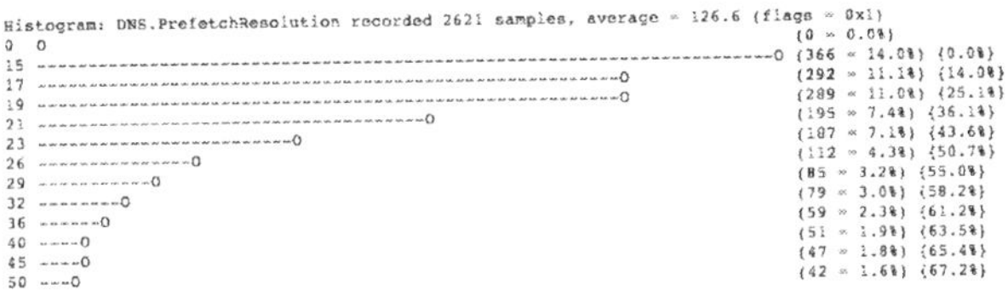

Figure 1.9: DNS prefetch histograms

The above histogram shows the distribution of latencies for DNS prefetch requests: roughly 50% (rightmost column) of the prefetch queries were finished within 20 ms (leftmost column). Note that this is data based on a recent browsing session (9869 samples), and is private to the user. If the user has opted in to report their usage stats in Chrome, then the summary of this data is anonymized and periodically beaconed back to the engineering team, which is then able to see the impact of their experiments and adjust accordingly.

Optimizing TCP Connection Management with Pre-connect

We have pre-resolved the hostname and we have a high likelihood navigation event that is about to happen, as estimated by the Omnibox, or the Chrome predictor. Why not go one step further, and also speculatively pre-connect to the destination host and complete the TCP handshake before the user dispatches the request? By doing so, we can eliminate another full round-trip of latency delay, which can easily save hundreds of milliseconds for the user. Well, that is exactly what TCP pre-connect is and how it works.

To see the hosts for which a TCP pre-connect has been triggered, open a new tab and visit `chrome://dns`.

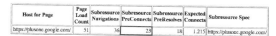

Figure 1.10: Showing hosts for which TCP pre-connects have been triggered

First, Chrome checks its socket pools to see if there is an available socket for the hostname, which it may be able to reuse—keep-alive sockets are kept in the pool for some period of time, to avoid the TCP handshake and slow-start penalties. If no socket is available, then it can initiate the TCP handshake, and place it in the pool. Then, when the user initiates the navigation, the HTTP request can be dispatched immediately.

For the curious, Chrome provides a utility at `chrome://net-internals#sockets` for exploring the state of all the open sockets in Chrome. A screenshot is shown in Figure 1.11.

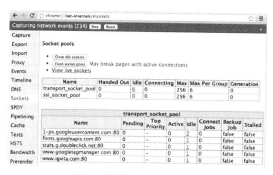

Figure 1.11: Open sockets

Note that you can also drill into each socket and inspect the timeline: connect and proxy times, arrival times for each packet, and more. Last but not least, you can also export this data for further analysis or a bug report. Having good instrumentation is key to any performance optimization, and `chrome://net-internals` is the nexus of all things networking in Chrome—if you have not explored it yet, you should!

Optimizing Resource Loading with Prefetch Hints

Sometimes the author of a page is able to provide additional navigation, or page context, based on the structure or the layout of their site, and help the browser optimize the experience for the user. Chrome supports two such hints, which can be embedded in the markup of the page:

```
<link rel="subresource" href="/javascript/myapp.js">
<link rel="prefetch"    href="/images/big.jpeg">
```

Subresource and prefetch look very similar, but have very different semantics. When a link resource specifies its relationship as "prefetch", it is an indication to the browser that this resource might be needed in a future navigation. In other words, it is effectively a cross-page hint. By contrast, when a resource specifies the relationship as a "subresource", it is an early indication to the browser that the resource will be used on a current page, and that it may want to dispatch the request before it encounters it later in the document.

As you would expect, the different semantics of the hints lead to very different behavior by the resource loader. Resources marked with prefetch are considered low priority and might be downloaded by the browser only once the current page has finished loading. Subresource resources are fetched with high priority as soon as they are encountered and will compete with the rest of the resources on the current page.

Both hints, when used well and in the right context, can help significantly with optimizing the user experience on your site. Finally, it is also important to note that prefetch is part of the HTML5 spec [19], and as of today supported by Firefox and Chrome, whereas subresource is currently only available in Chrome[20].

Optimizing Resource Loading with Browser Prefreshing

Unfortunately, not all site owners are able or willing to provide the browser with subresource hints in their markup. Further, even if they do, we must wait for the HTML document to arrive from the server before we are able to parse the hints and begin fetching the necessary subresources—depending on the server response time, as well as the latency between the client and the server, this could take hundreds and even thousands of milliseconds.

However, as we saw earlier, Chrome is already learning the hostnames of the popular resources to perform DNS prefetching. So, why couldn't it do the same, but go one step further and perform the DNS lookup, use TCP pre-connect, and then also speculatively prefetch the resource? Well, that is exactly what *prefreshing* could do:

- User initiates a request to a target URL
- Chrome queries its predictor for learned subresources associated with the target URL and initiates the sequence of DNS prefetch, TCP pre-connect, and resource prefreshing
- If the learned subresource is in the cache, then it is loaded from disk and into memory
- If the learned subresource is missing, or has expired, then a network request is made

Resource prefreshing is a great example of the workflow of every experimental optimization in Chrome—in theory, it should enable better performance, but there are many tradeoffs as well. There is only one way to reliably determine if it will make the cut and make it into Chrome: implement it and run it as an A/B experiment in some of the pre-release channels with real users, on real networks, with real browsing patterns.

As of early 2013, the Chrome team is in the early stages of discussing the implementation. If it makes the cut based on gathered results, we may see prefreshing in Chrome sometime later in the year. The process of improving Chrome network performance never stops—the team is always experimenting with new approaches, ideas, and techniques.

Optimizing Navigation with Prerendering

Each and every optimization we have covered up to now helps reduce the latency between the user's direct request for a navigation and the resulting page rendering in their tab. However, what would it take to have a truly instant experience? Based on the UX data we saw earlier, this interaction would

---
[19] http://www.whatwg.org/specs/web-apps/current-work/multipage/links.html#link-type-prefetch
[20] http://www.chromium.org/spdy/link-headers-and-server-hint/link-rel-subresource

have to happen in less than 100 ms, which does not leave much room for network latency at all. What could we do to deliver a rendered page in less than 100 ms?

Of course, you already know the answer, since this is a common pattern employed by many users: if you open multiple tabs then switching between tabs is instant and is definitely much faster than waiting for the navigation between the same resources in a single foreground tab. Well, what if the browser provided an API to do this?

```
<link rel="prerender" href="http://example.org/index.html">
```

You guessed it, that is prerendering in Chrome[21]. Instead of just downloading a single resource, as the "prefetch" hint would have done, the "prerender" attribute indicates to Chrome that it should, well, prerender the page in a hidden tab, along with all of its subresources. The hidden tab itself is invisible to the user, but when the user triggers the navigation, the tab is swapped in from the background for an "instant experience".

Curious to try it out? You can visit http://prerender-test.appspot.com for a hands-on demo, and see the history and status of the prerendered pages for your profile by visiting chrome://net-internals/\#prerender. (See Figure 1.12.)

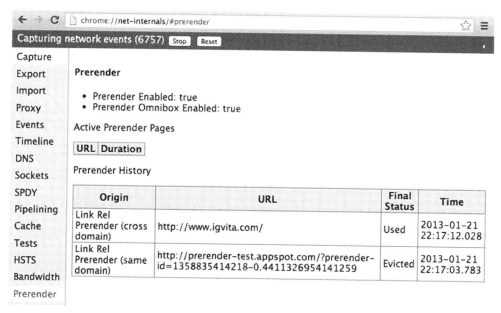

Figure 1.12: Prerendered pages for the current profile

As you would expect, rendering an entire page in a hidden tab can consume a lot of resources, both CPU and network, and hence should only be used in cases where we have high confidence that the hidden tab will be used. For example, when you are using the Omnibox, a prerender may be triggered for a high confidence suggestion. Similarly, Google Search sometimes adds the prerender hint to its markup if it estimates that the first search result is a high confidence destination (also known as Google Instant Pages):

Note that you can also add prerender hints to your own site. Before you do, note that prerendering has a number of restrictions and limitations, which you should keep in mind:

---

[21] https://developers.google.com/chrome/whitepapers/prerender

- At most one prerender tab is allowed across all processes
- HTTPS and pages with HTTP authentication are not allowed
- Prerendering is abandoned if the requested resource, or any of its subresources need to make a non-idempotent request (only GET requests allowed)
- All resources are fetched with lowest network priority
- The page is rendered with lowest CPU priority
- The page is abandoned if memory requirements exceed 100 MB
- Plugin initialization is deferred, and prerendering is abandoned if an HTML5 media element is present

In other words, prerendering is not guaranteed to happen and only applies to pages where it is safe. Additionally, since JavaScript and other logic may be executed within the hidden page, it is best practice to leverage the Page Visibility API[22] to detect if the page is visible—which is something you should be doing anyway[23].

1.8 Chrome Gets Faster as You Use It

Needless to say, Chrome's network stack is much more than a simple socket manager. Our whirlwind tour covered the many levels of potential optimizations that are performed transparently in the background, as you navigate the web. The more Chrome learns about the topology of the web and your browsing patterns, the better it can do its job. Almost like magic, Chrome gets faster as you use it. Except, it is not magic, because now you know how it works.

Finally, it is important to note that the Chrome team continues to iterate and experiment with new ideas to improve performance—this process never stops. By the time you read this, chances are there will be new experiments and optimizations being developed, tested, or deployed. Perhaps once we reach our target destination of instant page loads (< 100 ms), for each and every page, then we can take a break. Until then, there is always more work to do.

---

[22] https://developers.google.com/chrome/whitepapers/pagevisibility
[23] http://www.html5rocks.com/en/tutorials/pagevisibility/intro/

[chapter 2]

From SocialCalc to EtherCalc
Audrey Tang

EtherCalc[1] is an online spreadsheet system optimized toward simultaneous editing, using SocialCalc as its in-browser spreadsheet engine. Designed by Dan Bricklin (the inventor of spreadsheets), SocialCalc is part of the Socialtext platform, a suite of social collaboration tools for enterprise users.

For the Socialtext team, performance was the primary goal behind SocialCalc's development in 2006. The key observation was this: Client-side computation in JavaScript, while an order of magnitude slower than server-side computation in Perl, was still much faster than the network latency incurred during AJAX round trips.

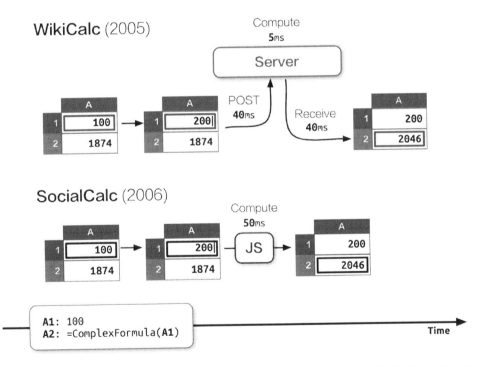

Figure 2.1: WikiCalc and SocialCalc's performance model. Since 2009, advances in JavaScript runtimes have reduced the 50 ms to less than 10 ms.

[1] http://ethercalc.net/

SocialCalc performs all of its computations in the browser; it uses the server only for loading and saving spreadsheets. Toward the end of the *Architecture of Open Source Applications* [BW11] chapter on SocialCalc, we introduced simultaneous collaboration on spreadsheets using a simple, chatroom-like architecture.

Multiplayer SocialCalc (2009)

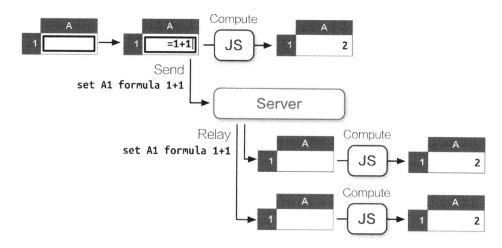

Figure 2.2: Multiplayer SocialCalc

However, as we began to test it for production deployment, we discovered several shortcomings in its performance and scalability characteristics, motivating a series of system-wide rewrites in order to reach acceptable performance. In this chapter, we'll see how we arrived at that architecture, how we used profiling tools, and how we made new tools to overcome performance problems.

Design Constraints

The Socialtext platform has both behind-the-firewall and on-the-cloud deployment options, imposing unique constraints on EtherCalc's resource and performance requirements.

At the time of this writing, Socialtext requires 2 CPU cores and 4 GB RAM for VMWare vSphere-based intranet deployment. For cloud-based hosting, a typical Amazon EC2 instance provides about twice that capacity, with 4 cores and 7.5 GB of RAM.

Behind-the-firewall deployment means that we can't simply throw hardware at the problem in the same way multi-tenant, hosted-only systems did (e.g., DocVerse, which later became part of Google Docs); we can assume only a modest amount of server capacity.

Compared to intranet deployments, cloud-hosted instances offer better capacity and on-demand extension, but network connections from browsers are usually slower and fraught with frequent disconnections and reconnections.

Therefore, the following resource constraints shaped EtherCalc's architecture directions:

Memory: An event-based server allows us to scale to thousands of concurrent connections with a small amount of RAM.

CPU: Based on SocialCalc's original design, we offload most computations and all content rendering to client-side JavaScript.
Network: By sending spreadsheet operations, instead of spreadsheet content, we reduce bandwidth use and allow recovering over unreliable network connections.

2.1 Initial Prototype

We started with a WebSocket server implemented in Perl 5, backed by Feersum[2], a libev[3]-based non-blocking web server developed at Socialtext. Feersum is very fast, capable of handling over 10,000 requests per second on a single CPU. On top of Feersum, we use the PocketIO[4] middleware to leverage the popular Socket.io JavaScript client, which provides backward compatibility for legacy browsers without WebSocket support.

The initial prototype closely resembles a chat server. Each collaborative session is a chatroom; clients sends their locally executed commands and cursor movements to the server, which relays them to all other clients in the same room.

The diagram below shows a typical flow of operation.

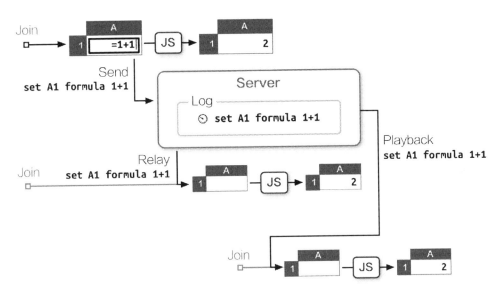

Figure 2.3: Prototype server with log and playback

The server logs each command with a timestamp. If a client drops and reconnects, it can resume by asking for a log of all requests since it was disconnected, then replay those commands locally to get to the same state as its peers.

This simple design minimized server-side CPU and RAM requirements, and demonstrates reasonable resiliency against network failure.

---
[2]https://metacpan.org/release/Feersum
[3]http://software.schmorp.de/pkg/libev.html
[4]https://metacpan.org/release/PocketIO

2.2 First Bottleneck

When we put the prototype to field testing in June 2011, we quickly discovered a performance problem with long-running sessions. Spreadsheets are long-lived documents, and a collaborative session can accumulate thousands of modifications over weeks of editing. When a client joins such an edit session under the naive backlog model, it must replay thousands of commands, incurring a significant startup delay before it can make any modifications.

To mitigate this issue, we implemented a snapshot mechanism. After every 100 commands sent to a room, the server will poll the states from each active client, and save the latest snapshot it receives next to the backlog. A freshly joined client receives the snapshot along with new commands entered after the snapshot was taken, so it only needs to replay 99 commands at most.

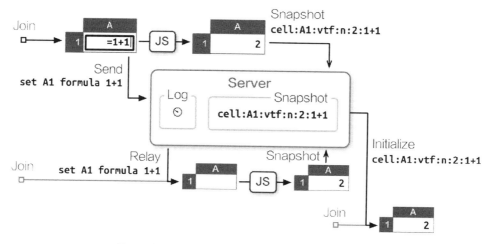

Figure 2.4: Prototype server with snapshot mechanism

This workaround solved the CPU issue for new clients, but created a network performance problem of its own, as it taxes each client's upload bandwidth. Over a slow connection, this delays the reception of subsequent commands from the client.

Moreover, the server has no way to validate the consistency of snapshots submitted by clients. Therefore, an erroneous—or malicious—snapshot can corrupt the state for all newcomers, placing them out of sync with existing peers.

An astute reader may note that both problems are caused by the server's inability to execute spreadsheet commands. If the server can update its own state as it receives each command, it would not need to maintain a command backlog at all.

The in-browser SocialCalc engine is written in JavaScript. We considered translating that logic into Perl, but that would have carried the steep cost of maintaining two code bases. We also experimented with embedded JS engines (V8[5], SpiderMonkey[6]), but they imposed their own performance penalties when running inside Feersum's event loop.

Finally, by August 2011, we resolved to rewrite the server in Node.js.

---

[5]https://metacpan.org/release/JavaScript-V8
[6]https://metacpan.org/release/JavaScript-SpiderMonkey

2.3 Porting to Node.js

The initial rewrite went smoothly because both Feersum and Node.js are based on the same libev event model, and Pocket.io's API matches Socket.io closely. It took us only an afternoon to code a functionally equivalent server in just 80 lines of code, thanks to the concise API offered by ZappaJS.[7]

Initial micro-benchmarking[8] showed that porting to Node.js cost us about one half of the maximum throughput. On a typical Intel Core i5 CPU in 2011, the original Feersum stack handled 5000 requests per second, while Express on Node.js maxed out at 2800 requests per second.

This performance degradation was deemed acceptable for our first JavaScript port, as it wouldn't significantly increase latency for users, and we expect that it will improve over time.

Subsequently, we continued the work to reduce client-side CPU use and minimize bandwidth use by tracking each session's ongoing state with server-side SocialCalc spreadsheets.

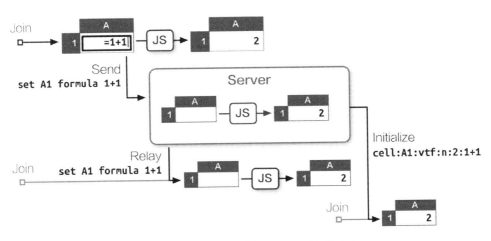

Figure 2.5: Maintaining spreadsheet state with Node.js server

2.4 Server-Side SocialCalc

The key enabling technology for our work is jsdom[9], a full implementation of the W3C document object model, which enables Node.js to load client-side JavaScript libraries within a simulated browser environment.

Using jsdom, it's trivial to create any number of server-side SocialCalc spreadsheets, each taking about 30 KB of RAM, running in its own sandbox:

```
require! <[ vm jsdom ]>
create-spreadsheet = ->
  document = jsdom.jsdom \<html><body/></html>
  sandbox  = vm.createContext window: document.createWindow! <<< {
    setTimeout, clearTimeout, alert: console.log
  }
```

---

[7] http://zappajs.com/
[8] http://c9s.github.com/BenchmarkTest/
[9] https://github.com/tmpvar/jsdom

```
vm.runInContext """
  #packed-SocialCalc-js-code
  window.ss = new SocialCalc.SpreadsheetControl
""" sandbox
```

Each collaboration session corresponds to a sandboxed SocialCalc controller, executing commands as they arrive. The server then transmits this up-to-date controller state to newly joined clients, removing the need for backlogs altogether.

Satisfied with benchmarking results, we coded a Redis[10]-based persistence layer and launched EtherCalc.org for public beta testing. For the next six months, it scaled remarkably well, performing millions of spreadsheet operations without a single incident.

In April 2012, after delivering a talk on EtherCalc at the OSDC.tw conference, I was invited by Trend Micro to participate in their hackathon, adapting EtherCalc into a programmable visualization engine for their real-time web traffic monitoring system.

For their use case we created REST APIs for accessing individual cells with GET/PUT as well as POSTing commands directly to a spreadsheet. During the hackathon, the brand-new REST handler received hundreds of calls per second, updating graphs and formula cell contents on the browser without any hint of slowdown or memory leaks.

However, at the end-of-day demo, as we piped traffic data into EtherCalc and started to type formulas into the in-browser spreadsheet, the server suddenly locked up, freezing all active connections. We restarted the Node.js process, only to find it consuming 100% CPU, locking up again soon after.

Flabbergasted, we rolled back to a smaller data set, which did work correctly and allowed us to finish the demo. But I wondered: what caused the lock-up in the first place?

2.5 Profiling Node.js

To find out where those CPU cycles went to, we needed a profiler.

Profiling the initial Perl prototype had been very straightforward, thanks largely to the illustrious NYTProf[11] profiler, which provides per-function, per-line, per-opcode and per-block timing information, with detailed call-graph visualization[12] and HTML reports. In addition to NYTProf, we also traced long-running processes with Perl's built-in DTrace support[13], obtaining real-time statistics on function entry and exit.

In contrast, Node.js's profiling tools leave much to be desired. As of this writing, DTrace support is still limited to illumos-based systems[14] in 32-bit mode, so we mostly relied on the Node Webkit Agent[15], which provides an accessible profiling interface, albeit with only function-level statistics.

A typical profiling session looks like this:

```
# "lsc" is the LiveScript compiler
# Load WebKit agent, then run app.js:
lsc -r webkit-devtools-agent -er ./app.js
# In another terminal tab, launch the profiler:
killall -USR2 node
```

---

[10] http://redis.io/
[11] https://metacpan.org/module/Devel::NYTProf
[12] https://metacpan.org/module/nytprofcg
[13] https://metacpan.org/module/perldtrace
[14] http://blog.nodejs.org/2012/04/25/profiling-node-js/
[15] https://github.com/c4milo/node-webkit-agent

```
# Open this URL in a WebKit browser to start profiling:
open http://tinyurl.com/node0-8-agent
```

To recreate the heavy background load, we performed high-concurrency REST API calls with the Apache benchmarking tool ab.[16] For simulating browser-side operations, such as moving cursors and updating formulas, we used Zombie.js[17], a headless browser also built with jsdom and Node.js.

Ironically, the bottleneck turned out to be in jsdom itself.

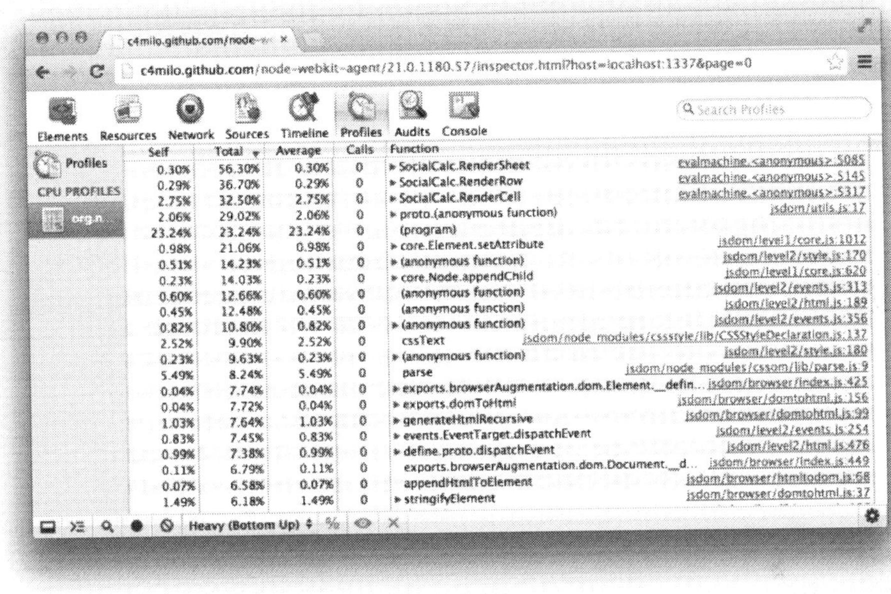

Figure 2.6: Profiler screenshot (with jsdom)

From the report in Figure 2.6, we can see that `RenderSheet` dominates the CPU use. Each time the server receives a command, it spends a few microseconds to redraw the `innerHTML` of cells to reflect the effect of each command.

Because all jsdom code runs in a single thread, subsequent REST API calls are blocked until the previous command's rendering completes. Under high concurrency, this queue eventually triggered a latent bug that ultimately resulted in server lock-up.

As we scrutinized the heap usage, we saw that the rendered result is all but unreferenced, as we don't really need a real-time HTML display on the server side. The only reference to it is in the HTML export API, and for that we can always reconstruct each cell's `innerHTML` rendering from the spreadsheet's in-memory structure.

So, we removed jsdom from the `RenderSheet` function, re-implemented a minimal DOM in 20 lines of LiveScript[18] for HTML export, then ran the profiler again (see Figure 2.7).

Much better! We have improved throughput by a factor of 4, HTML exporting is 20 times faster, and the lock-up problem is gone.

---

[16]http://httpd.apache.org/docs/trunk/programs/ab.html
[17]http://zombie.labnotes.org/
[18]https://github.com/audreyt/ethercalc/commit/fc62c0eb#L1R97

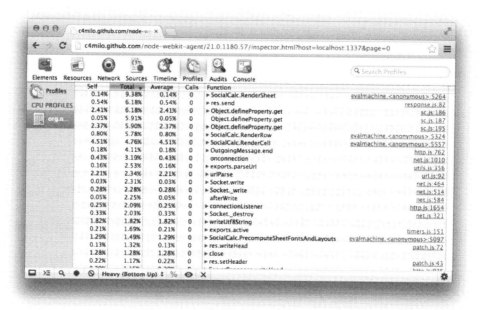

Figure 2.7: Updated profiler screenshot (without jsdom)

2.6 Multi-Core Scaling

After this round of improvement, we finally felt comfortable enough to integrate EtherCalc into the Socialtext platform, providing simultaneous editing for wiki pages and spreadsheets alike.

To ensure a fair response time on production environments, we deployed a reverse-proxying nginx server, using its `limit_req`[19] directive to put an upper limit on the rate of API calls. This technique proved satisfactory for both behind-the-firewall and dedicated-instance hosting scenarios.

For small and medium-sized enterprise customers, though, Socialtext provides a third deployment option: multi-tenant hosting. A single, large server hosts more than 35,000 companies, each averaging around 100 users.

In this multi-tenant scenario, the rate limit is shared by all customers making REST API calls. This makes each client's effective limit much more constraining—around 5 requests per second. As noted in the previous section, this limitation is caused by Node.js using only one CPU for all its computation.

Is there a way to make use of all those spare CPUs in the multi-tenant server?

For other Node.js services running on multi-core hosts, we utilized a pre-forking cluster server[20] that creates a process for each CPU.

However, while EtherCalc does support multi-server scaling with Redis, the interplay of Socket.io clustering[21] with RedisStore[22] in a single server would have massively complicated the logic, making debugging much more difficult.

---

[19]http://wiki.nginx.org/HttpLimitReqModule#limit_req
[20]https://npmjs.org/package/cluster-server
[21]http://stackoverflow.com/a/5749667
[22]https://github.com/LearnBoost/Socket.IO/wiki/Configuring-Socket.IO

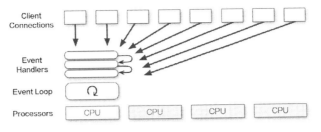

Figure 2.8: Event server (single-core)

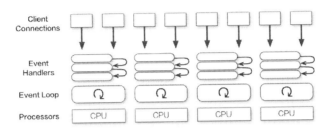

Figure 2.9: Event cluster server (multi-core)

Moreover, if all processes in the cluster are tied in CPU-bound processing, subsequent connections would still get blocked.

Instead of pre-forking a fixed number of processes, we sought a way to create one background thread for each server-side spreadsheet, thereby distributing the work of command execution among all CPU cores.

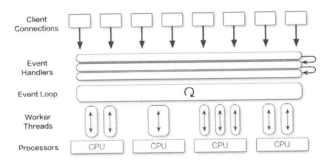

Figure 2.10: Event threaded server (multi-core)

For our purpose, the W3C Web Worker[23] API is a perfect match. Originally intended for browsers, it defines a way to run scripts in the background independently. This allows long tasks to be executed continuously while keeping the main thread responsive.

So we created webworker-threads[24], a cross-platform implementation of the Web Worker API for Node.js.

Using webworker-threads, it's very straightforward to create a new SocialCalc thread and communicate with it:

---

[23]http://www.w3.org/TR/workers/
[24]https://github.com/audreyt/node-webworker-threads

```
{ Worker } = require \webworker-threads
w = new Worker \packed-SocialCalc.js
w.onmessage = (event) -> ...
w.postMessage command
```

This solution offers the best of both worlds: It gives us the freedom to allocate more CPUs to EtherCalc whenever needed, and the overhead of background thread creation remains negligible on single-CPU environments.

2.7 Lessons Learned

Constraints are Liberating

In his book *The Design of Design*, Fred Brooks argues that by shrinking the designer's search space, constraints can help to focus and expedite a design process. This includes self-imposed constraints:

> Artificial constraints for one's design task have the nice property that one is free to relax them. Ideally, they push one into an unexplored corner of a design space, stimulating creativity.

During EtherCalc's development, such constraints were essential to maintain its *conceptual integrity* throughout various iterations.

For example, it might seem attractive to adopt three different concurrency architectures, each tailored to one of our server flavors (behind-the-firewall, on-the-cloud, and multi-tenant hosting). However, such premature optimization would have severely hampered the conceptual integrity.

Instead, I kept the focus on getting EtherCalc performing well without trading off one resource requirement for another, thereby minimizing its CPU, RAM and network uses at the same time. Indeed, since the RAM requirement is under 100 MB, even embedded platforms such as Raspberry Pi can host it easily.

This self-imposed constraint made it possible to deploy EtherCalc on PaaS environments (e.g., DotCloud, Nodejitsu and Heroku) where all three resources are constrained instead of just one. This made it very easy for people to set up a personal spreadsheet service, thus prompting more contributions from independent integrators.

Worst is Best

At the YAPC::NA 2006 conference in Chicago, I was invited to predict the open-source landscape, and this was my entry: [25]

> I think, but I cannot prove, that next year JavaScript 2.0 will bootstrap itself, complete self-hosting, compile back to JavaScript 1, and replace Ruby as the Next Big Thing on all environments.
>
> I think CPAN and JSAN will merge; JavaScript will become the common backend for all dynamic languages, so you can write Perl to run in the browser, on the server, and inside databases, all with the same set of development tools.
>
> Because, as we know, *worse is better*, so the *worst* scripting language is doomed to become the *best*.

---

[25] See http://pugs.blogs.com/pugs/2006/06/my_yapcna_light.html

The vision turned into reality around 2009 with the advent of new JavaScript engines running at the speed of native machine instructions. By the time of this writing, JavaScript has become a *"write once, run anywhere"* virtual machine—other major languages can compile to it with almost no performance penalty.[26]

In addition to browsers on the client side and Node.js on the server, JavaScript also made headway[27] into the Postgres database, enjoying a large collection of freely reusable modules[28] shared by these runtime environments.

What enabled such sudden growth in the community? During the course of EtherCalc's development, from participating in the fledgling NPM community, I reckoned that it was precisely because JavaScript prescribes very little and bends itself to the various uses, so innovators can focus on the vocabulary and idioms (e.g., jQuery and Node.js), each team abstracting their own *Good Parts* from a common, liberal core.

New users are offered a very simple subset to begin with; experienced developers are presented with the challenge to evolve better conventions from existing ones. Instead of relying on a core team of designers to get a complete language right for all anticipated uses, the grassroots development of JavaScript echoes Richard P. Gabriel's well-known maxim of Worse is Better.[29]

LiveScript, Redux

In contrast to the straightforward Perl syntax of Coro::AnyEvent[30], the callback-based API of Node.js necessitates deeply nested functions that are difficult to reuse.

After experimenting with various flow-control libraries, I finally solved this issue by settling on LiveScript[31], a new language that compiles to JavaScript, with syntax heavily inspired by Haskell and Perl.

In fact, EtherCalc was ported through a lineage of four languages: JavaScript, CoffeeScript, Coco and LiveScript. Each iteration brings more expressivity, while maintaining full back and forward compatibility, thanks to efforts such as js2coffee[32] and js2ls.[33]

Because LiveScript compiles to JavaScript rather than interpreting its own bytecode, it remains completely compatible with function-scoped profilers. Its generated code performs as good as hand-tuned JavaScript, taking full advantage of modern native runtimes.

On the syntactic side, LiveScript eliminated nested callbacks with novel constructs such as backcalls and cascades. It provides us with powerful syntactic tools for functional and object-oriented composition.

When I first encountered LiveScript, I remarked that it's like "a smaller language within Perl 6, struggling to get out"—a goal made much easier by adopting the same semantics as JavaScript itself and focusing strictly on syntactical ergonomics.

---

[26] http://asmjs.org
[27] http://pgre.st/
[28] https://npmjs.org/
[29] http://www.dreamsongs.com/WorseIsBetter.html
[30] https://metacpan.org/module/Coro::AnyEvent
[31] http://livescript.net/
[32] http://js2coffee.org/
[33] http://js2ls.org/

Conclusion

Unlike the SocialCalc project's well-defined specification and team development process, EtherCalc was a solo experiment from mid-2011 to late-2012 and served as a proving ground for assessing Node.js's readiness for production use.

This unconstrained freedom afforded an exciting opportunity to explore a wide variety of alternative languages, libraries, algorithms and architectures. I'm very grateful to all contributors, collaborators and integrators, and especially to Dan Bricklin and my Socialtext colleagues for encouraging me to experiment with these technologies. Thank you, folks!

[chapter 3]

Ninja
Evan Martin

Ninja is a build system similar to Make. As input you describe the commands necessary to process source files into *target* files. Ninja uses these commands to bring targets up to date. Unlike many other build systems, Ninja's main design goal was speed.

I wrote Ninja while working on Google Chrome. I started Ninja as an experiment to find out if Chrome's build could be made faster. To successfully build Chrome, Ninja's other main design goal followed: Ninja needed to be easily embedded within a larger build system.

Ninja has been quietly successful, gradually replacing the other build systems used by Chrome. After Ninja was made public others contributed code to make the popular CMake build system generate Ninja files—now Ninja is also used to develop CMake-based projects like LLVM and ReactOS. Other projects, like TextMate, target Ninja directly from their custom build.

I worked on Chrome from 2007 to 2012, and started Ninja in 2010. There are many factors contributing to the build performance of a project as large as Chrome (today around 40,000 files of C++ code generating an output binary around 90 MB in size). During my time I touched many of them, from distributing compilation across multiple machines to tricks in linking. Ninja primarily targets only one piece—the *front* of a build. This is the wait between starting the build and the time the first compile starts to run. To understand why that is important it is necessary to understand how we thought about performance in Chrome itself.

3.1 A Small History of Chrome

Discussion of all of Chrome's goals is out of scope here, but one of the defining goals of the project was speed. Performance is a broad goal that spans all of computer science, and Chrome uses nearly every trick available, from caching to parallelization to just-in-time compilation. Then there was startup speed—how long it the program took to show up on the screen after clicking the icon—which seems a bit frivolous in comparison.

Why care about startup speed? For a browser, a quick startup conveys a feeling of lightness, that doing something on the web is as trival an action as opening a text file. Further, the impact of latency on your happiness and on losing your train of thought is well-studied in human-computer interaction. Latency is especially a focus of web companies like Google or Amazon, who are in a good position to measure and experiment on the effect of latency—and who have done experiments that show that delays of even milliseconds have measurable effects on how frequently people use the site or make purchases. It's a small frustration that adds up subconsciously.

Chrome's approach to starting quickly was a clever trick by one of the first engineers on Chrome. As soon as they got their skeleton application to the point where it showed a window on the screen, they created a benchmark measuring that speed along with a continuous build that tracked it. Then, in Brett Wilson's words, "a very simple rule: this test can never get any slower."[1] As code was added to Chrome, maintenance of this benchmark demanded extra engineering effort[2]—in some cases work was delayed until it was truly needed, or data used during startup was precomputed—but the primary "trick" to performance, and the one that made the greatest impression on me, was simply to *do less work*.

I joined the Chrome team without any intention of working on build tools. My background and platform of choice was Linux, and I wanted to be the Linux guy. To limit scope the project was initially Windows-only; I took it as my role to help finish the Windows implementation so that I could then make it run on Linux.

When starting work on other platforms, the first hurdle was sorting out the build system. By that point Chrome was already large (complete, in fact—Chrome for Windows was released in 2008 before any ports had started), so efforts to switch even the Visual Studio-based Windows build to a different build system wholesale were conflicting with ongoing development. It felt like replacing the foundation of a building while it was in use.

Members of the Chrome team came up with an incremental solution called *GYP*[3] which could be used to generate, one subcomponent at a time, the Visual Studio build files already used by Chrome in addition to the build files that would be used on other platforms.

The input to GYP is simple: the desired name of the output accompanied by plain text lists of source files, the occasional custom rule like "process each IDL file to generate an additional source file", and some conditional behaviors (e.g., only use certain files on certain platforms). GYP then takes this high-level description and generates platform-native build files.[4]

On the Mac "native build files" meant Xcode project files. On Linux, however, there was no obvious single choice. The initial attempt used the Scons build system, but I was dismayed to discover that a GYP-generated Scons build could take 30 seconds to start while Scons computed which files had changed. I figured that Chrome was roughly the size of the Linux kernel so the approach taken there ought to work. I rolled up my sleeves and wrote the code to make GYP generate plain Makefiles using tricks from the kernel's Makefiles.

Thus I unintentionally began my descent into build system madness. There are many factors that make building software take time, from slow linkers to poor parallelization, and I dug into all of them. The Makefile approach was initially quite fast but as we ported more of Chrome to Linux, increasing the number of files used in the build, it grew slower.[5]

As I worked on the port I found one part of the build process especially frustrating: I would make a change to a single file, run make, realize I'd left out a semicolon, run make again, and each time the wait would be long enough that I would forget what I was working on. I thought back to how hard we fought against latency for end users. "How can this be taking so long," I'd wonder, "there can't be that much work to do." As an experiment I started Ninja, to see how simple I could make it.

---

[1] http://blog.chromium.org/2008/10/io-in-google-chrome.html
[2] http://neugierig.org/software/chromium/notes/2009/01/startup.html
[3] GYP stands for Generate Your Projects.
[4] This is the same pattern used by the Autotools: Makefile.am is a list of source files, which is then processed by the configure script to generate more concrete build instructions.
[5] Chrome itself also has grown rapidly. It currently grows at a rate of around 1000 commits a week, most of which are code additions.

3.2 The Design of Ninja

At a high level any build system performs three main tasks. It will (1) load and analyze build goals, (2) figure out which steps need to run in order to achieve those goals, and (3) execute those steps.

To make startup in step (1) fast, Ninja needed to do a minimal amount of work while loading the build files. Build systems are typically used by humans, which means they provide a convenient, high-level syntax for expressing build goals. It also means that when it comes time to actually build the project the build system must process the instructions further: for example, at some point Visual Studio must concretely decide based on the build configuration where the output files must go, or which files must be compiled with a C++ or C compiler.

Because of this, GYP's work in generating Visual Studio files was effectively limited to translating lists of source files into the Visual Studio syntax and leaving Visual Studio to do the bulk of the work. With Ninja I saw the opportunity to do as much work as possible in GYP. In a sense, when GYP generates Ninja build files, it does all of the above computation once. GYP then saves a snapshot of that intermediate state into a format that Ninja can quickly load for each subsequent build.

Ninja's build file language is therefore simple to the point of being inconvenient for humans to write. There are no conditionals or rules based on file extensions. Instead, the format is just a list of which exact paths produce which exact outputs. These files can be loaded quickly, requiring almost no interpretation.

This minimalist design counterintuitively leads to greater flexibility. Because Ninja lacks higher-level knowledge of common build concepts like an output directory or current configuration, Ninja is simple to plug into larger systems (e.g., CMake, as we later found) that have different opinions about how builds should be organized. For example, Ninja is agnostic as to whether build outputs (e.g., object files) are placed alongside the source files (considered poor hygiene by some) or in a separate build output directory (considered hard to understand by others). Long after releasing Ninja I finally thought of the right metaphor: whereas other build systems are compilers, Ninja is an assembler.

3.3 What Ninja Does

If Ninja pushes most of the work to the build file generator, what is there left to do? The above ideology is nice in principle but real world needs are always more complicated. Ninja grew (and lost) features over the course of its development. At every point, the important question was always "can we do less?" Here is a brief overview of how it works.

A human needs to debug the files when the build rules are wrong, so .ninja build files are plain text, similar to Makefiles, and they support a few abstractions to make them more readable.

The first abstraction is the "rule", which represents a single tool's command-line invocation. A rule is then shared between different build steps. Here is an example of the Ninja syntax for declaring a rule named "compile" that runs the gcc compiler along with two build statements that make use of it for specific files.

```
rule compile
  command = gcc -Wall -c $in -o $out
build out/foo.o: compile src/foo.c
build out/bar.o: compile src/bar.c
```

The second abstraction is the variable. In the example above, these are the dollar-sign-prefixed identifiers ($in and $out). Variables can represent both the inputs and outputs of a command and can be used to make short names for long strings. Here is an extended compile definition that makes use of a variable for compiler flags:

```
cflags = -Wall
rule compile
  command = gcc $cflags -c $in -o $out
```

Variable values used in a rule can be shadowed in the scope of a single `build` block by indenting their new definition. Continuing the above example, the value of `cflags` can be adjusted for a single file:

```
build out/file_with_extra_flags.o: compile src/baz.c
  cflags = -Wall -Wextra
```

Rules behave almost like functions and variables behave like arguments. These two simple features are dangerously close to a programming language—the opposite of the "do no work" goal. But they have the important benefit of reducing repeated strings which is not only useful for humans but also for computers, reducing the quantity of text to be parsed.

The build file, once parsed, describes a graph of dependencies: the final output binary depends on linking a number of objects, each of which is the result of compiling sources. Specifically it is a bipartite graph, where "nodes" (input files) point to "edges" (build commands) which point to nodes (output files)[6]. The build process then traverses this graph.

Given a target output to build, Ninja first walks up the graph to identify the state of each edge's input files: that is, whether or not the input files exist and what their modification times are. Ninja then computes a *plan*. The plan is the set of edges that need to be executed in order to bring the final target up to date, according to the modification times of the intermediate files. Finally, the plan is executed, walking down the graph and checking off edges as they are executed and successfully completed.

Once these pieces were in place I could establish a baseline benchmark for Chrome: the time to run Ninja again after successfully completing a build. That is the time to load the build files, examine the built state, and determine there was no work to do. The time it took for this benchmark to run was just under a second. This was my new startup benchmark metric. However, as Chrome grew, Ninja had to keep getting faster to keep that metric from regressing.

3.4 Optimizing Ninja

The initial implementation of Ninja was careful to arrange the data structures in order to allow a fast build, but wasn't particularly clever in terms of optimizations. Once the program worked, I reasoned, a profiler could reveal which pieces mattered.[7]

Over the years, profiling pointed at different pieces of the program. Sometimes the worst offender was a single hot function that could be micro-optimized. At other times, it suggested something more broad like being careful not to allocate or copy memory except when necessary. There were also cases where a better representation or data structure had the most impact. What follows is a walk through the Ninja implementation and some of the more interesting stories about its performance.

---

[6]This extra indirection allows builds to correctly model commands that have multiple outputs.
[7]Ninja has a large test suite of 164 test cases which itself runs in under a second, which means developers can have confidence that performance changes don't affect the correctness of the program.

Parsing

Initially Ninja used a hand-written lexer and a recursive descent parser. The syntax was simple enough, I thought. It turns out that for a large enough project like Chrome[8], simply parsing the build files (named with the extension .ninja) can take a surprising amount of time.

The original function to analyze a single character soon appeared in profiles:

```
static bool IsIdentifierCharacter(char c) {
  return
    ('a' <= c && c <= 'z') ||
    ('A' <= c && c <= 'Z') ||
    // and so on...
}
```

A simple fix—at the time saving 200 ms—was to replace the function with a 256-entry lookup table that could be indexed by the input character. Such a thing is trivial to generate using Python code like:

```
cs = set()
for c in string.ascii_letters + string.digits + r'+,-./\_$':
    cs.add(ord(c))
for i in range(256):
    print '%d,' % (i in cs),
```

This trick kept Ninja fast for quite a while. Eventually we moved to something more principled: re2c, the lexer generator used by PHP. It can generate more complex lookup tables and trees of unintelligible code. For example:

```
if (yych <= 'b') {
    if (yych == '`') goto yy24;
    if (yych <= 'a') goto yy21;
    // and so on...
```

It remains an open question as to whether treating the input as text in the first place is a good idea. Perhaps we will eventually require Ninja's input to be generated in some machine-friendly format that would let us avoid parsing for the most part.

Canonicalization

Ninja avoids using strings to identify paths. Instead, Ninja maps each path it encounters to a unique Node object and the Node object is used in the rest of the code. Reusing this object ensures that a given path is only ever checked on disk once, and the result of that check (i.e., the modification time) can be reused in other code.

The pointer to the Node object serves as a unique identity for that path. To test whether two Nodes refer to the same path it is sufficient to compare pointers rather than perform a more costly string comparison. For example, as Ninja walks up the graph of inputs to a build, it keeps a stack of dependendent Nodes to check for dependency loops: if A depends on B depends on C depends on A, the build can't proceed. This stack, representing files, can be implemented as a simple array of pointers, and pointer equality can be used to check for duplicates.

---

[8]Today's Chrome build generates over 10 MB of .ninja files.

To always use the same Node for a single file, Ninja must reliably map every possible name for a file into the same Node object. This requires a *canonicalization* pass on all paths mentioned in input files, which transforms a path like foo/../bar.h into just bar.h. Initially Ninja simply required all paths to be provided in canonical form but that ends up not working for a few reasons. One is that user-specified paths (e.g., the command-line ninja ./bar.h) are reasonably expected to work correctly. Another is that variables may combine to make non-canonical paths. Finally, the dependency information emitted by gcc may be non-canonical.

Thus most of what Ninja ends up doing is path processing, so canonicalizing paths is another hot point in profiles. The original implementation was written for clarity, not performance, so standard optimization techniques—like removing a double loop or avoiding memory allocation—helped considerably.

The Build Log

Often micro-optimizations like the above are less impactful than structural optimizations where you change the algorithm or approach. This was the case with Ninja's *build log*.

One part of the Linux kernel build system tracks the commands used to generate outputs. Consider a motivating example: you compile an input foo.c into an output foo.o, and then change the build file such that it should be rebuilt with different compilation flags. For the build system to know that it needs to rebuild the output, it must either note that foo.o depends on the build files themselves (which, depending on the organization of the project, might mean that a change to the build files would cause the entire project to rebuild), or record the commands used to generate each output and compare them for each build.

The kernel (and consequently the Chrome Makefiles and Ninja) takes the latter approach. While building, Ninja writes out a build log that records the full commands used to generate each output[9]. Then for each subsequent build, Ninja loads the previous build log and compares the new build's commands to the build log's commands to detect changes. This, like loading build files or path canonicalization, was another hot point in profiles.

After making a few smaller optimizations Nico Weber, a prolific contributor to Ninja, implemented a new format for the build log. Rather than recording commands, which are frequently very long and take a lot of time to parse, Ninja instead records a hash of the command. In subsequent builds, Ninja compares the hash of the command that is about to be run to the logged hash. If the two hashes differ, the output is out of date. This approach was very successful. Using hashes reduced the size of the build log dramatically—from 200 MB to less than 2 MB on Mac OS X—and made it over 20 times faster to load.

Dependency Files

There is an additional store of metadata that must be recorded and used across builds. To correctly build C/C++ code a build system must accomodate dependencies between header files. Suppose foo.c contains the line #include "bar.h" and bar.h itself includes the line #include "baz.h". All three of those files (foo.c, bar.h, baz.h) then affect the result of compilation. For example, changes to baz.h should still trigger a rebuild of foo.o.

Some build systems use a "header scanner" to extract these dependencies at build time, but this approach can be slow and is difficult to make exactly correct in the presence of #ifdef directives. Another alternative is to require the build files to correctly report all dependencies, including headers,

---

[9]It also stores when each command started and finished, which is useful for profiling builds of many files.

but this is cumbersome for developers: every time you add or remove an `#include` statement you need to modify or regenerate the build.

A better approach relies on the fact that at compile time gcc (and Microsoft's Visual Studio) can output which headers were used to build the output. This information, much like the command used to generate an output, can be recorded and reloaded by the build system so that the dependencies can be tracked exactly. For a first-time build, before there is any output, all files will be compiled so no header dependency is necessary. After the first compilation, modifications to any files used by an output (including modifications that add or remove additional dependencies) will cause a rebuild, keeping the dependency information up-to-date.

When compiling, gcc writes header dependencies in the format of a Makefile. Ninja then includes a parser for the (simplified subset) Makefile syntax and loads all of this dependency information at the next build. Loading this data is a major bottleneck. On a recent Chrome build, the dependency information produced by gcc sums to 90 MB of Makefiles, all of which reference paths which must be canonicalized before use.

Much like with the other parsing work, using `re2c` and avoiding copies where possible helped with performance. However, much like how work was shifted to GYP, this parsing work can be pushed to a time other than the critical path of startup. Our most recent work on Ninja (at the time of this writing, the feature is complete but not yet released) has been to make this processing happen eagerly during the build.

Once Ninja has started executing build commands, all of the performance-critical work has been completed and Ninja is mostly idle as it waits for the commands it executes to complete. In this new approach for header dependencies, Ninja uses this time to process the Makefiles emitted by gcc as they are written, canonicalizing paths and processing the dependencies into a quickly deserializable binary format. On the next build Ninja only needs to load this file. The impact is dramatic, particularly on Windows. (This is discussed further later in this chapter.)

The "dependency log" needs to store thousands of paths and dependencies between those paths. Loading this log and adding to it needs to be fast. Appending to this log should be safe, even in the event of an interruption such as a cancelled build.

After considering many database-like approaches I finally came up with a trivial implementation: the file is a sequence of records and each record is either a path or a list of dependencies. Each path written to the file is assigned a sequential integer identifier. Dependencies are then lists of integers. To add dependencies to the file, Ninja first writes new records for each path that doesn't yet have an identifier and then writes the dependency record using those identifiers. When loading the file on a subsequent run Ninja can then use a simple array to map identifiers to their Node pointers.

Executing a Build

Performance-wise the process of executing the commands judged necessary according to the dependencies discussed above is relatively uninteresting because the bulk of the work that needs to be done is performed in those commands (i.e., in the compilers, linkers, etc.), not in Ninja itself[10].

Ninja runs build commands in parallel by default, based on the number of available CPUs on the system. Since commands running simultaneously could have their outputs interleave, Ninja buffers

---

[10]One minor benefit of this is that users on systems with few CPU cores have noticed their end-to-end builds are faster due to Ninja consuming relatively little processing power while driving the build, which frees up a core for use by build commands.

all output from a command until that command completes before printing its output. The resulting output appears as if the commands were run serially.[11]

This control over command output allows Ninja to carefully control its total output. During the build Ninja displays a single line of status while running; if the build completes successfully the total printed output of Ninja is a single line.[12] This doesn't make Ninja run any quicker but it makes Ninja *feel* fast, which is almost as important to the original goal as real speed is.

Supporting Windows

I wrote Ninja for Linux. Nico (mentioned previously) did the work to make it function on Mac OS X. As Ninja became more widely used people started asking about Windows support.

At a superficial level supporting Windows wasn't too hard. There were some straightforward changes like making the path separator a backslash or changing the Ninja syntax to allow colons in a path (like c:\foo.txt). Once those changes were in place the larger problems surfaced. Ninja was designed with behavioral assumptions from Linux; Windows is different in small but important ways.

For example, Windows has a relatively low limit on the length of a command, an issue that comes up when constructing the command passed to a final link step that may mention most files in the project. The Windows solution for this is "response" files, and only Ninja (not the generator program in front of Ninja) is equipped to manage these.

A more important performance problem is that file operations on Windows are slow and Ninja works with a lot of files. Visual Studio's compiler emits header dependencies by simply printing them while compiling, so Ninja on Windows currently includes a tool that wraps the compiler to make it produce the gcc-style Makefile dependency list required by Ninja. This large number of files, already a bottleneck on Linux, is much worse on Windows where opening a file is much more costly. The aforementioned new approach to parsing dependencies at build time fits perfectly on Windows, allowing us to drop the intermediate tool entirely: Ninja is already buffering the command's output, so it can parse the dependencies directly from that buffer, sidestepping the intermediate on-disk Makefile used with gcc.

Getting the modification time of a file—GetFileAttributesEx() on Windows[13] and stat() on non-Windows platforms—seems to be about 100 times slower on Windows than it is on Linux.[14] It is possible this is due to "unfair" factors like antivirus software but in practice those factors exist on end-user systems so Ninja performance suffers. The Git version control system, which similarly needs to get the state of many files, can use multiple threads on Windows to execute file checks in parallel. Ninja ought to adopt this feature.

3.5 Conclusions and Alternative Designs

Occasionally on the mailing list someone will suggest that Ninja ought to work instead as a memory-resident daemon or server, especially one coupled with file modification monitors (e.g., inotify on Linux). All these concerns about the time taken to load data and the time to write it back out would not be an issue if Ninja just stayed around between builds.

---

[11]Most successful build commands don't have any output, so this only comes up when multiple commands fail in parallel: their error messages appear serially.
[12]This is the origin of the name "Ninja": quiet and strikes quickly.
[13]stat() on Windows is even slower than GetFileAttributesEx().
[14]This is when the disk cache is warm, so disk performance shouldn't be a factor.

In fact, that design was my original plan for Ninja. It was only after I saw the first build worked quickly that I realized it might be possible to make Ninja work without needing a server component. It may yet be necessary as Chrome continues to grow, but the simpler approach, where we gain speed by doing less work rather than more complex machinery, will always be the most appealing to me. It is my hope some other restructurings (like the changes we made to use a lexer generator or the new dependency format on Windows) will be enough.

Simplicity is a virtue in software; the question is always how far it can go. Ninja managed to cut much of the complexity from a build system by delegating certain expensive tasks to other tools (GYP or CMake), and because of this it is useful in projects other than the one it was made for. Ninja's simple code hopefully encouraged contributions— the majority of work for supporting OS X, Windows, CMake, and other features was done by contributors. Ninja's simple semantics have led to experiments by others to reimplement it in other languages (Scheme and Go, to my knowledge).

Do milliseconds really matter? Among the greater concerns of software it might be silly to worry about. However, having worked on projects with slower builds, I find more than productivity is gained; a quick turnaround gives a project a feeling of lightness that makes me happy to play with it. And code that is fun to hack on is the reason I write software in the first place. In that sense speed is of primary importance.

3.6 Acknowledgements

Special thanks are due to the many contributors to Ninja, some of whom you can find listed on Ninja's GitHub project page.[15]

---

[15] https://github.com/martine/ninja/contributors

[chapter 4]

Parsing XML at the Speed of Light
Arseny Kapoulkine

4.1 Preface

XML is a standardized markup language that defines a set of rules for encoding hierarchically structured documents in a human-readable text-based format. XML is in widespread use, with documents ranging from very short and simple (such as SOAP queries) to multi-gigabyte documents (OpenStreetMap) with complicated data relationships (COLLADA). In order to process XML documents, users typically need a special library: an XML parser, which converts the document from text to internal representation. XML is a compromise between parsing performance, human readability and parsing-code complexity—therefore a fast XML parser can make the choice of XML as an underlying format for application data model more preferable.

This chapter describes various performance tricks that allowed the author to write a very high-performing parser in C++: pugixml.[1] While the techniques were used for an XML parser, most of them can be applied to parsers of other formats or even unrelated software (e.g., memory management algorithms are widely applicable beyond parsers).

Since there are several substantially different approaches to XML parsing, and the parser has to do additional processing that even people familiar with XML do not know about, it is important to outline the entire task at hand first, before diving into implementation details.

4.2 XML parsing models

Each of the different models of XML parsing is appropriate in different situations, and each has implications for performance and memory consumption. The following models are in widespread use:

- With SAX (Simple API for XML) parsers, the user provides the parser with a document stream as an input and several callbacks such as "start of tag," "end of tag," "character data inside tag". The parser invokes the callbacks according to the data in the document. The context needed for parsing is limited by the tree depth of the current element, which means that the memory requirements are greatly reduced. This type of parsing can be used for streaming documents where only part of the document is available at any single time.
- Pull parsing is similar to SAX in the parsing process—that is, the document is processed one element at a time—but the control is inverted: in SAX, parsing is controlled by the parser

---
[1] http://pugixml.org

through callbacks, whereas in Pull parsing the user controls the parsing process through an iterator-like object.
- With DOM (Document Object Model) parsers, the user provides the parser with the entire document as a text stream/buffer, from which the parser generates a document object—an in-memory representation of the entire document tree, which has an individual object for each specific XML element or attribute, and a set of allowed operations (e.g., "get all child elements of this node"). Pugixml follows this model.

The choice of the parsing model usually depends on the document size and structure. Since pugixml is a DOM parser, it is effective for documents that:
- are small enough to fit in memory,
- have a complicated structure with references between nodes that need to be traversed, or
- need complicated document transformations.

4.3 Design choices in pugixml

Pugixml focuses on the problem of DOM parsing largely because, while fast and lightweight SAX parsers (such as Expat) were available, all production-ready XML DOM parsers at the time of pugixml's creation (2006) were either not very lightweight, not very fast or—usually—neither. Thus the main goal of pugixml is to be a very fast lightweight DOM-based XML manipulation library.

XML is defined by a W3C recommendation[2] that specifies two different types of parsing: validating and non-validating (in other words, non-validating parsers check XML syntax while validating parsers can check data semantics as well). Even a non-validating parser has to do some relatively resource-intensive validation work.

When performance is the primary goal, a compromise must be reached between performance and conformance. For pugixml the compromise is as follows: any well-formed XML document will be fully parsed, including all required transformations, with the exception of document type declarations.[3] Since only rules that are fast to verify are checked, a non-well-formed document can sometimes be parsed successfully.

The data in an XML document often has to be transformed in certain ways by the time it reaches the user. The transformations include end-of-line handling, attribute-value normalization and character reference expansion. These transformations have an associated performance cost; pugixml optimizes them as much as possible while providing a way to disable them for maximum performance.

The task at hand is to make a fast DOM parser that successfully parses conforming XML documents with required transformations, is as fast as reasonably possible, and is production ready. For performance purposes, "production ready" mainly means it offers resistance to malformed data. Sacrificing buffer overrun checks to improve performance is not feasible.

Next, we'll discuss the parsing process used by pugixml. The last sections will describe the data structure used by pugixml to store the document object model and the algorithm used by pugixml to allocate memory for this data structure.

---

[2] http://www.w3.org/TR/REC-xml/

[3] Document type (DOCTYPE) declarations are parsed but their contents are ignored. This decision is based on performance issues, implementation complexity and demand for the feature.

4.4 Parsing

The goal of a DOM parser is to take an input—a string that contains an XML document—and produce a tree of objects that represents the same document in memory. A parser typically consists of two stages: a lexer and a parser. A lexer is given an input character stream and produces a token stream. (For an XML parser the set of tokens can include open angle brackets, quotation marks, tag names, and attribute names.) The parser consumes the token stream and produces a syntax tree based on the grammar, using one of many parsing algorithms such as recursive descent. When encountering a token with string data, such as a tag name, the lexer or parser copies the string contents to a heap and stores a reference to the string inside a tree node.

To improve parsing performance, pugixml deviates from the typical approach in several ways.

Token stream vs. character stream

As mentioned before, parsers traditionally use lexers to convert the character stream into a token stream. This can improve performance in cases where a parser has to do a lot of backtracking, but for XML parsers a lexer stage is just an extra layer of complexity that increases the per-character overhead. Thus pugixml operates on a character stream instead of a token stream.

Normally a stream consists of UTF-8 characters, and pugixml reads the stream byte by byte. Due to UTF-8 structure there is no need to parse UTF-8 byte sequences unless you're looking for specific non-ASCII characters, because in valid UTF-8 streams all bytes below 128 are standalone ASCII characters (i.e., are not part of a UTF-8 character).[4]

In-place parsing

There are several inefficiencies in the typical implementation of a parser. One of them is copying string data to the heap. This involves allocating many blocks of varying sizes, from bytes to megabytes, and requires us to copy all strings from the original stream to the heap. Avoiding the copy operation allows us to eliminate both sources of overhead. Using a technique known as in-place (or *in situ*) parsing, the parser can use data from the stream directly. This is the parsing strategy used by pugixml.

A basic in-place parser takes an input string stored in a contiguous memory buffer, scans the string as a character stream, and creates the necessary tree structure. Upon encountering a string that is part of the data model, such as a tag name, the parser saves a pointer to the string and its length (instead of saving the whole string).[5]

As such, this is a tradeoff between performance and memory usage. In-place parsing is usually faster compared to parsing with copying strings to the heap, but it can consume more memory. An in-place parser needs to hold the original stream in memory in addition to its own data describing the document's structure. A non in-place parser can store relevant parts of the original stream instead.

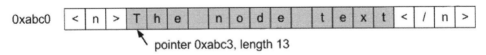

Figure 4.1: An example of basic in-place text parsing.

---

[4]Note that conforming XML parsers are required to reject certain Unicode codepoints. Pugixml sacrifices this analysis for increased performance.

[5]This creates a lifetime dependency—the entire source buffer must outlive all document nodes for the technique to work.

Most in-place parsers have to deal with additional issues. In the case of pugixml, there are two: simplifying string access and transforming XML data during parsing.

Accessing strings that are parsed in-place is difficult because they are not null-terminated. That is, the character after the string is not a null byte, but is instead the next character in the XML document, such as an open angle bracket (<). This makes it difficult to use standard C/C++ string functions that expect null-terminated strings.

To make sure we can use these functions we'll have to null-terminate the strings during parsing. Since we can't easily insert new characters, the character after the last character of each string will have to be overwritten with a null character. Fortunately, we can always do this in XML: a character that follows the end of a string is always a markup character and is never relevant to document representation in memory.

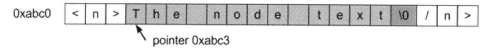

Figure 4.2: Adjusting in-place parsing for null-terminated strings.

The second issue is more complicated: often the string value and the representation in the XML file are different. A conforming parser is expected to perform decoding of the representation. Since doing this during node object access would make object access performance unpredictable, we prefer to do this at parsing time. Depending on the content type, an XML parser could be required to perform the following transformations:

- End-of-line handling: The input document can contain various types of line endings and the parser should normalize them as follows: any two-character sequence of one carriage return (ASCII 0xD) and one line feed (ASCII 0xA) and any free-standing carriage return should be replaced with a line feed character. For example, the line

  'line1\xD\xAline2\xDline3\xA\xA'

  should be transformed to

  'line1\xAline2\xAline3\xA\xA'.

- Character reference expansion: XML supports escaping characters using their Unicode code point with either decimal or hexadecimal representation. For example, a should expand to a and ø should expand to ø.
- Entity reference expansion: XML supports generic entity references, where &name; is replaced with the value of entity name. There are five predefined entities: < (<), > (>), " ("), ' (') and & (&).
- Attribute-value normalization: in addition to expanding references, the parser should perform whitespace normalization when parsing attribute values. All whitespace characters (space, tab, carriage return and line feed) should be replaced with a space. Additionally, depending on the type of the attribute, leading and trailing whitespaces should be removed and whitespace sequences in the middle of the string should be collapsed into a single space.

It is possible to support an arbitrary transformation in an in-place parser by modifying the string contents, given an important constraint: a transformation must never increase the length of the string.

If it does, the result might overlap with significant data in the document. Fortunately, all of the above transformations satisfy this requirement.[6]

General entity expansion does *not* satisfy this constraint. Since pugixml does not support DOCTYPE declarations, and it is impossible to specify custom entities without DOCTYPE, any supported document can be fully parsed using in-place parsing.[7]

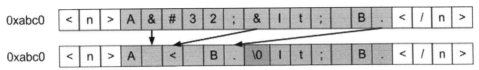

Figure 4.3: Text transformations with in-place text parsing.

Interestingly, in-place parsing can be used with memory-mapped file I/O.[8] Supporting null-termination and text transformation requires a special memory mapping mode known as *copy-on-write* to avoid modifying the file on disk.

Using memory mapped file I/O with in-place parsing has the following benefits:

- The kernel can usually map cache pages directly into the process address space, thus eliminating a memory copy that would have happened with standard file I/O.
- If the file is not already in the cache, the kernel can prefetch sections of the file from disk, effectively making I/O and parsing parallel.
- Since only modified pages need to allocate physical memory, memory consumption can be greatly decreased on documents with large text sections.

Optimizing character-wise operations

Eliminating string copies is not the only thing we can do to optimize parser performance. When comparing parser performance, a useful metric is the average number of processor cycles spent for each character. While this varies among documents and processor architectures, it is reasonably stable for documents of similar structure. Thus it makes sense to optimize for this metric, and an obvious place to start is in the operations performed for each character.

The most important operation is detecting character set membership: given a character from the input stream, does it belong to a certain set of characters?

A useful approach is to create a Boolean flag table, where for each character value a true/false value is stored depending on whether the character belongs to the set or not. Depending on the encoding, different table data structures and sizes make sense as follows:

- For encodings where each character occupies no more than 8 bits, a table of size 256 is sufficient.
- For UTF-8, we would like to use a byte-indexed table to avoid code point decoding; this works only if all characters with code points (i.e. numeric values) above 127 belong to the set or no characters with code points above 127 belong to the set. If either of these are true, then a table of size 256 is sufficient. The first 128 entries of the table are filled with true or false

---

[6]This is obvious for all transformations, except perhaps Unicode transformation. In that case, both UTF-8 and UTF-16 encodings are more compact than hexadecimal or decimal representation of Unicode code points, which is why replacing one with the other never increases the length.

[7]It is possible to support general entity references with in-place parsing by splitting every string with an entity reference into three nodes: prefix string before entity reference, a node of a special type that contains the reference id, and a suffix string, which may have to be split further. This approach is used by the Microsoft XML parser (for different reasons).

[8]See http://en.wikipedia.org/wiki/Memory-mapped_file.

(depending on whether the character is in the target set) and the last 128 entries of the table all share the same value. Because of the way UTF-8 encodes data, all code points above 127 will be represented as sequences of bytes with values above 127. Furthermore, the first character of the sequence will also be above 127.
- For UTF-16 or UTF-32, tables of large sizes are usually impractical. Given the same constraint as the one for optimized UTF-8, we can leave the table to be 128 or 256 entries large, and add an additional comparison to deal with values outside the range.

Note that we only need one bit to store the true/false value, so it might make sense to use bitmasks to store eight different character sets in one 256 byte table. Pugixml uses this approach to save cache space: on the x86 architecture, checking a boolean value usually has the same cost as checking a bit within a byte, provided that bit position is a compile-time constant. This C code demonstrates this approach:

```
enum chartype_t {
  ct_parse_pcdata  = 1, // \0, &, \\r, \<
  ct_parse_attr    = 2, // \0, &, \\r, ', "
  ct_parse_attr_ws = 4, // \0, &, \\r, ', ", \\n, tab
  // ...
};
static const unsigned char table[256] = {
  55, 0, 0, 0, 0, 0, 0, 0, 0, 12, 12, 0, 0, 63, 0, 0, // 0-15
  // ...
};
bool ischartype_utf8(char c, chartype_t ct) {
  // note: unsigned cast is important to
  // guarantee that the value is in 0..255 range
  return ct & table[(unsigned char)c];
}

bool ischartype_utf16_32(wchar_t c, chartype_t ct) {
  // note: unsigned cast is important to
  // guarantee that the value is not negative
  return ct & ((unsigned)c < 128 ? table[(unsigned)c] : table[128]);
}
```

If the tested range includes all characters in a certain interval, it might make sense to use a comparison instead of a table lookup. With careful use of unsigned arithmetics just one comparison is needed. For example, a test for a character being a digit:

```
bool isdigit(char ch) { return (ch >= '0' && ch <= '9'); }
```

can be rewritten using just one comparison:

```
bool isdigit(char ch) { return (unsigned)(ch - '0') < 10; }
```

If we work character by character, improving on the above approaches is usually impossible. However, it is sometimes possible to work on groups of characters and use vectorized checks. If the target system has some form of SIMD instructions available, you can usually use these instructions for fast operation on groups of 16 characters or more.

Even without resorting to platform-specific instruction sets it is sometimes possible to vectorize character operations. For example, here is one way to check if four consecutive bytes in a UTF-8 byte stream represent ASCII symbols[9]:

Finally, whatever you do, avoid is.*() functions from the standard library (such as isalpha()) for performance-sensitive code. Even the best implementations check whether the current locale is "C", which is more expensive than the table lookup itself, and the worst implementations can be two orders of magnitude slower than that.[10]

Optimizing string transformations

In pugixml, the reading and transformation of values is particularly time-consuming. For example, let's look at reading plain-character data (PCDATA); e.g., the text between the XML tags. Any standard conforming parser, as previously discussed, should perform reference expansion and end of line normalization during PCDATA content processing.[11]

For example, the following text in XML:

A < B.

should be transformed to

A < B.

The PCDATA parsing function takes a pointer to the start of PCDATA value, and proceeds by reading the rest of the value, converting the value data in-place and null-terminating the result.

Since there are two boolean flags, we have four variations of this function. In order to avoid expensive run-time checks, we're using boolean template arguments for these flags—thus we're compiling four variations of a function from a single template, and then using runtime dispatch to obtain the correct function pointer once before the parsing begins. The parser calls the function using this function pointer.

This allows the compiler to remove condition checks for flags and remove dead code for each specialization of the function. Importantly, inside the function's parsing loop we use a fast character set test to skip all characters that are part of the usual PCDATA content, and only process the characters we're interested in. Here's what the code looks like:

```
template <bool opt_eol, bool opt_escape> struct strconv_pcdata_impl {
  static char_t* parse(char_t* s) {
    gap g;
    while (true) {
      while (!PUGI__IS_CHARTYPE(*s, ct_parse_pcdata)) ++s;
      if (*s == '<') { // PCDATA ends here
        *g.flush(s) = 0;
```

---

[9]Of course, the data has to be suitably aligned for this to work; additionally, this technique violates strict aliasing rules of the C/C++ standard, which may or may not be a problem in practice.

$((const\ uint32\_t)data\ \&\ 0x80808080) == 0$

[10]See Chapter 12 for another example of this problem.

[11]Pugixml allows the user to turn either of these off at runtime for both performance and data preservation reasons. For example, you might be dealing with documents where it is important to preserve the exact type of newline sequences, or where entity references should be left unexpanded by the XML parser in order to be processed afterwards.

```
            return s + 1;
        } else if (opt_eol && *s == '\r') { // 0x0d or 0x0d 0x0a pair
          *s++ = '\n'; // replace first one with 0x0a
          if (*s == '\n') g.push(s, 1);
        } else if (opt_escape && *s == '&') {
          s = strconv_escape(s, g);
        } else if (*s == 0) {
          return s;
        } else {
          ++s;
        }
      }
    }
};
```

An additional function gets a pointer to a suitable implementation based on runtime flags; e.g., &strconv_pcdata_impl<false, true>::parse.

One unusual item in this code is the gap class instance. As shown before, if we do string transformations, the resulting string becomes shorter because some of the characters have to be removed. There are several ways of doing this.

One strategy (that pugixml *doesn't* use) is to keep separate read and write pointers that both point to the same buffer. In this case the read pointer tracks the current read position, and the write pointer tracks the current write position. At all times the invariant write <= read should hold. Any character that has to be a part of the resulting string must be explicitly written to the write pointer. This technique avoids the quadratic cost of naive character removal, but is still inefficient, since we now read and write all characters in the string every time, even if we don't need to modify the string.

An obvious extension of this idea is to skip the prefix of the original string that does not need to be modified and only start writing characters after that prefix—indeed, that's how algorithms like the one behind std::remove_if() commonly operate.

Pugixml follows a different approach (see Figure 4.4). At any time there is *at most one gap* in the string. The gap is a sequence of characters that are no longer valid because they are no longer part of the final string. When a new gap has to be added because another substitution was made (e.g., replacing " with " generates a gap of 5 characters), the existing gap (if one exists) is collapsed by moving the data between two gaps to the beginning of the first gap and then remembering the new gap. In terms of complexity, this approach is equivalent to the approach with read and write pointers; however it allows us to use faster routines to collapse gaps. (Pugixml uses memmove which can copy more efficiently compared to a character-wise loop, depending on the gap length and on C runtime implementation.)

Optimizing control flow

The pugixml parser itself can be thought of as a recursive-descent parser. However, the recursion is transformed into a loop to improve performance. A node cursor acts as a stack. When a start tag is encountered, a new node is appended to the cursor and becomes the new cursor; when an end tag is encountered, the cursor is moved to the parent of the current cursor. This makes stack space consumption constant regardless of the input document, which improves robustness, and avoids potentially expensive function calls.

The parser uses a dispatch loop that reads a character from the stream, reads zero or more characters past that (depending on the first character) to determine the tag type, and then proceeds

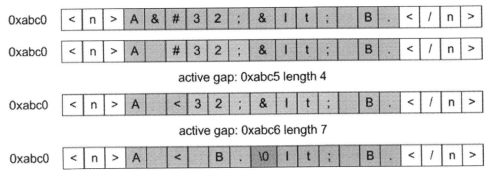

Figure 4.4: An example of gap operations during PCDATA conversion.

to the code that parses the relevant tag. For example, if the first character is <, we have to read at least one more character to differentiate between a start tag, end tag, comment, or other types of tags. Pugixml also uses `goto` statements to avoid going through the dispatch loop in certain cases — for example, text content parsing stops at the end of stream or the < character. However, if the next character is <, we don't have to go through the dispatch loop only to read the character again and check that it's <; we can jump straight to the code that does the tag parsing.

Two important optimizations for such code are branch ordering and code locality.

In the parser, various parts of the code handle various forms of inputs. Some of them (such as tag name or attribute parsing) execute frequently, while others (such as DOCTYPE parsing) rarely execute at all. Even within a small section of code, different inputs have different probabilities. For example, after the parser encounters an open angle bracket (<), the most likely character to appear next is a character of a tag name. Next most likely is /[12], followed by ! and ?.

With this in mind, it is possible to rearrange the code to yield faster execution. First, all "cold" code; that is, code that is unlikely to ever execute, or is unlikely to execute frequently—in the case of pugixml this includes all XML content except element tags with attributes and text content — has to be moved out of the parser loop into separate functions. Depending on the function's contents and the compiler, adding attributes such as `noinline`, or specifically marking extra functions as "cold" might help. The idea is to limit the amount of code inlined into the main parser function to the hot code. This helps the compiler optimize the function by keeping the control flow graphs small, and keeps all hot code as close together as possible to minimize instruction cache misses.

After this, in both hot and cold code it makes sense to order any conditional chains you have by condition probability. For example, code like this is not efficient for typical XML content:

```
if (data[0] == '<')
{
  if (data[1] == '!') { ... }
  else if (data[1] == '/') { ... }
  else if (data[1] == '?') { ... }
  else { /* start-tag or unrecognized tag */ }
}
```

A better version would look like this:

```
if (data[0] == '<')
```

---

[12] The reason / is less probable than a tag name character is that for every end tag there is a start tag, but there are also empty-element tags such as <node/>.

```
{
  if (PUGI__IS_CHARTYPE(data[1], ct_start_symbol)) { /* start-tag */ }
    else if (data[1] == '/') { ... }
    else if (data[1] == '!') { ... }
    else if (data[1] == '?') { ... }
    else { /* unrecognized tag */ }
}
```

In this version the branches are sorted by probability from most-frequent to least-frequent. This minimizes the average amount of condition tests and conditional jumps performed.

Ensuring memory safety

Memory safety is an important concern for a parser. On any input (including malformed input), the parser must never read or write memory beyond the end of the input buffer. There are two ways to implement this. The first option is to make sure the parser checks the current read position against the end position everywhere. The second option is to use a null-terminated string as an input and make sure the parser handles the null terminator accordingly. Pugixml uses an extended variant of the latter.

Additional read position checks incur a noticeable performance overhead, whereas the null terminator is often naturally included in existing checks. For example, the loop

```
while (PUGI__IS_CHARTYPE(*s, ct_alpha))
  ++s;
```

skips a run of alphabetical characters and stops at the null terminator or the next non-alphabetic character without requiring extra checks. Storing the buffer end position everywhere also reduces the overall speed because it usually requires an extra register. Function calls also get more expensive since you need to pass two pointers (current position and end position) instead of one.

However, requiring null-terminated input is less convenient for library users: often XML data gets read into a buffer that might not have space for an extra null terminator. From the client's point of view a memory buffer should be a pointer and a size with no null terminator.

Since the internal memory buffer has to be mutable for in-place parsing to work, pugixml solves this problem in a simple way. Before parsing, it replaces the last character in the buffer with a null terminator and keeps track of the value of the old character. That way, the only places it has to account for the value of the last character are places where it is valid for the document to end. For XML, there are not many[13], so the approach results in a net win.[14]

This summarizes the most interesting tricks and design decisions that help keep pugixml parser fast for a wide range of documents. However, there is one last performance-sensitive component of the parser that is worth discussing.

---

[13] For example, if a tag name scan stopped at the null terminator, then the document is invalid because there are no valid XML documents where the character before the last one is a part of tag name.

[14] Of course, the parsing code becomes more complicated, since some comparisons need to account for the value of the last character, and all others need to skip it for performance reasons. A unit test suite with good coverage and fuzz testing helps keep the parser correct for all document inputs.

4.5 Data structures for the document object model

An XML document is a tree-like structure. It contains one or more nodes; each node can contain one or more nodes; nodes can represent different types of XML data, such as elements or text; and element nodes can also contain one or more attributes.

Every representation of node data is usually a tradeoff between memory consumption and the performance of various operations. For example, *semantically* a node contains a collection of child nodes; this collection can be represented in the data structure. Specifically, this data can be stored as an array or as a linked list. An array representation would allow for fast index-based access; a linked list representation would allow for constant-time insertions or removals.[15]

Pugixml chooses to represent both node and attribute collections as a linked list. Why not as arrays? The two main benefits of arrays are fast index-based access (which is not particularly important for pugixml) and memory locality (which can be achieved through different means).

Fast index-based access is usually not needed because the code that processes the XML tree either needs to iterate through all child nodes or get a specific node that is identified by the value of an attribute (e.g. "get the child node with an 'id' attribute equal to 'X' ").[16] Index-based access is also fragile in a mutable XML document: for example, adding XML comments alters the indices of subsequent nodes in the same subtree.

Memory locality depends on the allocation algorithm. With the right algorithm, linked lists can be as efficient as arrays if list nodes are allocated sequentially. (More on this later.)

The basic tree data structure with children stored in an array (which is *not* what pugixml uses) usually looks like this:[17]

The basic tree data structure that uses linked lists (which is not *exactly* what pugixml uses) looks like this:

```
struct Node {
  Node* first_child;
  Node* last_child;
  Node* prev_sibling;
  Node* next_sibling;
};
```

Here, the `last_child` pointer is necessary to support backwards iteration and appending in O(1) time.

Note that with this design it is easy to support different node types to reduce memory consumption; for example, an element node needs an attribute list but a text node does not. The array approach forces us to keep the size of all node types the same, which prevents such optimization from being effective.

Pugixml uses a linked list-based approach. That way, node modification is always O(1). Furthermore, the array approach would force us to allocate blocks of varying sizes, ranging from tens of bytes to megabytes in case of a single node with a lot of children; whereas in the linked list approach

---

[15]Tree modification is important—while there are ways to represent immutable trees much more efficiently compared to what pugixml is doing, tree mutation is a much needed feature both for constructing documents from scratch and for modifying existing documents.

[16]More complex logic can be used as well.

[17]The capacity field is required to implement an amortized constant-time addition. See http://en.wikipedia.org/wiki/Dynamic_array for more information.

struct Node { Node* children; size_t children_size; size_t children_capacity; };

there are only a few different allocation sizes needed for node structure. Designing a fast allocator for fixed size allocations is usually easier than designing a fast allocator for arbitrary allocations which is another reason pugixml chooses this strategy.

To keep memory consumption closer to the array-based approach, pugixml omits the `last_child` pointer, but keeps access to the last child available in O(1) time by making the sibling list partially cyclic with `prev_sibling_cyclic`:

```
struct Node {
  Node* first_child;
  Node* prev_sibling_cyclic;
  Node* next_sibling;
};
```

This data structure is organized as follows:

1. `first_child` points to the first child of the node, or NULL if node has no children.
2. `prev_sibling_cyclic` points to the left sibling of the node (a child of node's parent that is immediately before the node in the document). If the node is the leftmost one (i.e., if the node is the first child of its parent), `prev_sibling_cyclic` points to the last child of the node's parent, or to itself if it is the only child. `prev_sibling_cyclic` cannot be NULL.
3. `next_sibling` points to the right sibling of the node or NULL if the node is the last child of its parent.

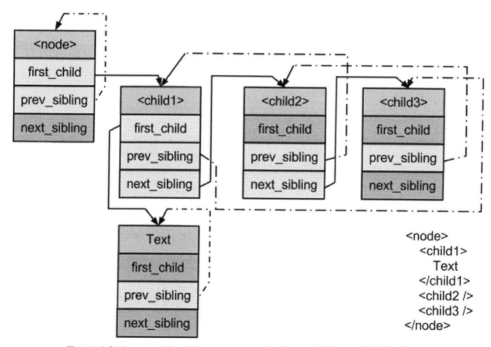

Figure 4.5: An example subtree, represented using partially-cyclic linked lists.

With this structure, all of the following operations are constant-time:

```
Node* last_child(Node* node) {
  return (node->first_child) ?
```

54 Parsing XML at the Speed of Light

```
        node->first_child->prev_sibling_cyclic : NULL;
}

Node* prev_sibling(Node* node) {
  return (node->prev_sibling_cyclic->next_sibling) ?
      node->prev_sibling_cyclic : NULL;
}
```

The array-based approach and the linked list approach with the partially-cyclic-sibling-list trick become equivalent in terms of memory consumption. Using 32-bit types for size/capacity makes the array-based node smaller on 64-bit systems.[18] In the case of pugixml, other benefits of linked lists outweigh the costs.

With the data structures in place, it is time to talk about the last piece of the puzzle—the memory allocation algorithm.

4.6 Stack-based memory allocation

A fast memory allocator is critical for the performance of a DOM parser. In-place parsing eliminates allocation for string data, but DOM nodes still need to be allocated. String allocations of varying sizes are also needed to support tree mutation. Preserving allocation locality is important for tree traversal performance: if successive allocation requests return adjacent memory blocks, it becomes easy to ensure tree locality during construction. Finally, destruction speed is important: in addition to deletion in constant time, the ability to quickly deallocate all memory allocated for the document without deleting each node individually can significantly improve the time it takes to destroy large documents.

Before discussing the allocation scheme that pugixml uses, let's discuss a scheme that it *could* have used.

Since DOM nodes have a small set of required allocation sizes, it would be possible to use a standard memory pool based on free lists for each size. For such a pool, there would be a single linked list of free blocks where each block is the same size. During an allocation request, if the free list is empty, a new page with an array of blocks is allocated. The blocks are linked together to form a single linked list, which then becomes the free list of the allocator. If a free list is not empty, the first block is removed from the list and returned to the user. A deallocation request simply prepends the block to the free list.

This allocation scheme is very good at reusing memory—allocating a node after freeing some other node would reuse the memory immediately. However, adding support for releasing memory pages back to the heap requires additional per-page tracking of used blocks. The locality of the allocations also varies on the prior usage of the allocator, which may end up decreasing traversal performance.

Since pugixml supports tree mutation, it requires support for allocations of arbitrary size. It was unclear whether this allocator could be easily extended to support arbitrarily sized allocations and other required features of pugixml without impacting the parsing performance. Employing a complicated general-purpose allocation scheme akin to the algorithms implemented in dlmalloc and other general-purpose memory allocators was also not an option—such allocators tend to be somewhat slower than simple free lists, not to mention more complex. Pugixml needed something simple and fast.

---

[18]This assumes a limit of 2^{32} child nodes.

It turns out that the simplest allocation scheme possible is the stack allocator. This allocator works as follows: given a memory buffer and an offset inside that buffer, an allocation only requires increasing that offset by the allocation size. Of course, it is impossible to predict the memory buffer size in advance, so an allocator has to be able to allocate new buffers on demand.

This code illustrates the general idea:

```
const size_t allocator_page_size = 32768;
struct allocator_page {
  allocator_page* next_page;
  size_t offset;
  char data[allocator_page_size];
};
struct allocator_state {
  allocator_page* current;
};

void* allocate_new_page_data(size_t size) {
  size_t extra_size = (size > allocator_page_size) ?
    size - allocator_page_size : 0;
  return malloc(sizeof(allocator_page) + extra_size);
}

void* allocate_oob(allocator_state* state, size_t size) {
  allocator_page* page = (allocator_page*)allocate_new_page_data(size);
  // add page to page list
  page->next_page = state->current;
  state->current = page;
  // user data is located at the beginning of the page
  page->offset = size;
  return page->data;
}

void* allocate(allocator_state* state, size_t size) {
  if (state->current->offset + size <= allocator_page_size) {
    void* result = state->current->data + state->current->offset;
    state->current->offset += size;
    return result;
  }
  return allocate_oob(state, size);
}
```

Supporting allocations that are larger than page size is easy. We just allocate a larger memory block, but treat it in the same way as we would treat a small page.[19]

This allocator is very fast. It's probably the fastest allocator possible, given the constraints. Benchmarks show it to be faster than a free list allocator, which has to do more work to determine the correct list based on page size and has to link all blocks in a page together. Our allocator also exhibits almost perfect memory locality. The only case where successive allocations are not adjacent is when it allocates a new page.

---

[19]For performance reasons this implementation does not adjust the offset to be aligned. Instead it expects that all stored types need pointer type alignment, and that all allocation requests specify size aligned to a pointer size.

In case of small allocations this allocator does not waste memory. However, it is possible to devise a hypothetical memory allocation pattern (that might arise in practice) where it does waste memory. A sequence of allocation sizes alternating between 64 and 65536 would cause a new page allocation on every call, resulting in 30% wasted space. For this reason, the implementation of this allocator in pugixml behaves slightly differently: if an allocation is larger than a quarter of the default page size, it allocates an entire page for it, and instead of adding it to the front of the page list, it adds it after the first entry. That way, the small allocations that happen after a large one still go into the page in progress.

Note that `allocate_oob()` is "cold" code—that is, it only gets executed once we exhaust the current page, which should be a rare event. For this reason, explicitly forbidding the compiler to inline it can improve performance.[20] This also means that having more complicated logic in `allocate_oob()`—for example, logic that treats large allocations differently—does not have any effect on the overall performance of the allocator.

Finally, since all allocations are contained in some page and the allocator keeps the entire page list as a state, it's very easy to destroy the entire page list and thereby free all allocated memory. This is very fast since it only touches headers of each page in memory.

4.7 Supporting deallocation in a stack-based allocator

The implementation discussed in the previous section does not have any way to release or reuse memory.

Interestingly, for a lot of use cases this is actually not a big deal. Since we can release the memory on document destruction by removing all pages[21], parsing a document or creating a new document does not consume extra memory. However, a problem arises when we delete a substantial portion of the document and then proceed to add more nodes to the document. Since we never reuse memory, peak memory consumption can become very significant.

Implementing fine-grained reuse while preserving the allocation performance seems impossible. However, a compromise can be reached. During allocation, we'll count the number of allocations made in each respective page. Deallocation requests then have to get a reference to the page of the destroyed pointer and decrease this counter. If this counter reaches zero, the page is not needed any more and can be removed.

For this to be possible, we need to know what page each object was allocated in. This is possible without storing a pointer to the page, but it is difficult.[22] For this reason, pugixml resorts to storing a page pointer alongside each allocation.

Pugixml uses two different approaches to reducing the memory overhead associated with storing a page pointer with each allocation.

The first approach is to store a page pointer in a single pointer-sized field with several bits of unrelated data which we would have to store anyway. The allocator makes sure that all pages are aligned to 32 bytes, so this means that the five least significant bits of every page pointer are zero; as such they can be used to store arbitrary data. Five bits is a good number because the metadata of

---

[20]This improvement is measurable in pugixml.

[21]This, of course, means that nodes or attributes cannot exist without the document—which, in C++, is a reasonable design decision for node ownership.

[22]It is possible to do this without storing extra data using a page alignment that is larger than the page size (i.e., allocate all pages using a 64k allocations with 64k alignment), but it is not possible to use large allocation alignments in a portable way without huge memory overhead.

an XML node fits: three bits are used for a node type, and two bits are used to specify whether the node's name and value reside in the in-place buffer.

The second approach is to store the offset of the allocated element relative to the beginning of the page, which allows us to get the address of the page pointer in the following way:

```
(allocator_page*)((char*)(object) -
    object->offset - offsetof(allocator_page, data))
```

If our page size is limited by $2^{16} = 65536$ bytes, this offset fits in 16 bits, so we can spend 2 bytes instead of 4 storing it. Pugixml uses this approach for heap-allocated strings.

An interesting feature of the resulting algorithm is that it respects the locality of reference exhibited by the code that uses the allocator. Locality of allocation requests eventually leads to locality of allocated data in space. Locality of *deallocation* requests in space leads to successfully released memory. This means, in the case of tree storage, that deletion of a large subtree usually releases most of the memory that is used by the subtree.

Of course, for certain usage patterns nothing is ever deleted until the entire document is destroyed. For example, if a page size is 32000 bytes, we can do one million 32-byte allocations, thus allocating 1000 pages. If we keep every 1000th object alive and delete the remaining objects, each page will have exactly one object left, which means that, although the cumulative size of live objects is now $1000 \cdot 32 = 32000$ bytes, we still keep all pages in memory (consuming 32 million bytes). This results in an extremely high memory overhead. However, such usage is extremely unlikely, and the benefits of the algorithm outweigh this problem for pugixml.

4.8 Conclusion

Optimizing software is hard. In order to be successful, optimization efforts almost always involve a combination of low-level micro-optimizations, high-level performance-oriented design decisions, careful algorithm selection and tuning, balancing among memory, performance, implementation complexity, and more. Pugixml is an example of a library that needs all of these approaches to deliver a very fast production-ready XML parser—even though compromises had to be made to achieve this. A lot of the implementation details can be adapted to different projects and tasks, be it another parsing library or something else entirely. The author hopes that the presented tricks were entertaining and that some of them will be useful for other projects.

[chapter 5]

MemShrink
Kyle Huey

5.1 Introduction

Firefox has long had a reputation for using too much memory. The accuracy of that reputation has varied over the years but it has stuck with the browser. Every Firefox release in the past several years has been met by skeptical users with the question "Did they fix the memory leak yet?" We shipped Firefox 4 in March 2011 after a lengthy beta cycle and several missed ship dates—and it was met by the same questions. While Firefox 4 was a significant step forward for the web in areas such as open video, JavaScript performance, and accelerated graphics, it was unfortunately a significant step backwards in memory usage.

The web browser space has become very competitive in recent years. With the rise of mobile devices, the release of Google Chrome, and Microsoft reinvesting in the web, Firefox has found itself having to contend with a number of excellent and well-funded competitors instead of just a moribund Internet Explorer. Google Chrome in particular has gone to great lengths to provide a fast and slim browsing experience. We began to learn the hard way that being a good browser was no longer good enough; we needed to be an excellent browser. As Mike Shaver, at the time VP of Engineering at Mozilla and a longtime Mozilla contributor, said, "this is the world we wanted, and this is the world we made."

That is where we found ourselves in early 2011. Firefox's market share was flat or declining while Google Chrome was enjoying a fast rise to prominence. Although we had begun to close the gap on performance, we were still at a significant competitive disadvantage on memory consumption as Firefox 4 invested in faster JavaScript and accelerated graphics often at the cost of increased memory consumption. After Firefox 4 shipped, a group of engineers led by Nicholas Nethercote started the MemShrink project to get memory consumption under control. Today, nearly a year and a half later, that concerted effort has radically altered Firefox's memory consumption and reputation. The "memory leak" is a thing of the past in most users' minds, and Firefox often comes in as one of the slimmest browsers in comparisons. In this chapter we will explore the efforts we made to improve Firefox's memory usage and the lessons we learned along the way.

5.2 Architecture Overview

You will need a basic grasp of what Firefox does and how it works to make sense of the problems we encountered and the solutions we found.

A modern web browser is fundamentally a virtual machine for running untrusted code. This code is some combination of HTML, CSS, and JavaScript (JS) provided by third parties. There is also code from Firefox add-ons and plugins. The virtual machine provides capabilities for computation, layout and styling of text, images, network access, offline storage, and even access to hardware-accelerated graphics. Some of these capabilities are provided through APIs designed for the task at hand; many others are available through APIs that have been repurposed for entirely new uses. Because of the way the web has evolved, web browsers must be very liberal in what they accept, and what browsers were designed to handle 15 years ago may no longer be relevant to providing a high-performance experience today.

Firefox is powered by the Gecko layout engine and the Spidermonkey JS engine. Both are primarily developed for Firefox, but are separate and independently reusable pieces of code. Like all widely used layout and JS engines, both are written in C++. Spidermonkey implements the JS virtual machine including garbage collection and multiple flavors of just-in-time compilation (JIT). Gecko implements most APIs visible to a web page including the DOM, graphical rendering via software or hardware pipelines, page and text layout, a full networking stack, and much more. Together they provide the platform that Firefox is built on. The Firefox user interface, including the address bar and navigation buttons, is just a series of special web pages that run with enhanced privileges. These privileges allow them access to all sorts of features that normal web pages cannot see. We call these special, built-in, privileged pages *chrome* (no relation to Google Chrome) as opposed to *content*, or normal web pages.

For our purposes, the most interesting details about Spidermonkey and Gecko are how they manage memory. We can categorize memory in the browser based on two characteristics: how it is allocated and how it is freed. Dynamically allocated memory (the *heap*) is obtained in large chunks from the operating system and divided into requested quantities by the heap allocator. There are two main heap allocators: the specialized garbage-collected heap allocator used for the garbage-collected memory (the *GC heap*) in Spidermonkey, and jemalloc, which is used by everything else in Spidermonkey and Gecko. There are also three methods of freeing memory: manually, via reference counting, and via garbage collection.

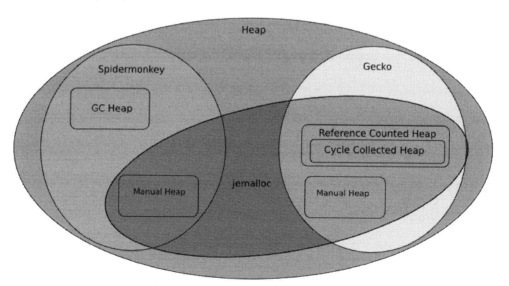

Figure 5.1: Memory management in Firefox

The GC heap in Spidermonkey contains objects, functions, and most of the other things created by running JS. We also store implementation details whose lifetimes are linked to these objects in the GC heap. This heap uses a fairly standard incremental mark-and-sweep collector that has been heavily optimized for performance and responsiveness. This means that every now and then the garbage collector wakes up and looks at all the memory in the GC heap. Starting from a set of "roots" (such as the global object of the page you are viewing) it "marks" all the objects in the heap that are reachable. It then "sweeps" all the objects that are not marked and reuses that memory when needed.

In Gecko most memory is reference counted. With reference counting the number of references to a given piece of memory is tracked. When that number reaches zero the memory is freed. While reference counting is technically a form of garbage collection, for this discussion we distinguish it from garbage collection schemes that require specialized code (i.e., a *garbage collector*) to periodically reclaim memory. Simple reference counting is unable to deal with cycles, where one piece of memory A references another piece of memory B, and vice versa. In this situation both A and B have reference counts of 1, and are never freed. Gecko has a specialized tracing garbage collector specifically to collect these cycles which we call the *cycle collector*. The cycle collector manages only certain classes that are known to participate in cycles and opt in to cycle collection, so we can think of the cycle collected heap as a subset of the reference counted heap. The cycle collector also works with the garbage collector in Spidermonkey to handle cross-language memory management so that C++ code can hold references to JS objects and vice versa.

There is also plenty of manually managed memory in both Spidermonkey and Gecko. This encompasses everything from the internal memory of arrays and hashtables to buffers of image and script source data. There are also other specialized allocators layered on top of manually managed memory. One example is an arena allocator. Arenas are used when a large number of separate allocations can all be freed simultaneously. An arena allocator obtains chunks of memory from the main heap allocator and subdivides them as requested. When the arena is no longer needed the arena returns those chunks to the main heap without having to individually free the many smaller allocations. Gecko uses an arena allocator for page layout data, which can be thrown away all at once when a page is no longer needed. Arena allocation also allows us to implement security features such as *poisoning*, where we overwrite the deallocated memory so it cannot be used in a security exploit.

There are several other custom memory management systems in small parts of Firefox, used for a variety of different reasons, but they are not relevant to our discussion. Now that you have a brief overview of Firefox's memory architecture, we can discuss the problems we found and how to fix them.

5.3 You Make What You Measure

The first step of fixing a problem is figuring out what the problem is. The strict definition of a memory leak, allocating memory from the operating system (OS) and not releasing it back to the OS, does not cover all the situations we are interested in improving. Some situations that we encounter that are not "leaks" in the strict sense:

- A data structure requires twice as much memory as it needs to.
- Memory that is no longer used is not released until a timer expires.
- Many copies of the same large buffer (strings, image data, etc.) exist throughout the program.

This is all complicated even further by the fact that most of the memory in Firefox's heap is subject to some form of garbage collection and so memory that is no longer used will not be released until the next time the GC runs. We have taken to using the term "leak" very loosely to encompass any situation that results in Firefox being less memory-efficient than it could reasonably be. This is consistent with the way our users employ the term as well: most users and even web developers cannot tell if high memory usage is due to a true leak or any number of other factors at work in the browser.

When MemShrink began we did not have much insight into the browser's memory usage. Identifying the nature of memory problems often required using complex tools like Massif or lower-level tools like GDB. These tools have several disadvantages:

- They are designed for developers and are not easy to use.
- They are not aware of Firefox internals (such as the implementation details of the various heaps).
- They are not "always on"—you have to be using them when the problem happens.

In exchange for these disadvantages you get some very powerful tools. To address these disadvantages over time we built a suite of custom tools to gain more insight with less work into the behavior of the browser.

The first of these tools is about:memory. First introduced in Firefox 3.6, it originally displayed simple statistics about the heap, such as the amount of memory mapped, and committed. Later measurements for some things of interest to particular developers were added, such as the memory used by the embedded SQLite database engine and the amount of memory used by the accelerated graphics subsystem. We call these measurements *memory reporters*. Other than these one-off additions about:memory remained a primitive tool presenting a few summary statistics on memory usage. Most memory did not have a memory reporter and was not specifically accounted for in about:memory. Even so, about:memory can be used by anyone without a special tool or build of Firefox just by typing it into the browser's address bar. This would become the "killer feature".

Well before MemShrink was a gleam in anyone's eye the JavaScript engine in Firefox was refactored to split the monolithic global GC heap into a collection of smaller subheaps called compartments. These compartments separate things like chrome and content (privileged and unprivileged code, respectively) memory, as well as the memory of different web sites. The primary motivation for this change was security, but it turned out to be very useful for MemShrink. Shortly after this was implemented we prototyped a tool called about:compartments that displayed all of the compartments, how much memory they use, and how they use that memory. about:compartments was never integrated directly into Firefox, but after MemShrink started it was modified and combined into about:memory.

While adding this compartment reporting to about:memory, we realized that incorporating similar reporting for other allocations would enable useful heap profiling without specialized tools like Massif. about:memory was changed so that instead of producing a series of summary statistics it displayed a tree breaking down memory usage into a large number of different uses. We then started to add reporters for other types of large heap allocations such as the layout subsystem. One of our earliest metric-driven efforts was driving down the amount of *heap-unclassified*, memory that was not covered by a memory reporter. We picked a pretty arbitrary number, 10% of the total heap, and set out to get heap-unclassified down to that amount in average usage scenarios. Ultimately it would turn out that 10% was too low a number to reach. There are simply too many small one-off allocations in the browser to get heap-unclassified reliably below approximately 15%. Reducing the amount of heap-unclassified increases the insight into how memory is being used by the browser.

To reduce the amount of heap-unclassified we wrote a tool, christened the Dark Matter Detector (DMD), that helped track down the unreported heap allocations. It works by replacing the heap allocator and inserting itself into the about:memory reporting process and matching reported memory blocks to allocated blocks. It then summarizes the unreported memory allocations by call site.

Running DMD on a Firefox session produces lists of call sites responsible for heap-unclassified. Once the source of the allocations was identified, finding the responsible component and a developer to add a memory reporter for it proceeded quickly. Within a few months we had a tool that could tell you things like "all the Facebook pages in your browser are using 250 MB of memory, and here is the breakdown of how that memory is being used."

We also developed another tool (called *Measure and Save*) for debugging memory problems once they were identified. This tool dumps representations of both the JS heap and the cycle-collected C++ heap to a file. We then wrote a series of analysis scripts that can traverse the combined heap and answer questions like "what is keeping this object alive?" This enabled a lot of useful debugging techniques, from just examining the heap graph for links that should have been broken to dropping into a debugger and setting breakpoints on specific objects of interest.

A major benefit of these tools is that, unlike with a tool such as Massif, you can wait until the problem appears before using the tool. Many heap profilers (including Massif) must be started when the program starts, not partway through after a problem appears. Another benefit that these tools have is that the information can be analyzed and used without having the problem reproduced in front of you. Together they allow users to capture information for the problem they are seeing and send it to developers when those developers cannot reproduce the problem. Expecting users of a web browser, even those sophisticated enough to file bugs in a bug tracker, to use GDB or Massif on the browser is usually asking too much. But loading about:memory or running a small snippet of JavaScript to get data to attach to a bug report is a much less arduous task. Generic heap profilers capture a lot of information, but come with a lot of costs. We were able to write a set of tools tailored to our specific needs that offered us significant benefits over the generic tools.

It is not always worth investing in custom tooling; there is a reason we use GDB instead of writing a new debugger for each piece of software we build. But for those situations where the existing tools cannot deliver you the information you need in the way you want it, we found that custom tooling can be a big win. It took us about a year of part-time work on about:memory to get to a point where we considered it complete. Even today we are still adding new features and reporters when necessary. Custom tools are a significant investment. An extensive digression on the subject is beyond the scope of this chapter, but you should consider carefully the benefits and costs of custom tools before writing them.

5.4 Low-Hanging Fruit

The tools that we built provided us significantly more visibility into memory usage in the browser than we had previously. After using them for a while we began to get a feel for what was normal and what was not. Spotting things that were not normal and were possibly bugs became very easy. Large amounts of heap-unclassified pointed to usage of more arcane web features that we had not yet added memory reporters for or leaks in Gecko's internals. High memory usage in strange places in the JS engine could indicate that the code was hitting some unoptimized or pathological case. We were able to use this information to track down and fix the worst bugs in Firefox.

One anomaly we noticed early on was that sometimes a compartment would stick around for a page that had already been closed, even after forcing the garbage collector to run repeatedly. Sometimes these compartments would eventually go away on their own and sometimes they would last indefinitely. We named these leaks *zombie compartments*. These were some of our most serious leaks, because the amount of memory a web page can use is unbounded. We fixed a number of these bugs in both Gecko and the Firefox UI code, but it soon became apparent that the largest source of zombie compartments was add-ons. Dealing with leaks in add-ons stymied us for several months before we found a solution that is discussed later in this chapter. Most of these zombie compartments, both in Firefox and in add-ons, were caused by long-lived JS objects maintaining references to short-lived JS objects. The long-lived JS objects are typically objects attached to the browser window, or even global singletons, while the short-lived JS objects might be objects from web pages.

Because of the way the DOM and JS work, a reference to a single object from a web page will keep the entire page and its global object (and anything reachable from that) alive. This can easily add up to many megabytes of memory. One of the subtler aspects of a garbage collected system is that the GC only reclaims memory when it is unreachable, not when the program is done using it. It is up to the programmer to ensure that memory that will not be used again is unreachable. Failing to remove all references to an object has even more severe consequences when the lifetime of the referrer and the referent are expected to differ significantly. Memory that should be reclaimed relatively quickly (such as the memory used for a web page) is instead tied to the lifetime of the longer lived referrer (such as the browser window or the application itself).

Fragmentation in the JS heap was also a problem for us for a similar reason. We often saw that closing a lot of web pages did not cause Firefox's memory usage, as reported by the operating system, to decline significantly. The JS engine allocates memory from the operating system in megabyte-sized chunks and subdivides that chunk amongst different compartments as needed. These chunks can only be released back to the operating system when they are completely unused. We found that allocation of new chunks was almost always caused by web content demanding more memory, but that the last thing keeping a chunk from being released was often a chrome compartment. Mixing a few long-lived objects into a chunk full of short-lived objects prevented us from reclaiming that chunk when web pages were closed. We solved this by segregating chrome and content compartments so that any given chunk has either chrome or content allocations. This significantly increased the amount of memory we could return to the operating system when tabs are closed.

We discovered another problem caused in part by a technique to reduce fragmentation. Firefox's primary heap allocator is a version of jemalloc modified to work on Windows and Mac OS X. Jemalloc is designed to reduce memory loss due to fragmentation. One of the techniques it uses to do this is rounding allocations up to various size classes, and then allocating those size classes in contiguous chunks of memory. This ensures that when space is freed it can later be reused for a similar size allocation. It also entails wasting some space for the rounding. We call this wasted space *slop*. The worst case for certain size classes can involve wasting almost 50% of the space allocated. Because of the way jemalloc size classes are structured, this usually happens just after passing a power of two (e.g., 17 rounds up to 32 and 1025 rounds up to 2048).

Often when allocating memory you do not have much choice in the amount you ask for. Adding extra bytes to an allocation for a new instance of a class is rarely useful. Other times you have some flexibility. If you are allocating space for a string you can use extra space to avoid having to reallocate the buffer if later the string is appended to. When this flexibility presents itself, it makes sense to ask for an amount that exactly matches a size class. That way memory that would have been "wasted" as slop is available for use at no extra cost. Usually code is written to ask for powers of two because those fit nicely into pretty much every allocator ever written and do not require special knowledge of the allocator.

We found lots of code in Gecko that was written to take advantage of this technique, and several places that tried to and got it wrong. Multiple pieces of code attempted to allocate a nice round chunk of memory, but got the math slightly wrong, and ended up allocating just beyond what they intended. Because of the way jemalloc's size classes are constructed, this often led to wasting nearly

50% of the allocated space as slop. One particularly egregious example was in an arena allocator implementation used for layout data structures. The arena attempted to get 4 KB chunks from the heap. It also tacked on a few words for bookkeeping purposes which resulted in it asking for slightly over 4 KB, which got rounded to 8 KB. Fixing that mistake saved over 3 MB of slop on GMail alone. On a particularly layout-heavy test case it saved over 700 MB of slop, reducing the browser's total memory consumption from 2 GB to 1.3 GB.

We encountered a similar problem with SQLite. Gecko uses SQLite as the database engine for features such as history and bookmarks. SQLite is written to give the embedding application a lot of control over memory allocation, and is very meticulous about measuring its own memory usage. To keep those measurements it adds a couple words which pushes the allocation over into the next size class. Ironically the instrumentation needed to keep track of memory consumption ends up doubling consumption while causing significant underreporting. We refer to these sorts of bugs as "clownshoes" because they are both comically bad and result in lots of wasted empty space, just like a clown's shoes.

5.5 Not Your Fault Does Not Mean Not Your Problem

Over the course of several months we made great strides in improving memory consumption and fixing leaks in Firefox. Not all of our users were seeing the benefits of that work though. It became clear that a significant number of the memory problems our users were seeing were originating in add-ons. Our tracking bug for leaky add-ons eventually counted over 100 confirmed reports of add-ons that caused leaks.

Historically Mozilla has tried to have it both ways with add-ons. We have marketed Firefox as an extensible browser with a rich selection of add-ons. But when users report performance problems with those add-ons we simply tell users not to use them. The sheer number of add-ons that caused memory leaks made this situation untenable. Many Firefox add-ons are distributed through Mozilla's addons.mozilla.org (AMO). AMO has review policies intended to catch common problems in add-ons. We began to get an idea of the scope of the problem when AMO reviewers started testing add-ons for memory leaks with tools like about:memory. A number of tested add-ons proved to have problems such as zombie compartments. We began reaching out to add-on authors, and we put together a list of best practices and common mistakes that caused leaks. Unfortunately this had rather limited success. While some add-ons did get fixed by their authors, most did not.

There were a number of reasons why this proved ineffective. Not all add-ons are regularly updated. Add-on authors are volunteers with their own schedules and priorities. Debugging memory leaks can be hard, especially if you cannot reproduce the problem in the first place. The heap dumping tool we described earlier is very powerful and makes gathering information easy but analyzing the output is still complicated and too much to expect add-on authors to do. Finally, there were no strong incentives to fix leaks. Nobody wants to ship bad software, but you can't always fix everything. People may also be more interested in doing what *they* want to do than what *we* want them to do.

For a long time we talked about creating incentives for fixing leaks. Add-ons have caused other performance problems for Mozilla too, so we have discussed making add-on performance data visible in AMO or in Firefox itself. The theory was that being able to inform users of the performance effects the add-ons they have installed or are about to install would help them make informed decisions about the add-ons they use. The first problem with this is that users of consumer-facing software like web browsers are usually not capable of making informed decisions about those tradeoffs. How many of Firefox's 400 million users understand what a memory leak is and can evaluate whether it is worth suffering through it to be able to use some random add-on? Second, dealing with performance impacts of add-ons this way required buy-in from a lot of different parts of the Mozilla community. The people who make up the add-on community, for example, were not thrilled about the idea of smacking add-ons with a banhammer. Finally, a large percentage of Firefox add-ons are not installed through AMO at all, but are bundled with other software. We have very little leverage over those add-ons short of trying to block them. For these reasons we abandoned our attempts to create those incentives.

The other reason we abandoned creating incentives for add-ons to fix leaks is that we found a completely different way to solve the problem. We ultimately managed to find a way to "clean up" after leaky add-ons in Firefox. For a long time we did not think that this was feasible without breaking lots of add-ons, but we kept experimenting with it anyways. Eventually we were able to implement a technique that reclaimed memory without adversely affecting most add-ons. We leveraged the boundaries between compartments to "cut" references from chrome compartments to content compartments when a the page is navigated or the tab is closed. This leaves an object floating around in the chrome compartment that no longer references anything. We originally thought that this would be a problem when code tried to use these objects, but we found that most times these objects are not used later. In effect add-ons were accidentally and pointlessly caching things from webpages, and cleaning up after them automatically had little downside. We had been looking for a social solution to a technical problem.

5.6 Eternal Persistence is the Price of Excellence

The MemShrink project has made considerable progress on Firefox's memory issues, but much work still remains to be done. Most of the easy problems have been fixed by this point—what remains requires a substantial quantity of engineering effort. We have plans to continue to reduce our JS heap fragmentation with a moving garbage collector that can consolidate the heap. We are reworking the way we handle images to be more memory efficient. Unlike many of the completed changes, these require extensive refactoring of complex subsystems.

Equally important is that we do not regress the improvements we have already made. Mozilla has had a strong culture of regression testing since 2006. As we made progress on slimming down Firefox's memory usage, our desire for a regression testing system for memory usage increased. Testing performance is harder than testing features. The hardest part of building this system was coming up with a realistic workload for the browser. Existing memory tests for browsers fail pretty spectacularly on realism. MemBuster, for instance, loads a number of wikis and blogs into a new browser window every time in rapid succession. Most users use tabs these days instead of new windows, and browse things more complex than wikis and blogs. Other benchmarks load all the pages into the same tab which is also completely unrealistic for a modern web browser. We devised a workload that we believe is reasonably realistic. It loads 100 pages into a fixed set of 30 tabs with delays between loads to approximate a user reading the page. The pages used are those from Mozilla's existing *Tp5* pageset. Tp5 is a set of pages from the Alexa Top 100 that are used to test pageload performance in our existing performance testing infrastructure. This workload has proven to be useful for our testing purposes.

The other aspect of testing is figuring out what to measure. Our testing system measures memory consumption at three different points during the test run: before loading any pages, after loading all the pages, and after closing all tabs. At each point we also take measurements after 30 seconds of no activity and after forcing the garbage collector to run. These measurements help to see if any of the problems we have encountered in the past recur. For example, a significant difference between the +30 second measurement and the measurement after forcing garbage collection may indicate that our garbage collection heuristics are too conservative. A significant difference between the measurement taken before loading anything and the measurement taken after closing all tabs may indicate that we are leaking memory. We measure a number of quantities at all of these points including the resident set size, the "explicit" size (the amount of memory that has been asked for via `malloc()`, `mmap()`, etc.), and the amount of memory that falls into certain categories in `about:memory` such as heap-unclassified.

Once we put this system together we set it up to run regularly on the latest development versions of Firefox. We also ran it on previous versions of Firefox back to roughly Firefox 4. The result is pseudo-continuous integration with a rich set of historical data. With some nice webdev work we ended up with `areweslimyet.com`, a public web based interface to all of the data gathered by our memory testing infrastructure. Since it was finished `areweslimyet.com` has detected several regressions caused by work on different parts of the browser.

5.7 Community

A final contributing factor to the success of the MemShrink effort has been the support of the broader Mozilla community. While most (but certainly not all) of the engineers working on Firefox are employed by Mozilla these days, Mozilla's vibrant volunteer community contributes support in the forms of testing, localization, QA, marketing, and more, without which the Mozilla project would grind to a halt. We intentionally structured MemShrink to receive community support and that has paid off considerably. The core MemShrink team consisted of a handful of paid engineers, but the support from the community that we received through bug reporting, testing, and add-on fixing has magnified our efforts.

Even within the Mozilla community, memory usage has long been a source of frustration. Some have experienced the problems first hand. Others have friends or family who have seen the problems. Those lucky enough to have avoided that have undoubtedly seen complaints about Firefox's memory usage or comments asking "is the leak fixed yet?" on new releases that they worked hard on. Nobody enjoys having their hard work criticized, especially when it is for things that you do not work on. Addressing a long-standing problem that most community members can relate to was an excellent first step towards building support.

Saying we were going to fix things was not enough though. We had to show that we were serious about getting things done and we could make real progress on the problems. We held public weekly meetings to triage bug reports and discuss the projects we were working on. Nicholas also blogged a progress report for each meeting so that people who were not there could see what we were doing. Highlighting the improvements that were being made, the changes in bug counts, and the new bugs being filed clearly showed the effort we were putting into MemShrink. And the early improvements we were able to get from the low-hanging fruit went a long way to showing that we could tackle these problems.

The final piece was closing the feedback loop between the wider community and the developers working on MemShrink. The tools that we discussed earlier turned bugs that would have been closed as unreproducible and forgotten into reports that could be and were fixed. We also turned complaints, comments, and responses on our progress report blog posts into bug reports and tried to gather the necessary information to fix them. All bug reports were triaged and given a priority. We also put forth an effort to investigate all bug reports, even those that were determined to be unimportant to fix.

That investigation made the reporter's effort feel more valued, and also aimed to leave the bug in a state where someone with more time could come along and fix it later. Together these actions built a strong base of support in the community that provided us with great bug reports and invaluable testing help.

5.8 Conclusions

Over the two years that the MemShrink project has been active we have made great improvements in Firefox's memory usage. The MemShrink team has turned memory usage from one of the most common user complaints to a selling point for the browser and significantly improved the user experience for many Firefox users.

I would like to thank Justin Lebar, Andrew McCreight, John Schoenick, Johnny Stenback, Jet Villegas, Timothy Nikkel for all of their work on MemShrink and the other engineers who have helped fix memory problems. Most of all I thank Nicholas Nethercote for getting MemShrink off the ground, working extensively on reducing Spidermonkey's memory usage, running the project for two years, and far too many other things to list. I would also like to thank Jet and Andrew for reviewing this chapter.

[chapter 6]

Applying Optimization Principle Patterns to Component Deployment and Configuration Tools

Doug C. Schmidt, William R. Otte, and Aniruddha Gokhale

6.1 Introduction

Distributed, real-time and embedded (DRE) systems are an important class of applications that share properties of both enterprise distributed systems and resource-constrained real-time and embedded systems. In particular, applications in DRE systems are similar to enterprise applications, i.e., they are distributed across a large domain. Moreover, like real-time and embedded systems, applications in DRE systems are often mission-critical and carry stringent safety, reliability, and *quality of service* (QoS) requirements.

In addition to the complexities described above, deployment of application and infrastructure components in DRE systems incurs its own set of unique challenges. First, applications in DRE system domains may have particular dependencies on the target environment, such as particular hardware/software (e.g., GPS, sensors, actuators, particular real-time operating systems, etc.). Second, the deployment infrastructure of a DRE system must contend with strict resource requirements in environments with finite resources (e.g., CPU, memory, network bandwidth, etc.).

Component-Based Software Engineering (CBSE) [HC01] is increasingly used as a paradigm for developing applications in both enterprise [ATK05] and DRE systems [SHS+06]. CBSE facilitates systematic software reuse by encouraging developers to create black box components that interact with each other and their environment through well-defined interfaces. CBSE also simplifies the deployment of highly complex distributed systems [WDS+11] by providing standardized mechanisms to control the configuration and lifecycle of applications. These mechanisms enable the composition of large-scale, complex applications from smaller, more manageable units of functionality, e.g., commercial off-the-shelf components and preexisting application building-blocks. These applications can be packaged along with descriptive and configuration metadata, and made available for deployment into a production environment.

Building on expertise gleaned from the development of *The ACE ORB* (TAO) [SNG+02]—an open-source implementation of the *Common Object Request Broker Architecture* (CORBA) standard—we have been applying CBSE principles to DRE systems over the past decade. As a result of these efforts, we have developed a high-quality open-source implementation of the OMG *CORBA Component Model* (CCM), which we call the *Component Integrated ACE ORB* (CIAO) [Insty].

CIAO implements the so-called *Lightweight CCM* [OMG04] specification, which is a subset of the full CCM standard that is tuned for resource-constrained DRE systems.

In the context of our work on applying CBSE principles to DRE systems, we have also been researching the equally challenging problem of facilitating deployment and configuration of component-based systems in these domains. Managing deployment and configuration of component-based applications is a challenging problem for the following reasons:

- *Component dependency and version management.* There may be complex requirements and relationships amongst individual components. Components may depend on one another for proper operation, or specifically require or exclude particular versions. If these relationships are not described and enforced, component applications may fail to deploy properly; even worse, malfunction in subtle and pernicious ways.
- *Component configuration management.* A component might expose configuration hooks that change its behavior, and the deployment infrastructure must manage and apply any required configuration information. Moreover, several components in a deployment may have related configuration properties, and the deployment infrastructure should ensure that these properties remain consistent across an entire application.
- *Distributed connection and lifecycle management.* In the case of enterprise systems, components must be installed and have their connection and activation managed on remote hosts.

To address the challenges outlined above, we began developing a deployment engine for CIAO in 2005. This tool, which we call the *Deployment and Configuration Engine* (DAnCE) [DBO$^+$05], is an implementation of the OMG *Deployment and Configuration* (D&C) specification [OMG06]. For most of its history, DAnCE served primarily as a research vehicle for graduate students developing novel approaches to deployment and configuration, which had two important impacts on its implementation:

- As a research vehicle, DAnCE's development timeline was largely driven by paper deadlines and feature demonstrations for sponsors. As a result, its tested use cases were relatively simple and narrowly focused.
- Custodianship of DAnCE changed hands several times as research projects were completed and new ones started. As a result, there was often not a unified architectural vision for the entire infrastructure.

These two factors had several impacts on DAnCE. For example, narrow and focused use-cases often made evaluating end-to-end performance on real-world application deployments a low priority. Moreover, the lack of a unified architectural vision combined with tight deadlines often meant that poor architectural choices were made in the name of expediency, and were not later remedied. These problems were brought into focus as we began to work with our commercial sponsors to apply DAnCE to larger-scale deployments, numbering in the hundreds to thousands of components on tens to hundreds of hardware nodes. While the smaller, focused uses cases would have acceptable deployment times, these larger deployments would take unacceptably long amounts of time, on the order of an hour or more to fully complete.

In response to these problems, we undertook an effort to comprehensively evaluate the architecture, design, and implementation of DAnCE and create a new implementation that we call *Locality-Enabled DAnCE* (LE-DAnCE) [OGS11] [OGST13]. This chapter focuses on documenting and applying optimization principle patterns that form the core of LE-DAnCE to make it suitable for DRE systems. Table 6.1 summarizes common optimization patterns [Var05], many of which we apply in LE-DAnCE. An additional goal of this paper was to supplement this catalog with new patterns we identified in our work on LE-DAnCE.

Title	Principle	Examples from Networking
Avoiding Waste	Avoid obvious waste	zero-copy [PDZ00]
Shifting in Time	Shift computation in time (precompute, lazy evaluation, sharing expenses, batching)	copy-on-write [ABB+86, NO88], integrated layer processing [CT90]
Relaxing Specifications	Relax specifications (trading off certainty for time, trading off accuracy for time, and shifting computation in time)	fair queuing [SV95], IPv6 fragmentation
Leveraging other Components	Leverage other system components (exploiting locality, trading memory for speed, exploiting hardware)	Lulea IP lookups [DBCP97], TCP checksum
Adding Hardware	Add hardware to improve performance	Pipelined IP lookup [HV05], counters
Efficient Routines	Create efficient routines	UDP lookups
Avoiding Generality	Avoid unnecessary generality	Fbufs [DP93]
Specification vs Implementation	Don't confuse specification and implementation	Upcalls [HP88]
Passing Hints	Pass information like hints in interfaces	Packet filters [MJ93, MRA87, EK96]
Passing Information	Pass information in protocol headers	Tag switching [RDR+97]
Expected Use Case	Optimize the expected case	Header prediction [CJRS89]
Exploiting State	Add or exploit state to gain speed	Active VC list
Degrees of Freedom	Optimize degrees of freedom	IP trie lookups [SK03]
Exploit Finite Universes	Use special techniques for finite universes	Timing wheels [VL97]
Efficient Data Structures	Use efficient data structures	Level-4 switching

Table 6.1: Catalog of Optimization Principles and Known Use Cases in Networking [Var05]

The remainder of this chapter is organized as follows: Section 6.2 provides an overview of the OMG D&C specification; Section 6.3 identifies the most significant sources of DAnCE performance problems (parsing deployment information from XML, analysis of deployment information at run-time, and serialized execution of deployment steps) and uses them as case studies to identify optimization principles that (1) are generally applicable to DRE systems and (2) we applied to LE-DAnCE; and Section 6.4 presents concluding remarks.

6.2 Overview of DAnCE

The OMG D&C specification provides standard interchange formats for metadata used throughout the component-based application development lifecycle, as well as runtime interfaces used for packaging and planning. These runtime interfaces deliver deployment instructions to the middleware deployment infrastructure via a *component deployment plan*, which contains the complete set of deployment and configuration information for component instances and their associated connection information. During DRE system initialization this information must be parsed, components deployed to physical hardware resources, and the system activated in a timely manner.

This section presents a brief summary of the core architectural elements and processes that must be provided by a standards-compliant D&C implementation. We use this summary as a basis to discuss substantial performance and scalability problems in DAnCE, which is our open-source implementation of the OMG *Deployment and Configuration* (D&C) specification [OMG06], as outlined in Section 6.1. This summary is split into three sections: (1) *the DAnCE runtime architecture*, which describes the daemons and actors that are present in the system, the (2) *data model*, which describes the structure of the "deployment plans" that describe component applications, and (3) the *deployment process*, which provides a high level overview of the process by which a deployed distributed application is realized.

Runtime D&C Architecture

The runtime interfaces defined by the OMG D&C specification for deployment and configuration of components consists of the two-tier architecture shown in Figure 6.1.

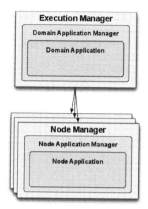

Figure 6.1: OMG D&C architectural overview and separation of concerns

This architecture consists of (1) a set of global (system-wide) entities used to coordinate deployment and (2) a set of local (node-level) entities used to instantiate component instances and configure their connections and QoS properties. Each entity in these global and local tiers correspond to one of the following three major roles:

Manager This role (known as the *ExecutionManager* at the global-level and as the *NodeManager* at the node-level) is a singleton daemon that coordinates all deployment entities in a single context. The Manager serves as the entry point for all deployment activity and as a factory for implementations of the *ApplicationManager* role.

ApplicationManager This role (known as the *DomainApplicationManager* at the global-level and as the *NodeApplicationManager* at the node-level entity) coordinates the lifecycle for running instances of a component-based application. Each ApplicationManager represents exactly one component-based application and is used to initiate deployment and teardown of that application. This role also serves as a factory for implementations of the *Application* role.

Application This role (known as the *DomainApplication* at the global-level and the *NodeApplication* at the node-level entity) represents a deployed instance of a component-based application. It is used to finalize the configuration of the associated component instances that comprise an application and begin execution of the deployed component-based application.

D&C Deployment Data Model

In addition to the runtime entities described above, the D&C specification also contains an extensive data model that is used to describe component applications throughout their deployment lifecycle. The metadata defined by the specification is intended for use as:

- An interchange format between various tools (e.g., development tools, application modeling and packaging applications, and deployment planning tools) applied to create the applications and
- Directives that describe the configuration and deployment used by the runtime infrastructure.

Most entities in the D&C metadata contain a section where configuration information may be included in the form of a sequence of name/value pairs, where the value may be an arbitrary data type. This configuration information can be used to describe everything from basic configuration information (such as shared library entry points and component/container associations) to more complex configuration information (such as QoS properties or initialization of component attributes with user-defined data types).

This metadata can broadly be grouped into three categories: *packaging*, *domain*, and *deployment*. Packaging descriptors are used from the beginning of application development to specify component interfaces, capabilities, and requirements. After implementations have been created, this metadata is further used to group individual components into assemblies, describe pairings with implementation artifacts, such as shared libraries (also known as dynamically linked libraries), and create packages containing both metadata and implementations that may be installed into the target environment. Domain descriptors are used by hardware administrators to describe capabilities (e.g., CPU, memory, disk space, and special hardware such as GPS receivers) present in the domain.

OMG D&C Deployment Process

Component application deployments are performed in a four phase process codified by the OMG D&C standard. The *Manager* and *ApplicationManager* are responsible for the first two phases and the *Application* is responsible for the final two phases, as described below:

1. *Plan preparation.* In this phase, a deployment plan is provided to the *ExecutionManager*, which (1) analyzes the plan to determine which nodes are involved in the deployment and (2) splits the plans into "locality-constrained" plans, one for each node containing information only for the corresponding node. These locality-constrained plans have only instance and connection information for a single node. Each *NodeManager* is then contacted and provided with its locality-constrained plan, which causes the creation of *NodeApplicationManagers* whose reference is returned. Finally, the *ExecutionManager* creates a *DomainApplicationManager* with these references.
2. *Start launch.* When the *DomainApplicationManager* receives the start launch instruction, it delegates work to the *NodeApplicationManagers* on each node. Each *NodeApplicationManager* creates a *NodeApplication* that loads all component instances into memory, performs preliminary configuration, and collects references for all endpoints described in the deployment plan. These references are then cached by a *DomainApplication* instance created by the *DomainApplicationManager*.
3. *Finish launch.* This phase is started by an operation on the *DomainApplication* instance, which apportions its collected object references from the previous phase to each *NodeApplication* and causes them to initiate this phase. All component instances receive final configurations and all connections are then created.
4. *Start.* This phase is again initiated on the *DomainApplication*, which delegates to the *NodeApplication* instances and causes them to instruct all installed component instances to begin execution.

6.3 Applying Optimization Principle Patterns to DAnCE

This section examines three of the most problematic performance problems we identified when applying DAnCE to component-based applications in a large-scale production DRE system. We first describe a case study that highlights many of these performance challenges. We then identify the causes of performance degradation and use this discussion to present optimization principles, which are guidelines that may be applied in other situations and applications to remedy or prevent performance problems.

Overview of the SEAMONSTER Platform

An example DRE system that revealed significant performance issues with DAnCE was a collaboration with the University of Alaska on the *South East Alaska MOnitoring Network for Science, Telecommunications, Education, and Research* (SEAMONSTER) platform. SEAMONSTER is a glacier and watershed sensor web hosted at the University of Alaska Southeast (UAS) [FHHC07]. This sensor web monitors and collects data regarding glacier dynamics and mass balance, watershed hydrology, coastal marine ecology, and human impact/hazards in and around the Lemon Creek watershed and Lemon Glacier. The collected data is used to study the correlations between glacier velocity, glacial lake formation and drainage, watershed hydrology, and temperature variation.

The SEAMONSTER sensor web includes sensors and weatherized computer platforms that are deployed on the glacier and throughout the watershed to collect data of scientific interest. The data collected by the sensors is relayed via wireless networks to a cluster of servers that filter, correlate, and analyze the data. Effective deployment of data collection and filtering applications on SEAMONSTER field hardware and dynamic adaptation to changing environmental conditions and resource availability present significant software challenges for efficient operation of SEAMONSTER. While SEAMONSTER servers provide significant computational resources, the field hardware is computationally constrained.

Field nodes in a sensor web often have a large number of observable phenomena in their area of interest. The type, duration, and frequency of observation of these phenomena may change over time, based on changes in the environment, occurrence of transient events in the environment, and changing goals and objectives in the science mission of the sensor web. Moreover, limited power, processing capability, storage, and network bandwidth constrain the ability of these nodes to continually perform observations at the desired frequency and fidelity. Dynamic changes in environmental conditions coupled with limited resource availability requires individual nodes of the sensor web to rapidly revise current operations and future plans to make the best use of their resources.

To address these challenges, we proposed to transition the data collection and processing tasks to a middleware platform built on top of the CIAO and DAnCE middleware described in Section 6.1 and Section 6.2, respectively. We developed a run-time planner [KOS+08] that analyzed the physical observations of the sensor nodes. Based on that information—as well as the operational goals of the network—the planner generates deployment plans describing desired software configuration.

Using DAnCE to apply the deployment changes requested by the run-time planner, however, revealed a number of shortcomings in its performance. These shortcomings were exacerbated by the limited performance of the field hardware, relative slowness of the network linking the nodes, and the stringent real-time requirements of the system. Each of these shortcomings is described below.

Optimizing Deployment Plan Parsing

Context

Component application deployments for OMG D&C are described by a data structure that contains all the relevant configuration metadata for the component instances, their mappings to individual nodes, and any connection information required. This deployment plan is serialized on disk in a XML file whose structure is described by an XML Schema defined by the D&C specification. This XML document format presents significant advantages by providing a simple interchange format for exchanging deployment plan files between modeling tools [GNS+02].

For example, in the SEAMONSTER case study this format provided a convenient interchange format between the planning front end and the deployment infrastructure. This format is also easy to generate and manipulate using widely available XML modules for popular programming languages. Moreover, it enables simple modification and data mining by text processing tools such as perl, grep, sed, and awk.

Problem

Processing these deployment plan files during deployment and even runtime, however, can lead to substantial performance penalties. These performance penalties stem from the following sources:

- XML deployment plan file sizes grow substantially as the number of component instances and connections in the deployment increases, which causes significant I/O overhead to load the plan into memory and to validate the structure against the schema to ensure that it is well-formed.
- The XML document format cannot be directly used by the deployment infrastructure because the infrastructure is a CORBA application that implements OMG *Interface Definition Language* (IDL) interfaces. Hence, the XML document must first be converted into the IDL format used by the runtime interfaces of the deployment framework.

In DRE systems, component deployments that number in the thousands are not uncommon. Moreover, component instances in these domains will exhibit a high degree of connectivity. Both these factors contribute to large plans. Plans need not be large, however, to significantly impact the operation of a system. Though the plans were significantly smaller in the SEAMONSTER case study described above the extremely limited computational resources meant that the processing overhead for even smaller plans was often too time consuming.

Optimization Principle Patterns in Parsing Configuration Metadata

There are two general approaches to resolving the challenge of XML parsing outlined in Section 6.3.

1. Optimize the XML-to-IDL processing capability. DAnCE uses a vocabulary-specific XML data binding [WKNS05] tool called the *XML Schema Compiler* (XSC). XSC reads D&C XML schemas and generates a C++-based interface to XML documents built atop the *Document Object Model* (DOM) XML programming API. DOM is a time/space-intensive approach since the entire document must first be processed to construct a tree-based representation of the document prior to initiating the XML-to-IDL translation process. Since deployment plan data structures contain extensive internal cross-referencing, an alternative to DOM including event-based mechanisms to process deployment plans, such as the *Simple API for XML* (SAX), would not yield substantial gains either.

The C++ data binding generated by XSC creates a number of classes (based on the content of the XML schema) that provide strongly-typed object-oriented access to the data in the XML document. Moreover, this interface leverages features of the C++ STL to help programmers write compact and efficient code to interact with their data. The general process for populating these wrappers is to 1) parse the XML document using a DOM XML parser; 2) parse the DOM tree to populate the generated class hierarchy. In order to enhance compatibility with STL algorithms and functors, XSC stores its data internally inside STL container classes.

Initial versions of the XSC data binding were highly inefficient. Even relatively modest deployments numbering as few as several hundred to a thousand components would take nearly half an hour to process. After analyzing the execution of this process using tools such as Rational Quantify revealed a very straightforward problem: the generated XSC code was individually inserting elements into its internal data structures (in this case, std::vector) in a naive manner. As a result, exorbitant amounts of time were spent re-allocating and copying data inside these containers for each additional element inserted.

Below we present specific guidelines that developers must be aware of:

- *Be aware of the cost of your abstractions.* High level abstractions, such as the container classes that are available in the C++ STL can greatly simplify programs by reducing the need to reproduce complex and error-prone lower level (largely boilerplate) code. It is important to characterize and document (when writing abstractions) and understand (when using them) what hidden costs may be incurred by using the higher level operations provided by your abstraction.
- *Use appropriate abstractions for your use case.* Often, there is a choice to be made between abstractions that provide similar functionality. An example may be the choice between std::vector and std::list; each presents its own advantages. In XSC, std::vector was initially used because we desired random access to elements in the data binding; the cost was extremely poor performance when parsing the XML document due to poor insertion performance. Our use case, however, only required sequential access, so the much better insertion performance of std::list was in the end much more desirable.

By understanding the specific requirements of the particular use case of our generated XML data binding—in particular that most nodes are visited a single time and can be visited in order—we are able to apply the pattern *Expected Use Case* through the application of two other optimization patterns. The *Avoiding Generality* pattern is applicable in this case because we consciously avoid generality by generating the data binding without random access containers. We then chose to use the most efficient data structure (*Efficient Data Structures* pattern) to satisfy that lack of generality.

2. Preprocess the XML files for latency-critical deployments. While optimizing the XML to IDL conversion process yielded conversion times that were tractable, this step in the deployment process still consumed a large fraction of the total time required for deployment.

This yet-unresolved overhead could be avoided by applying another optimization principle pattern: *When possible, perform costly computations outside of the critical path.* In many cases, the result of costly procedures and computations can be pre-computed and stored for later retrieval. This is especially true in cases such as the XML deployment plan, which is unlikely to change between when it is generated, and when the application deployment is requested.

This optimization approach applies the optimization pattern *Shifting in Time* by shifting the costly conversion of the deployment plan to a more efficient binary format outside of the critical path of application deployment. In applying this pattern, we first convert the deployment plan into its runtime IDL representation. We then serialize the result to disk using the *Common Data Representation* (CDR) [OMG08] binary format defined by the CORBA specification. The SEAMONSTER online planner could take advantage of this optimization by producing these binary plans in lieu of XML-based deployment plans, significantly reducing latency.

The platform-independent CDR binary format used to store the deployment plan on disk is the same format used to transmit the plan over the network at runtime. The advantage of this approach is that it leverages the heavily optimized de-serialization handlers provided by the underlying CORBA implementation. These handlers create an in-memory representation of the deployment plan data structure from the on-disk binary stream.

Optimizing Plan Analysis

Context

After a component deployment plan has been loaded into an in-memory representation, it must be analyzed by the middleware deployment infrastructure before any subsequent deployment activity is performed. This analysis occurs during the plan preparation phase described in Section 6.2. The goal of this analysis is to determine (1) the number of deployment sub-problems that are part of the deployment plan and (2) which component instances belong to each sub-problem.

As mentioned in Section 6.2, the output of this analysis process is a set of "locality-constrained" sub-plans. A locality-constrained sub-plan contains all the necessary metadata to execute a deployment successfully. It therefore contains copies of the information contained in the original plan (described in Section 6.2).

The runtime plan analysis is actually conducted twice during the plan preparation phase of deployment: once at the global level and again on each node. Global deployment plans are split according to the node that the individual instances are assigned to. This two-part analysis results in a new sub-plan for each node that only contains the instances, connections, and other component metadata necessary for that node.

The algorithm for splitting plans used by our DAnCE implementation of the D&C specification is straightforward. For each instance to be deployed in the plan, the algorithm determines which sub-plan should contain it and retrieve the appropriate (or create a new) sub-plan data structure. As this relationship is determined, all metadata necessary for that component instance is copied to the sub-plan, including connections, metadata describing executables, shared library dependencies, etc.

Problem

While this approach is conceptually simple, it is fraught with accidental complexities that yield the following inefficiencies in practice:

1. *Reference representation in IDL.* Deployment plans are typically transmitted over networks, so they must obey the rules of the CORBA IDL language mapping. Since IDL does not have any concept of references or pointers, some alternative mechanism must be used to describe the relationships between plan elements. The deployment plan stores all the major elements in sequences, so references to other entities can be represented with simple indices into these sequences. While this implementation can follow references in constant time, it also means these references become invalidated when plan entities are copied to sub-plans, as their position in deployment plan sequences will most likely be different. It is also impossible to determine if the target of a reference has already been copied without searching the sub-plan, which is time-consuming.

2. *Memory allocation in deployment plan sequences.* The CORBA IDL mapping requires that sequences be stored in consecutive memory addresses. If a sequence is resized, therefore, its contents will most likely be copied to another location in memory to accommodate the increased sequence size. With the approach summarized above, substantial copying overhead will occur as plan sizes grow. This overhead is especially problematic in resource-constrained systems (such as our SEAMONSTER case study), whose limited run-time memory must be conserved for application components. If the deployment infrastructure is inefficient in its use of this resource, either it will exhaust the available memory, or cause significant thrashing of any virtual memory available (both impacting deployment latency and the usable life of flash-based storage).

3. *Inefficient parallelization of plan analysis.* The algorithm described above would appear to benefit greatly from parallelization, as the process of analyzing a single component and determining which elements must be copied to a sub-plan is independent of all other components. Multi-threading this algorithm, however, would likely not be effective because access to sub-plans to copy instance metadata must be serialized to avoid data corruption. In practice, component instances in the deployment plan are usually grouped according to the node and/or process since deployment plans are often generated from modeling tools. As a result, multiple threads would likely compete for a lock on the same sub-plan, which would cause the "parallelized" algorithm to run largely sequentially. While parallelization has historically been viewed as non-applicable to resource-constrained DRE systems (such as SEAMONSTER), the advent of multi-core processors in single-board computers is motivating more parallelism in these environments.

Optimization Principle Patterns in Analysis of Deployment Plans

This performance challenge could potentially be resolved by applying the *Specification vs Implementation* pattern, and leveraging some of the same optimization principles described earlier for the XSC tool, especially *being aware of the cost of abstractions*, and *using appropriate containers for the use case*. For example, pointers/references could be used instead of sequence indices to refer to related data structures, potentially removing the need to carefully rewrite references when plan entities are copied between plans. Likewise, an associative container (such as an STL map) instead of a sequence could store plan objects, thereby increasing the efficiency of inserting plan entities into sub-plans.

While these and other similar options are tempting, there are some inherent complexities in the requirements of the D&C standard that make these optimizations less attractive. Since this data must be transmitted to other entities as part of the deployment process, using a more efficient representation for analysis would introduce yet another conversion step into the deployment process. This conversion would potentially overwhelm any gains attained by this new representation.

A more attractive result is to apply a different set of optimization principles to this problem, outlined below:

- *Cache previously calculated results for later use.* This is an example of the patterns *Shifting in Time* and *Exploiting State*. It is possible to perform a simple pre-analysis step to pre-calculate values that will be more time consuming to perform later. In this case, iterating over the plan first to determine the final sizes necessary to contain the calculated sub-plans and cache that state for later use.
- *Where possible, pre-allocate any data structures.* As a result of the additional state gleaned through the pre-analysis step described above, we can apply the *Avoiding Waste* and avoid gratuitous waste by pre-allocating the sequences which were previously being re-allocated each time a new plan element was discovered.
- *Design your algorithms to take advantage of parallelization.* While this can be seen as an application of the *Adding Hardware*, this pattern speaks more to taking advantage of intrinsic properties of hardware such as word size caching effects. Moreover, this pattern speaks to adding special purpose hardware to perform specialized calculations.

Taking advantage of multiple general-purpose processors is an l important emerging principle. Since multi-core computers are pervasive in desktop and server domains, and are becoming increasingly common even in embedded domains, it is increasingly important to design for this important hardware feature. We therefore propose an additional pattern which we will call *Design for Parallelization*, wherein one optimizes design of algorithms and interfaces for parallelization, shown in Table 6.2.

- *Structure shared data access to avoid necessary use of synchronization.* Synchronization, e.g., using mutexes to protect access to shared data, is tedious and error prone to use. Moreover, overzealous use of synchronization can often entirely negate any parallelization of your algorithms. A much more preferable approach is to structure your algorithms to eliminate the need for synchronization entirely; requiring only shared *read* access to data, instead of shared *write* access.

This optimization principle is not only an important companion to *Design for Parallelization* proposed above, but is also a wise programming practice in general: deadlocks and race conditions caused by incorrect synchronization are pernicious and difficult to diagnose bugs. Indeed, our recent work in software frameworks intended for fractionated spacecraft has proposed a component model that eliminates synchronization from application code entirely [DEG$^+$12]. To that end, we propose another optimization pattern which we call *Avoid Synchronization*, wherein one should avoid overzealous synchronization and locking, shown in Table 6.2 below.

These principles can be applied to the algorithm described above to create a version that is far more amenable to optimization; the new algorithm (along with how the above principles influenced the design, is described below.

1. *Phase 1: Determine the number of sub-plans to produce.* In this phase, a single thread iterates over all component instances contained in the deployment plan to determine the number of necessary sub-plans. When this operation is performed at the global level, it simply requires a constant time operation per instance. When performed at the local level, it requires that locality constraints (described in Section 6.2) be evaluated. Since this phase is potentially time consuming the results are cached for later use. This is an example of *Shifting in Time* and *Exploiting State*.

2. *Phase 2: Preallocate data structures for sub-plans.* Using information gleaned in phase 1 above, preallocate data structures necessary to assemble sub-plans. As part of this preallocation it is possible to reserve memory for each sequence in the sub-plan data structure to avoid repeated resizing and copying. Statistics are collected in phase 1 to estimate these lengths efficiently. This is an example of *Avoiding Waste*

3. *Phase 3: Assemble node-specific sub-plans.* This phase of the new analysis process is similar to the algorithm described at the beginning of this section. The main difference is that the cached results of the pre-analysis phase are used to guide the creation of sub-plans. Instead of considering each instance in order (as the original DAnCE implementation did), LE-DAnCE fully constructs one sub-plan at a time, by processing instances on a per-node basis. This approach simplifies parallelizing this phase by dedicating a single thread per sub-plan and eliminates any shared state between threads, except for read-only access to the original plan. It is therefore unnecessary to use any locking mechanism to protect access to the sub-plans. This is an example of *Design for Parallelization* and *Avoid Synchronization*.

The revised algorithm above is a much more efficient implementation of plan analysis, and can show improvement even on the single-core embedded processors that were typical of the SEAMONSTER use-case: the above is far more memory efficient, both in terms of space used and the amount of re-allocation that is necessary. The use of multi-core embedded processors would substantially improve run-time performance over the old algorithm.

Optimization Through Reduction in Serialized Execution of Deployment Tasks

Context

The complexities presented below involve the serial (non-parallel) execution of deployment tasks. The related sources of latency in DAnCE exist at both the global and node level. At the global level, this lack of parallelism results from the underlying CORBA transport used by DAnCE. The lack of parallelism at the local level, however, results from the lack of specificity in terms of the interface of the D&C implementation with the target component model that is contained in the D&C specification.

The D&C deployment process presented in Section 6.2 enables global entities to divide the deployment process into a number of node-specific subtasks. Each subtask is dispatched to individual nodes using a single remote invocation, with any data produced by the nodes passed back to the global entities via "out" parameters that are part of the operation signature described in IDL. Due to the synchronous (request/response) nature of the CORBA messaging protocol used to implement DAnCE, the conventional approach is to dispatch these subtasks serially to each node. This approach is simple to implement in contrast to the complexity of using the CORBA *asynchronous method invocation* (AMI) mechanism [AOS+00].

Problem

To minimize initial implementation complexity, we used synchronous invocation in an (admittedly shortsighted) design choice in the initial DAnCE implementation. This global synchronicity worked fine for relatively small deployments with less than about 100 components. As the number of nodes and instances assigned to those nodes scaled up, however, this global/local serialization imposed a substantial cost in deployment latency.

This serialized execution yielded the most problematic performance degradation in our SEA-MONSTER case study, i.e., the limited computational resources available on the field hardware would often take several minutes to complete. Such latency at the node level can quickly becomes disastrous. In particular, even relatively modest deployments involving tens of nodes quickly escalates the deployment latency of the system to a half hour or more.

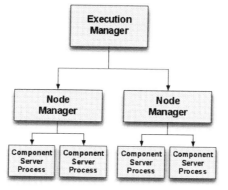

Figure 6.2: Simplified, serialized DAnCE architecture

This serialization problem, however, is not limited only to the global/local task dispatching; it exists in the node-specific portion of the infrastructure, as well. The D&C specification provides no guidance in terms of how the NodeApplication should interface with the target component model, such as the CORBA Component Model (CCM), instead leaving such an interface as an implementation detail.

In DAnCE, the D&C architecture was implemented using three processes, as shown in Figure 6.2.

The ExecutionManager and NodeManager processes instantiate their associated ApplicationManager and Application instances in their address spaces. When the NodeApplication installs concrete component instances it spawns one (or more) separate application processes as needed. These application processes use an interface derived from an older version of the CCM specification that allows the NodeApplication to instantiate containers and component instances individually. This approach is similar to that taken by CARDAMOM [Obj06] (which is another open-source CCM implementation) that is tailored for enterprise DRE systems, such as air-traffic management systems.

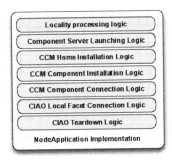

Figure 6.3: Previous DAnCE NodeApplication implementation

The DAnCE architecture shown in Figure 6.2 was problematic with respect to parallelization since its NodeApplication implementation integrated all logic necessary for installing, configuring, and connecting instances directly (as shown in Figure 6.3), rather than performing only some processing and delegating the remainder of the concrete deployment logic to the application process. This tight integration made it hard to parallelize the node-level installation procedures for the following reasons:

- The amount of data shared by the *generic deployment logic* (the portion of the NodeApplication implementation that interprets the plan) and the *specific deployment logic* (the portion which has specific knowledge of how to manipulate components) made it hard to parallelize their installation in the context of a *single* component server since that data must be modified during installation.
- Groups of components installed to separate application processes were considered as separate deployment sub-tasks, so these groupings were handled sequentially one after the other.

Optimization Principle Patterns in Reducing Serialized Phasing

In a similar vein to the analysis problem described earlier, this is a problem wherein excessive serialization is impacting performance. In this case, however, instead of re-evaluating the algorithmic approach to the *deployment process*, we will re-consider the *architectural design* of the system instead. In order to address the performance challenge in this case, we applied the following optimization principles to DAnCE:

1. *Don't let specifications overly constrain your design.* When implementing a system or software framework according to the specification, it is often natural to model your design along the strictures and implicit assumptions of the specification. It is often possible to architect your

implementation in order to introduce architectural elements or behavior that remain within the strictures of the specification. This is an example of both the *Specification vs. Implementation* pattern and the *Degrees of Freedom* pattern.

2. *Maintain strict separation of concerns.* Ensure that your system operates in *layers* or *modules* that interact through well-defined interfaces. This helps to ensure that the state for each layer or module is well-contained, simplifying interactions between logically distinct portions of your applications and making it easier to apply the *Design for Parallelization* pattern. Moreover, ensuring that the state for each layer is self contained helps to apply the *Avoid Synchronization* pattern.

   Moreover, modularizing your software design can often reveal ways that other optimization principle patterns can be applied. As such, we propose another principle pattern, *Separate Concerns*, leveraging separation of concern to modularize architecture (summarized in Table 6.2. Although traditionally a level of indirection may be frowned upon because it could lead to performance penalties, sometimes it can reveal new opportunities or help apply other optimizations.

3. *Ensure that these layers or modules can interact asynchronously.* If the modules or layers in your architecture have interfaces that assume synchronous operation, it becomes difficult to leverage parallel operation to improve performance. Even if the interface is itself synchronous, it is often possible to use other techniques, such as leveraging abstractions that allow you to interact with a synchronous interface in an asynchronous manner. Avoiding synchronous interactions between is another important application of the *Design for Parallelization* pattern.

Applying these principles at the global level (e.g., the ExecutionManager described in Section 6.2) the separation of concerns is maintained by virtue of the fact that it and the node-level resources are in separate processes, and likely the different physical nodes. Asynchrony in this context is also easy to achieve, as we were able to leverage the CORBA Asynchronous Method Invocation (AMI) to allow the client (in this case, the global infrastructure) to interact asynchronously with the synchronous server interface (in this case, the node level infrastructure), and dispatch multiple requests to individual nodes in parallel. This is an example of *Degrees of Freedom* in that the specification does not reject the notion of asynchronous interaction between these entities.

Applying these principles in the node level infrastructure, however, was more challenging. As described above, our initial implementation had poor separation of concerns, making it extremely difficult to apply multiple threads of execution in order to parallelize deployment activity at the node level. To support this, we created a new abstraction at the node level that we called the Locality Manager, which was the result of applying the above optimization principles.

Overview of the LE-DAnCE Locality Manager. The LE-DAnCE node-level architecture (e.g., NodeManager, NodeApplicationManager, and NodeApplication) now functions as a node-constrained version of the global portion of the OMG D&C architecture. Rather than having the NodeApplication directly triggering installation of concrete component instances, this responsibility is now delegated to LocalityManager instances. The node-level infrastructure performs a second "split" of the plan it receives from the global level by grouping component instances into one or more application processes. The NodeApplication then spawns a number of LocalityManager processes and delegates these "process-constrained" (*i.e.*, containing only components and connections apropos to a single process) plans to each application process in parallel.

The Locality Manager is an example of the *Specification vs. Implementation* pattern. The specification would suggest that the NodeApplication is the final entity that interacts with the component middleware; by recognizing that our implementation could introduce another layer of abstraction, we've been able to apply a number of other optimization patterns.

Unlike the previous DAnCE NodeApplication implementation, the LE-DAnCE LocalityManager functions as a generic application process that strictly separates concerns between the general deployment logic needed to analyze the plan and the specific deployment logic needed to install and manage the lifecycle of concrete component middleware instances. This separation is achieved using entities called *Instance Installation Handlers*, which provide a well-defined interface for managing the lifecycle of a component instance, including installation, removal, connection, disconnection, and activation. Installation Handlers are also used in the context of the NodeApplication to manage the life-cycle of LocalityManager processes.

The genesis of these installation handlers is an example of the *Degrees of Freedom* pattern; by under specifying the explicit interaction with the component middleware, it has left us free to design our own interaction. In doing do, we have applied the *Separate Concerns* pattern.

Using the Locality Manager to reduce serialized execution of deployment steps. LE-DAnCE's new LocalityManager and Installation Handlers make it substantially easier to parallelize than DAnCE. Parallelism in both the LocalityManager and NodeApplication is achieved using an entity called the *Deployment Scheduler*, which is shown in Figure 6.4.

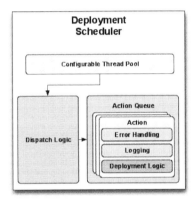

Figure 6.4: DAnCE Deployment Scheduler

The Deployment Scheduler combines the Command pattern [GHJV95] and the Active Object pattern [SSRB00]. Individual deployment actions (e.g., instance installation, instance connection, *etc.*) are encased inside an Action object, along with any required metadata. Each individual deployment action is an invocation of a method on an Installation Handler, so these actions need not be rewritten for each potential deployment target. Error handling and logging logic is also fully contained within individual actions, further simplifying the LocalityManager.

Individual actions (e.g., install a component or create a connection) are scheduled for execution by a configurable thread pool. This pool can provide user-selected, single-threaded, or multi-threaded behavior, depending on application requirements. This thread pool can also be used to implement more sophisticated scheduling behavior, e.g., a priority-based scheduling algorithm that dynamically reorders the installation of component instances based on metadata present in the plan.

The LocalityManager determines which actions to perform during each particular phase of deployment and creates one Action object for each instruction. These actions are then passed to the deployment scheduler for execution while the main thread of control waits on a completion signal from the Deployment Scheduler. Upon completion, the LocalityManager reaps either return values or error codes from the completed actions and completes the deployment phase.

To provide parallelism between LocalityManager instances on the same node, the LE-DAnCE Deployment Scheduler is also used in the implementation of the NodeApplication, along with an

Installation Handler for LocalityManager processes. Using the Deployment Scheduler at this level helps overcome a significant source of latency whilst conducting node-level deployments. Spawning LocalityManager instances can take a significant amount of time compared to the deployment time required for component instances, so parallelizing this process can achieve significant latency savings when application deployments have many LocalityManager processes per node.

Taken together, the dynamic re-ordering of deployment events and parallel installation of LocalityManager instances is a promising approach to improve deployment latency in the SEAMONSTER domain. By attaching high priority to critical deployment events, such as the activation or change in configuration of a sensor observing a present natural phenomena, DAnCE can help ensure that critical mission needs are met in a timely fashion. Moreover, the parallelism enabled by this design can reduce latency by allowing other LocalityManager instances to execute while one is blocked on I/O as it loads new component implementations, or by taking advantage of newer multicore embedded processors.

6.4 Concluding Remarks

This chapter provided an overview of the *Deployment And Configuration Engine* (DAnCE), an implementation of the OMG *Deployment and Configuration* specification. As a research tool, DAnCE was used to demonstrate novel techniques for the deployment and configuration (D&C) of component-based applications in DRE systems. While its performance was satisfactory for the narrow and focused demonstrations required for publications and demonstration, its performance was not satisfactory when applied to larger-scale production DRE systems. A number of factors, including changing architectural ownership and the demo-focused nature of DAnCE's development, caused a number of poor design choices early on to become entrenched in its architecture and design, seriously impeding performance.

A typical use case of DAnCE, in this case the *South East Alaska MOnitoring Network for Science, Telecommunications, Education, and Research* (SEAMONSTER) platform, was described to highlight many of the optimization opportunities present in DAnCE. Motivated by this use case, this paper described how we applied a catalog of optimization principles from the domain of networking to re-evaluate and re-engineer the design and implementation of DAnCE to remedy the deficiencies outlined above. In addition, we described three additional optimization principles: dealing with parallelization, synchronization, and separation of concerns. These additional patterns—in conjunction with those described in the initial catalog—were used to develop LE-DAnCE, which substantially improved the performance and reliability of DAnCE. A summary of the original pattern catalog, along with our additions, is shown in Table 6.2. Likewise, a thorough quantitative discussion of the performance enhancement results is described in [OGST13].

Based on our experiences applying the optimizations described in this chapter to LE-DAnCE and observing the results, we have learned the following lessons:

- *Taking advantage of parallelization is a critical optimization opportunity.* As multicore processors become a standard feature of even embedded devices, it is critically important that algorithms and processes be designed to take advantage of this capability. When optimizing algorithms and processes for parallelization, be judicious in applying synchronization since improper use of locks can cause parallel systems to operate in a serial fashion, or worse, malfunction in subtle ways.
- *When possible, shift time consuming operations out of the critical path.* While our optimizations to the plan analysis portion of the D&C process (described in Section 6.3) were effective in

Pattern	Explanation	Example in DaNCE
Avoiding Waste	Avoid obvious waste	Pre-allocate memory when parsing deployment plans.
Shifting in Time	Shift computation in time (pre-compute, lazy evaluation, sharing expenses, batching)	Pre-convert deployment plan to binary format, *potentially pre-compute plan splits*.
Relaxing Specifications	Relax specifications (trading off certainty for time, trading off accuracy for time, and shifting computation in time)	*Potentially pre-compute plan splits*.
Leveraging Other Components	Leverage other system components (exploiting locality, trading memory for speed, exploiting hardware)	(n/a)?
Adding Hardware	Add hardware to improve performance	(n/a)
Efficient Routines	Create efficient routines	XML-IDL Data Binding
Avoiding Generality	Avoid unnecessary generality	Optimize plan parsing
Specification vs Implementation	Don't confuse specification and implementation	LocalityManager
Passing Hints	Pass information like hints in interfaces	*Potentially used to pre-compute plan splits*
Passing Information	Pass information in protocol headers	(n/a)
Expected Use Case	Optimize the expected case	XML-IDL Data Binding
Exploiting State	Add or exploit state to gain speed	Pre-allocate child plans during plan analysis.
Degrees of Freedom	Optimize degrees of freedom	LocalityManager Installation Handlers
Exploit Finite Universes	Use special techniques for finite universes	(n/a)
Efficient Data Structures	Use efficient data structures	Optimize XML-IDL data binding
Design for Parallelization	Optimize design for parallelization	Process child plans in parallel
Avoid Synchronization	Avoid synchronization and locking	Unsynchronized access to parent plan during plan analysis.
Separate Concerns	Use strict separation of concerns to modularize architecture	Locality Manager

Table 6.2: Catalog of optimization principles and known use cases in LE-DAnCE

reducing the total deployment latency for large scale deployments, additional improvement is possible by further applying the *Shifting in Time* pattern Like the XML parsing problem described in Section 6.3, the result of this operation is likely fixed at the point that the XML plan is generated. This process could be similarly pre-computed and provided to the D&C infrastructure for additional latency savings. Passing these pre-computed plans (both for the global split and the local split) would be an example application of the *Passing Hints* optimization pattern.

- *Serialized execution of processes is a major source of performance problems in DRE systems.* Executing tasks in a serial fashion when designing distributed systems offers significant conceptual and implementation simplicity. This simplicity, however, often comes with a significant performance penalty. Often, the additional complexity of asynchronous interaction is well worth the additional complexity.

- *Lack of clear architectural and technical leadership is detrimental to open source projects.* Developers often contribute to an open source project to solve a narrow problem and leave soon after. Without clear leadership, poor architectural and technical decisions made by individual contributors eventually snowball into a nearly unusable project.

TAO, CIAO, and LE-DAnCE are available in open-source form from download.dre.vanderbilt.edu.

[chapter 7]

Infinispan
Manik Surtani

7.1 Introduction

Infinispan[1] is an open source data grid platform. It is a distributed, in-memory key-value NoSQL store. Software architects typically use data grids like Infinispan either as a performance-enhancing distributed in-memory cache in front of an expensive, slow data store such as a relational database, or as a distributed NoSQL data store to replace a relational database. In either case, the main reason to consider a data grid in any software architecture is performance. The need for fast and low-latency access to data is becoming increasingly common.

As such, performance is Infinispan's sole raison d'être. Infinispan's code base is, in turn, extremely performance sensitive.

7.2 Overview

Before digging into Infinispan's depths, let us consider how Infinispan is typically used. Infinispan falls into a category of software called middleware. According to Wikipedia, middleware "can be described as software glue"—the components that sit on servers, in between applications, such as websites, and an operating system or database. Middleware is often used to make an application developer more productive, more effective and able to turn out—at a faster pace—applications that are also more maintainable and testable. All of this is achieved by modularisation and component reuse. Infinispan specifically is often placed in between any application processing or business logic and the data-storage tier. Data storage (and retrieval) are often the biggest bottlenecks, and placing an in-memory data grid in front of a database often makes things much faster. Further, data storage is also often a single point of contention and potential failure. Again, making use of Infinispan in front of (or even in place of) a more traditional data store, applications can achieve greater elasticity and scalability.

Who Uses Infinispan?

Infinispan has been used in several industries, ranging from telecoms to financial services, high-end e-commerce to manufacturing systems, gaming and mobile platforms. Data grids in general have always been popular in the financial services industry due to their stringent requirements around

---
[1] http://www.infinispan.org

extremely fast access to large volumes of data in a way that isolates them from individual machine failure. These requirements have since spread into other industries, which contributes to Infinispan's popularity across such a broad range of applications.

As a Library or as a Server

Infinispan is implemented in Java (and some Scala) and can be used in two different ways. First, it can be used as a library, embedded into a Java application, by including Infinispan JAR files and referencing and instantiating Infinispan components programmatically. This way, Infinispan components sit in the same JVM as the application and a part of the application's heap memory is allocated as a data grid node.

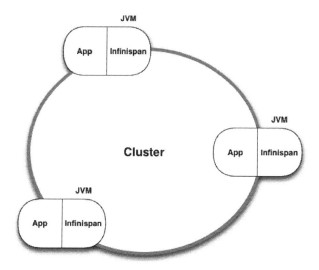

Figure 7.1: Infinispan as a library

Second, it can be used as a remote data grid by starting up Infinispan instances and allowing them to form a cluster. A client can then connect to this cluster over a socket from one of the many client libraries available. This way, each Infinispan node exists within its own isolated JVM and has the entire JVM heap memory at its disposal.

Peer-to-Peer Architecture

In both cases, Infinispan instances detect one another over a network, form a cluster, and start sharing data to provide applications with an in-memory data structure that transparently spans all the servers in a cluster. This allows applications to theoretically address an unlimited amount of in-memory storage as nodes are added to the cluster, increasing overall capacity.

Infinispan is a peer-to-peer technology where each instance in the cluster is equal to every other instance in the cluster. This means there is no single point of failure and no single bottleneck. Most importantly, it provides applications with an elastic data structure that can scale horizontally by adding more instances. And that can also scale back in, by shutting down some instances, all the while allowing the application to continue operating with no loss of overall functionality.

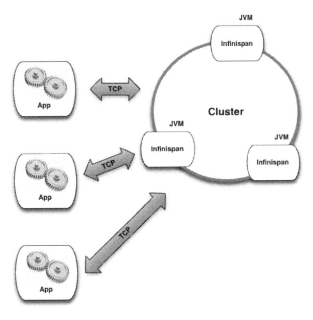

Figure 7.2: Infinispan as a remote data grid

7.3 Benchmarking Infinispan

The biggest problem when benchmarking a distributed data structure like Infinispan is the tooling. There is precious little that will allow you to measure the performance of storing and retrieving data while scaling out and back in. There is also nothing that offers comparative analysis, to be able to measure and compare performance of different configurations, cluster sizes, etc. To help with this, Radar Gun was created.

Radar Gun is covered in more depth in Section 7.4. The other tools mentioned here—the Yahoo Cloud Serving Benchmark, The Grinder and Apache JMeter—are not covered in as much depth, despite still being very important in benchmarking Infinispan. A lot of literature about these tools already exists online.

Radar Gun

Radar Gun[2] is an open source benchmarking framework that was designed to perform comparative (as well as competitive) benchmarks, to measure scalability and to generate reports from data points collected. Radar Gun is specifically targeted at distributed data structures such as Infinispan, and has been used extensively during the development of Infinispan to identify and fix bottlenecks. See Section 7.4 for more information on Radar Gun.

---

[2]https://github.com/radargun/radargun/wiki

Yahoo Cloud Serving Benchmark

The Yahoo Cloud Serving Benchmark[3] (YCSB) is an open source tool created to test latency when communicating with a remote data store to read or write data of varying sizes. YCSB treats all data stores as a single remote endpoint, so it doesn't attempt to measure scalability as nodes are added to or removed from a cluster. Since YCSB has no concept of a distributed data structure, it is only useful to benchmark Infinispan in client/server mode.

The Grinder and Apache JMeter

The Grinder[4] and Apache JMeter[5] are two simple open source load generators that can be used to test arbitrary servers listening on a socket. These are highly scriptable and, just like YCSB, useful for benchmarking Infinispan when used in client/server mode.

7.4 Radar Gun

Early Days

Created by the Infinispan core development team, Radar Gun started as a project on Sourceforge called the Cache Benchmarking Framework[6] and was originally designed to benchmark embedded Java caches running in different modes, in various configurations. It is designed to be comparative, so it would automatically run the same benchmark against various caching libraries—or various versions of the same library, to test for performance regressions.

Since its creation, it has gained a new name (Radar Gun), a new home on GitHub[7] and a host of new features.

Distributed Features

Radar Gun soon expanded to cover distributed data structures. Still focused on embedded libraries, Radar Gun is able to launch multiple instances of the framework on different servers, which in turn would launch instances of the distributed caching library. The benchmark is then run in parallel on each node in the cluster. Results are collated and reports are generated by the Radar Gun controller. The ability to automatically bring up and shut down nodes is crucial to scalability testing, as it becomes infeasible and impractical to manually run and re-run benchmarks on clusters of varying sizes, from two nodes all the way to hundreds or even thousands of nodes.

Fast and Wrong is No Good!

Radar Gun then gained the ability to perform status checks before and after running each stage of the benchmark, to ensure the cluster is still in a valid state. This allowed for early detection of incorrect results, and allowed for re-running of a benchmark without waiting for manual intervention at the end of a run—which could take many hours.

---

[3] https://github.com/brianfrankcooper/YCSB/wiki
[4] http://grinder.sourceforge.net/
[5] http://jmeter.apache.org/
[6] http://sourceforge.net/projects/cachebenchfwk/
[7] http://github.com/radargun

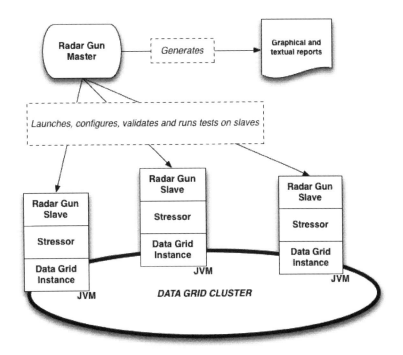

Figure 7.3: Radar Gun

Profiling

Radar Gun is also able to start and attach profiler instances to each data grid node and take profiler snapshots, for more insight into the goings on in each node when under load.

Memory Performance

Radar Gun also has the ability to measure the state of memory consumption of each node, to measure memory performance. In an in-memory data store, performance isn't all about how fast you read or write data, but also how well the structure performs with regards to memory consumption. This is particularly important in Java-based systems, as garbage collection can adversely affect the responsiveness of a system. Garbage collection is discussed in more detail later.

Metrics

Radar Gun measures performance in terms of transactions per second. This is captured for each node and then aggregated on the controller. Both reads and writes are measured and charted separately, even though they are performed simultaneously (to ensure a realistic test where such operations are interleaved). Radar Gun also captures means, medians, standard deviation, maximum and minimum values for read and write transactions, and these too are logged although they may not be charted. Memory performance is also captured, by way of a footprint for any given iteration.

Extensibility

Radar Gun is an extensible framework. It allows you to plug in your own data access patterns, data types and sizes. Further, it also allows you to add adapters to any data structure, caching library or NoSQL database that you would like to test.

End-users are often encouraged to use Radar Gun too when attempting to compare the performance of different configurations of a data grid.

7.5 Prime Suspects

There are several subsystems of Infinispan that are prime suspects for performance bottlenecks, and as such, candidates for close scrutiny and potential optimization. Let's look at each of these in turn.

The Network

Network communication is the single most expensive part of Infinispan, whether used for communication between peers or between clients and the grid itself.

Peer Network

Infinispan makes use of JGroups[8], an open source peer-to-peer group communication library for inter-node communication. JGroups can make use of either TCP or UDP network protocols, including UDP multicast, and provides high level features such as message delivery guarantees, retransmission and message ordering even over unreliable protocols such as UDP.

It becomes crucially important to tune the JGroups layer correctly, to match the characteristics of your network and application, such as time-to-live, buffer sizes, and thread pool sizes. It is also important to account for the way JGroups performs bundling—the combining of multiple small messages into single network packets—or fragmentation—the reverse of bundling, where large messages are broken down into multiple smaller network packets.

The network stack on your operating system and your network equipment (switches and routers) should also be tuned to match this configuration. Operating system TCP send and receive buffer sizes, frame sizes, jumbo frames, etc. all play a part in ensuring the most expensive component in your data grid is performing optimally.

Tools such as `netstat` and `wireshark` can help analyse packets, and Radar Gun can help drive load through a grid. Radar Gun can also be used to profile the JGroups layer of Infinispan to help locate bottlenecks.

Server Sockets

Infinispan makes use of the popular Netty[9] framework to create and manage server sockets. Netty is a wrapper around the asynchronous Java NIO framework, which in turn makes use of the operating system's asynchronous network I/O capabilities. This allows for efficient resource utilization at the expense of some context switching. In general, this performs very well under load.

---

[8] http://www.jgroups.org
[9] http://www.netty.io

Netty offers several levels of tuning to ensure optimal performance. These include buffer sizes, thread pools and the like, and should also be matched up with operating system TCP send and receive buffers.

Data Serialization

Before putting data on the network, application objects need to be serialized into bytes so that they can be pushed across a network, into the grid, and then again between peers. The bytes then need to be de-serialized back into application objects, when read by the application. In most common configurations, about 20% of the time spent in processing a request is spent in serialization and de-serialization.

Default Java serialization (and de-serialization) is notoriously slow, both in terms of CPU cycles and the bytes that are produced—they are often unnecessarily large, which means more data to push around a network.

Infinispan uses its own serialization scheme, where full class definitions are not written to the stream. Instead, magic numbers are used for known types where each known type is represented by a single byte. This greatly improves not just serialization and de-serialization speed, but also produces a much more compact byte stream for transmission across a network. An externalizer is registered for each known data type, registered against a magic number. This externalizer contains the logic to convert object to bytes and vice versa.

This technique works well for known types, such as internal Infinispan objects that are exchanged between peer nodes. Internal objects—such as commands, envelopes, etc.—have externalizers and corresponding unique magic numbers. But what about application objects? By default, if Infinispan encounters an object type it is unaware of, it falls back to default Java serialization for that object. This allows Infinispan to work out of the box—albeit in a less efficient manner when dealing with unknown application object types.

To get around this, Infinispan allows application developers to register externalizers for application data types as well. This allows powerful, fast, efficient serialization of application objects too, as long as the application developer can write and register externalizer implementations for each application object type.

This externalizer code has been released as a separate, reusable library, called JBoss Marshalling.[10] It is packaged with Infinispan and included in Infinispan distributions, but it is also used in various other open source projects to improve serialization performance.

Writing to Disk

In addition to being an in-memory data structure, Infinispan can also optionally persist to disk.

Persistence can either be for durability—to survive restarts or node failures, in which case everything in memory also exists on disk—or it can be configured as an overflow when Infinispan runs out of memory, in which case it acts in a manner similar to an operating system paging to disk. In the latter case, data is only written to disk when data needs to be evicted from memory to free up space.

When persisting for durability, persistence can either be online, where the application thread is blocked until data is safely written to disk, or offline, where data is flushed to disk periodically and asynchronously. In the latter case, the application thread is not blocked on the process of persistence, in exchange for uncertainty as to whether the data was successfully persisted to disk at all.

---

[10]http://www.jboss.org/jbossmarshalling

Infinispan supports several pluggable cache stores—adapters that can be used to persist data to disk or any form of secondary storage. The current default implementation is a simplistic hash bucket and linked list implementation, where each hash bucket is represented by a file on the filesystem. While easy to use and configure, this isn't the best-performing implementation.

Two high-performance, filesystem-based native cache store implementations are currently on the roadmap. Both will be written in C, with the ability to make system calls and use direct I/O where available (such as on Unix systems), to bypass kernel buffers and caches.

One of the implementations will be optimized for use as a paging system, and will therefore need to have random access, possibly a b-tree structure.

The other will be optimized as a durable store, and will mirror what is stored in memory. As such, it will be an append-only structure, designed for fast writing but not necessarily for fast reading/seeking.

Synchronization, Locking and Concurrency

As with most enterprise-class middleware, Infinispan is heavily biased towards modern, multi-core systems. To make use of the parallelism we have available with the large number of hardware threads in multi-core and SMP systems, as well as non-blocking, asynchronous I/O when dealing with network and disk communication, Infinispan's core data structures make use of software transactional memory techniques for concurrent access to shared data. This minimizes the need for explicit locks, mutexes and other forms of synchronization, preferring techniques like compare-and-set operations within a loop to achieve correctness when updating shared data structures. Such techniques have been proven to improve CPU utilization in multi-core and SMP systems, and despite the increased code complexity, has paid off in overall performance when under load.

In addition to the benefits of using software transactional memory approaches, this also future-proofs Infinispan to harness the power of synchronization support instructions in CPUs—hardware transactional memory—when such CPUs become commonplace, with minimal change to Infinispan's design.

Several data structures used in Infinispan are straight out of academic research papers. In fact, the non-blocking, lock-free dequeue[11] used in Infinispan was the structure's first Java implementation. Other examples include novel designs for lock amortization[12] and adaptive eviction policies.[13]

Threads and Context Switching

Various Infinispan subsystems make use of asynchronous operations that happen on separate threads. For example, JGroups allocates threads to monitor a network socket, which then decode messages and pass them to a message delivery thread. This may in turn attempt to store data in a cache store on disk—which may also be asynchronous and use a separate thread. Listeners may be notified of changes as well, and this can be configured to be asynchronous.

When dealing with thread pools to process such asynchronous tasks, there is always a context switching overhead. That threads are not cheap resources is also noteworthy. Allocating appropriately sized and configured thread pools is important to any installation making use of any of the asynchronous features of Infinispan.

---

[11]http://www.md.chalmers.se/~tsigas/papers/Lock-Free-Deques-Doubly-Lists-JPDC.pdf
[12]http://dl.acm.org/citation.cfm?id=1546683.1547428
[13]http://dl.acm.org/citation.cfm?id=511334.511340

Specific areas to look at are the asynchronous transport thread pool (if using asynchronous communications) and ensuring this thread pool is at least as large as the expected number of concurrent updates each node is expected to handle. Similarly, when tuning JGroups, the OOB^{14} and incoming thread pools should be at least as big as the expected number of concurrent updates.

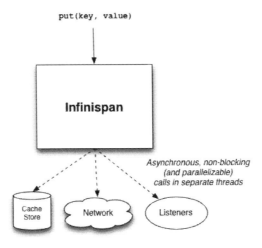

Figure 7.4: Threading in Infinispan

Garbage Collection

General good practices with regards to working with JVM garbage collectors is an important consideration for any Java-based software, and Infinispan is no exception. If anything, it is all the more important for a data grid, since container objects may survive for long periods of time while lots of transient objects—related to a specific operation or transaction—are also created. Further, garbage collection pauses can have adverse effects on a distributed data structure, as they can render a node unresponsive and cause the node to be marked as failed.

These have been taken into consideration when designing and building Infinispan, but at the same time there is a lot to consider when configuring a JVM to run Infinispan. Each JVM is different. However, some analysis[15] has been done on the optimal settings for certain JVMs when running Infinispan. For example, if using OpenJDK[16] or Oracle's HotSpot JVM[17], using the Concurrent Mark and Sweep collector[18] alongside large pages[19] for JVMs given about 12 GB of heap each appears to be an optimal configuration.

Further, pauseless garbage collectors—such as C4[20], used in Azul's Zing JVM[21]—are worthwhile considering cases where garbage collection pauses become a noticeable issue.

---

[14] http://www.jgroups.org/manual/html/user-advanced.html#d0e3284
[15] http://howtojboss.com/2013/01/08/data-grid-performance-tuning/
[16] http://openjdk.java.net/
[17] http://www.oracle.com/technetwork/java/javase/downloads/index.html
[18] http://www.oracle.com/technetwork/java/javase/gc-tuning-6-140523.html#cms
[19] http://www.oracle.com/technetwork/java/javase/tech/largememory-jsp-137182.html
[20] http://www.azulsystems.com/technology/c4-garbage-collector
[21] http://www.azulsystems.com/products/zing/virtual-machine

7.6 Conclusions

Performance-centric middleware like Infinispan has to be architected, designed and developed with performance in mind every step of the way. From using the best non-blocking and lock-free algorithms to understanding the characteristics of garbage being generated, to developing with an appreciation for JVM context switching overhead, to being able to step outside the JVM where needed (writing native persistence components, for example) are all important parts of the mindset needed when developing Infinispan. Further, the right tools for benchmarking and profiling, as well as running benchmarks in a continuous integration style, helps ensure performance is never sacrificed as features are added.

[chapter 8]

Talos
Clint Talbert and Joel Maher

At Mozilla, one of our very first automation systems was a performance testing framework we dubbed Talos. Talos had been faithfully maintained without substantial modification since its inception in 2007, even though many of the original assumptions and design decisions behind Talos were lost as ownership of the tool changed hands.

In the summer of 2011, we finally began to look askance at the noise and the variation in the Talos numbers, and we began to wonder how we could make some small modification to the system to start improving it. We had no idea we were about to open Pandora's Box.

In this chapter, we will detail what we found as we peeled back layer after layer of this software, what problems we uncovered, and what steps we took to address them in hopes that you might learn from both our mistakes and our successes.

8.1 Overview

Let's unpack the different parts of Talos. At its heart, Talos is a simple test harness which creates a new Firefox profile, initializes the profile, calibrates the browser, runs a specified test, and finally reports a summary of the test results. The tests live inside the Talos repository and are one of two types: a single page which reports a single number (e.g., startup time via a web page's onload handler) or a collection of pages that are cycled through to measure page load times. Internally, a Firefox extension is used to cycle the pages and collect information such as memory and page load time, to force garbage collection, and to test different browser modes. The original goal was to create as generic a harness as possible to allow the harness to perform all manner of testing and measure some collection of performance attributes as defined by the test itself.

To report its data, the Talos harness can send JSON to *Graph Server*: an in-house graphing web application that accepts Talos data as long as that data meets a specific, predefined format for each test, value, platform, and configuration. Graph Server also serves as the interface for investigating trends and performance regressions. A local instance of a standard Apache web server serve the pages during a test run.

The final component of Talos is the regression reporting tools. For every check-in to the Firefox repository, several Talos tests are run, these tests upload their data to Graph Server, and another script consumes the data from Graph Server and ascertains whether or not there has been a regression. If a regression is found (i.e., the script's analysis indicates that the code checked in made performance on this test significantly worse), the script emails a message to a mailing list as well as to the individual that checked in the offending code.

While this architecture—summarized in Figure 8.1—seems fairly straightforward, each piece of Talos has morphed over the years as Mozilla has added new platforms, products, and tests. With minimal oversight of the entire system as an end to end solution, Talos wound up in need of some serious work:

- Noise—the script watching the incoming data flagged as many spikes in test noise as actual regressions and was impossible to trust.
- To determine a regression, the script compared each check-in to Firefox with the values for three check-ins prior and three afterward. This meant that the Talos results for your check-in might not be available for several hours.
- Graph Server had a hard requirement that all incoming data be tied to a previously defined platform, branch, test type, and configuration. This meant that adding new tests was difficult as it involved running a SQL statement against the database for each new test.
- The Talos harness itself was hard to run because it took its requirement to be generic a little too seriously—it had a "configure" step to generate a configuration script that it would then use to run the test in its next step.

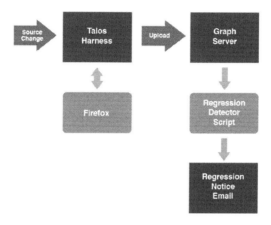

Figure 8.1: Talos architecture

While hacking on the Talos harness in the summer of 2011 to add support for new platforms and tests, we encountered the results from Jan Larres's master's thesis, in which he investigated the large amounts of noise that appeared in the Talos tests. He analyzed various factors including hardware, the operating system, the file system, drivers, and Firefox that might influence the results of a Talos test. Building on that work, Stephen Lewchuk devoted his internship to trying to statistically reduce the noise we saw in those tests.

Based on their work and interest, we began forming a plan to eliminate or reduce the noise in the Talos tests. We brought together harness hackers to work on the harness itself, web developers to update Graph Server, and statisticians to determine the optimal way to run each test to produce predictable results with minimal noise.

8.2 Understanding What You Are Measuring

When doing performance testing, it is important to have useful tests which provide value to the developers of the product and help customers to see how this product will perform under certain conditions. It is also important to have a repeatable environment so you can reproduce results as needed. But, what is most important is understanding what tests you have and what you measure from those tests.

A few weeks into our project, we had all been learning more about the entire system and started experimenting with various parameters to run the tests differently. One recurring question was "what do the numbers mean?" This was not easily answered. Many of the tests had been around for years, with little to no documentation.

Worse yet, it was not possible to produce the same results locally that were reported from an automated test run. It became evident that the harness itself performed calculations, (it would drop the highest value per page, then report the average for the rest of the cycles) and Graph Server did as well (drop the highest page value, then average the pages together). The end result was that no historical data existed that could provide much value, nor did anybody understand the tests we were running.

We did have some knowledge about one particular test. We knew that this test took the top 100 websites snapshotted in time and loaded each page one at a time, repeating 10 times. Talos loaded the page, waited for the `mozAfterPaint` event, (a standard event which is fired when Firefox has painted the canvas for the webpage) and then recorded the time from loading the page to receiving this event. Looking at the 1000 data points produced from a single test run, there was no obvious pattern. Imagine boiling those 10,000 points down to a single number and tracking that number over time. What if we made CSS parsing faster, but image loading slower? How would we detect that? Would it be possible to see page 17 slow down if all 99 other pages remained the same? To showcase how the values were calculated in the original version of Talos, consider the following numbers.

For the following page load values:

- Page 1: 570, 572, 600, 503, 560
- Page 2: 780, 650, 620, 700, 750
- Page 3: 1220, 980, 1000, 1100, 1200

First, the Talos harness itself would drop the first value and calculate the median:

- Page 1: 565.5
- Page 2: 675
- Page 3: 1050

These values would be submitted to Graph Server. Graph Server would drop the highest value and calculate the mean using these per page values and it would report that one value:

$$\frac{565.5 + 675}{2} = 620.25$$

This final value would be graphed over time, and as you can see it generates an approximate value that is not good for anything more than a coarse evaluation of performance. Furthermore, if a regression is detected using a value like this, it would be extremely difficult to work backwards and see which pages caused the regression so that a developer could be directed to a specific issue to fix.

We were determined to prove that we could reduce the noise in the data from this 100 page test. Since the test measured the time to load a page, we first needed to isolate the test from other influences in the system like caching. We changed the test to load the same page over and over again, rather than cycling between pages, so that load times were measured for a page that was mostly cached. While this approach is not indicative of how end users actually browse the web, it reduced some of the noise in the recorded data. Unfortunately, looking at only 10 data points for a given page was not a useful sample size.

By varying our sample size and measuring the standard deviation of the page load values from many test runs, we determined that noise was reduced if we loaded a page at least 20 times. After much experimentation, this method found a sweet spot with 25 loads and ignoring the first 5 loads. In other words, by reviewing the standard deviation of the values of multiple page loads, we found that 95% of our noisy results occurred within the first five loads. Even though we do not use those first 5 data points, we do store them so that we can change our statistical calculations in the future if we wish.

All this experimentation led us to some new requirements for the data collection that Talos was performing:

- All data collected needs to be stored in the database, not just averages of averages.
- A test must collect at least 20 useful data points per test (in this case, per page).
- To avoid masking regressions in one page by improvements in another page, each page must be calculated independently. No more averaging values across pages.
- Each test that is run needs to have a developer who owns the test and documentation on what is being collected and why.
- At the end of a test, we must be able to detect a regression for any given page at the time of reporting the results.

Applying these new requirements to the entire Talos system was the right thing to do, but with the ecosystem that had grown up around Talos it would be a major undertaking to switch to this new model. We had a decision to make as to whether we would refactor or rewrite the system.

8.3 Rewrite vs. Refactor

Given our research into what had to change on Talos, we knew we would be making some drastic changes. However, all historical changes to Talos at Mozilla had always suffered from a fear of "breaking the numbers." The many pieces of Talos were constructed over the years by well-intentioned contributors whose additions made sense at the time, but without documentation or oversight into the direction of the tool chain, it had become a patchwork of code that was not easy to test, modify, or understand.

Given our fear of the undocumented dark matter in the code base, combined with the issue that we would need to verify our new measurements against the old measurements, we began a refactoring effort to modify Talos and Graph Server in place. However, it was quickly evident that without a massive re-architecture of the database schema, The Graph Server system would never be able to ingest the full set of raw data from the performance tests. Additionally, we had no clean way to apply our newly-researched statistical methods into Graph Server's backend. Therefore, we decided to rewrite Graph Server from scratch, creating a project called Datazilla. This was not a decision made lightly, as other open source projects had forked the Graph Server code base for their own performance automation. On the Talos harness side of the equation, we also did a prototype from scratch. We even had a working prototype that ran a simple test and was about 2000 lines of code lighter.

While we rewrote Graph Server from scratch, we were worried about moving ahead with our new Talos test runner prototype. Our fear was that we might lose the ability to run the numbers "the old way" so that we could compare the new approach with the old. So, we abandoned our prototype and modified the Talos harness itself piecemeal to transform it into a data generator while leaving the existing pieces that performed averages to upload to the old Graph Server system. This was a singularly bad decision. We should have built a separate harness and then compared the new harness with the old one.

Trying to support the original flow of data and the new method for measuring data for each page proved to be difficult. On the positive side, it forced us to restructure much of the code internal to the framework and to streamline quite a few things. But, we had to do all this piecemeal on a running piece of automation, which caused us several headaches in our continuous integration rigs.

It would have been far better to develop both Talos the framework and Datazilla its reporting system in parallel from scratch, leaving all of the old code behind. Especially when it came to staging, it would have been far easier to stage the new system without attempting to wire in the generation of development data for the upcoming Datazilla system in running automation. We had thought it was necessary to do this so that we could generate test data with real builds and real load to ensure that our design would scale properly. In the end, that build data was not worth the complexity of modifying a production system. If we had known at the time that we were embarking on a year long project instead of our projected six month project, we would have rewritten Talos and the results framework from scratch.

8.4 Creating a Performance Culture

Being an open source project, we need to embrace the ideas and criticisms from other individuals and projects. There is no director of development saying how things will work. In order to get the most information possible and make the right decision, it was a requirement to pull in many people from many different teams. The project started off with two developers on the Talos framework, two on Datazilla/Graph Server, and two statisticians on loan from our metrics team. We opened up this project to our volunteers from the beginning and pulled in many fresh faces to Mozilla as well as others who used Graph Server and some Talos tests for their own projects. As we worked together, slowly understanding what permutations of test runs would give us less noisy results, we reached out to include several Mozilla developers in the project. Our first meetings with them were understandably rocky, due to the large changes we were proposing to make. The mystery of "Talos" was making this a hard sell for many developers who cared a lot about performance.

The important message that took a while to settle in was why rewriting large components of the system was a good idea, and why we couldn't simply "fix it in place." The most common feedback was to make a few small changes to the existing system, but everyone making that suggestion had no idea how the underlying system worked. We gave many presentations, invited many people to our meetings, held special one-off meetings, blogged, posted, tweeted, etc. We did everything we could to get the word out. Because the only thing more horrible than doing all this work to create a better system would be to do all the work and have no one use it.

It has been a year since our first review of the Talos noise problem. Developers are looking forward to what we are releasing. The Talos framework has been refactored so that it has a clear internal structure and so that it can simultaneously report to Datazilla and the old Graph Server. We have verified that Datazilla can handle the scale of data we are throwing at it (1 TB of data per six months) and have vetted our metrics for calculation results. Most excitingly, we have found a way to deliver a regression/improvement analysis in real time on a per-change basis to the Mozilla trees, which is a big win for developers.

So, now when someone pushes a change to Firefox, here is what Talos does:

- Talos collects 25 data points for each page.
- All of those numbers are uploaded to Datazilla.

- Datazilla performs the statistical analysis after dropping the first five data points. (95% of noise is found in the first 5 data points.)
- A Welch's T-Test is then used to analyze the numbers and detect if there are any outliers in the per-page data as compared to previous trends from previous pushes.[1]
- All results of the T-Test analysis are then pushed through a False Discovery Rate filter which ensures that Datazilla can detect any false positives that are simply due to noise.[2]
- Finally, if the results are within our tolerance, Datazilla runs the results through an exponential smoothing algorithm to generate a new trend line.[3] If the results are not within our tolerance, they do not form a new trend line and the page is marked as a failure.
- We determine overall pass/fail metrics based on the percentage of pages passing. 95% passing is a "pass".

The results come back to the Talos harness in real time, and Talos can then report to the build script whether or not there is a performance regression. All of this takes place with 10-20 Talos runs completing every minute (hence the 1 TB of data) while updating the calculations and stored statistics at the same time.

Taking this from a working solution to replacing the existing solution requires running both systems side by side for a full release of Firefox. This process ensures that we look at all regressions reported by the original Graph Server and make sure they are real and reported by Datazilla as well. Since Datazilla reports on a per-page basis instead of at the test suite level, there will be some necessary acclimation to the new UI and way we report regressions.

Looking back, it would have been faster to have replaced the old Talos harness up front. By refactoring it, however, Mozilla brought many new contributors into the Talos project. Refactoring has also forced us to understand the tests better, which has translated into fixing a lot of broken tests and turning off tests with little to no value. So, when considering whether to rewrite or refactor, total time expended is not the only metric to review.

8.5 Conclusion

In the last year, we dug into every part of performance testing automation at Mozilla. We have analyzed the test harness, the reporting tools, and the statistical soundness of the results that were being generated. Over the course of that year, we used what we learned to make the Talos framework easier to maintain, easier to run, simpler to set up, easier to test experimental patches with, and less error prone. We have created Datazilla as an extensible system for storing and retrieving all of our performance metrics from Talos and any future performance automation. We have rebooted our performance statistical analysis and created statistically viable, per-push regression/improvement detection. We have made all of these systems easier to use and more open so that any contributor anywhere can take a look at our code and even experiment with new methods of statistical analysis on our performance data. Our constant commitment to reviewing the data again and again at each milestone of the project and our willingness to throw out data that proved inconclusive or invalid helped us retain our focus as we drove this gigantic project forward. Bringing in people from across teams at Mozilla as well as many new volunteers helped lend the effort validity and also helped to establish a resurgence in performance monitoring and data analysis across several areas of Mozilla's efforts, resulting in an even more data-driven, performance-focused culture.

---

[1] https://github.com/mozilla/datazilla/blob/2c39a3/vendor/dzmetrics/ttest.py
[2] https://github.com/mozilla/datazilla/blob/2c369a/vendor/dzmetrics/fdr.py
[3] https://github.com/mozilla/datazilla/blob/2c369a/vendor/dzmetrics/data_smoothing.py

[chapter 9]

Zotonic
Arjan Scherpenisse and Marc Worrell

9.1 Introduction to Zotonic

Zotonic is an open source framework for doing full-stack web development, all the way from frontend to backend. Consisting of a small set of core functionalities, it implements a lightweight but extensible Content Management System on top. Zotonic's main goal is to make it easy to create well-performing websites "out of the box", so that a website scales well from the start.

While it shares many features and functionalities with web development frameworks like Django, Drupal, Ruby on Rails and Wordpress, its main competitive advantage is the language that Zotonic is powered by: Erlang. This language, originally developed for building phone switches, allows Zotonic to be fault tolerant and have great performance characteristics.

Like the title says, this chapter focusses on the performance of Zotonic. We'll look at the reasons why Erlang was chosen as the programming platform, then inspect the HTTP request stack, then dive in to the caching strategies that Zotonic employs. Finally, we'll describe the optimisations we applied to Zotonic's submodules and the database.

9.2 Why Zotonic? Why Erlang?

The first work on Zotonic was started in 2008, and, like many projects, came from "scratching an itch". Marc Worrell, the main Zotonic architect, had been working for seven years at Mediamatic Lab, in Amsterdam, on a Drupal-like CMS written in PHP/MySQL called Anymeta. Anymeta's main paradigm was that it implemented a "pragmatic approach to the Semantic Web" by modeling everything in the system as generic "things". Though successful, its implementations suffered from scalability problems.

After Marc left Mediamatic, he spent a few months designing a proper, Anymeta-like CMS from scratch. The main design goals for Zotonic were that it had to be easy to use for frontend developers; it had to support easy development of real-time web interfaces, simultaneously allowing long-lived connections and many short requests; and it had to have well-defined performance characteristics. More importantly, it had to solve the most common problems that limited performance in earlier Web development approaches—for example, it had to withstand the "Shashdot Effect" (a sudden rush of visitors).

Problems with the Classic PHP+Apache Approach

A classic PHP setup runs as a module inside a container web server like Apache. On each request, Apache decides how to handle the request. When it's a PHP request, it spins up mod_php5, and then the PHP interpreter starts interpreting the script. This comes with startup latency: typically, such a spin-up already takes 5 ms, and then the PHP code still needs to run. This problem can partially be mitigated by using PHP accelerators which precompile the PHP script, bypassing the interpreter. The PHP startup overhead can also be mitigated by using a process manager like PHP-FPM.

Nevertheless, systems like that still suffer from a *shared nothing* architecture. When a script needs a database connection, it needs to create one itself. Same goes any other I/O resource that could otherwise be shared between requests. Various modules feature persistent connections to overcome this, but there is no general solution to this problem in PHP.

Handling long-lived client connections is also hard because such connections need a separate web server thread or process for every request. In the case of Apache and PHP-FPM, this does not scale with many concurrent long-lived connections.

Requirements for a Modern Web Framework

Modern web frameworks typically deal with three classes of HTTP request. First, there are dynamically generated pages: dynamically served, usually generated by a template processor. Second, there is static content: small and large files which do not change (e.g., JavaScript, CSS, and media assets). Third, there are long-lived connections: WebSockets and long-polling requests for adding interactivity and two-way communication to pages.

Before creating Zotonic, we were looking for a software framework and programming language that would allow us to meet our design goals (high performance, developer friendliness) and sidestep the bottlenecks associated with traditional web server systems. Ideally the software would meet the following requirements.

- Concurrent: it needs to support many concurrent connections that are not limited by the number of unix processes or OS threads.
- Shared resources: it needs to have a mechanism to share resources cheaply (e.g., caching, db connections) between requests.
- Hot code upgrades: for ease of development and the enabling of hot-upgrading production systems (keeping downtime to a minimum), it would be nice if code changes could be deployed in a running system, without needing to restart it.
- Multi-core CPU support: a modern system needs to scale over multiple cores, as current CPUs tend to get scale in number of cores as opposed to increased clock speed.
- Fault tolerant: the system needs to be able to handle exceptional situations, "badly behaving" code, anomalies or resource starvation. Ideally, the system would achieve this by having some kind of supervision mechanism to restart the failing parts.
- Distributed: ideally, a system has built-in and easy to set up support for distribution over multiple nodes, to allow for better performance and protection against hardware failure.

Erlang to the Rescue

To our knowledge, Erlang was the only language that met these requirements "out of the box". The Erlang VM, combined with its Open Telecom Platform (OTP), provided the system that gave and continues to give us all the necessary features.

Erlang is a (mostly) functional programming language and runtime system. Erlang/OTP applications were originally developed for telephone switches, and are known for their fault-tolerance and their concurrent nature. Erlang employs an actor-based concurrency model: each actor is a lightweight "process" (green thread) and the only way to share state between processes is to pass messages. The Open Telecom Platform is the set of standard Erlang libraries which enable fault tolerance and process supervision, amongst others.

Fault tolerance is at the core of its programming paradigm: *let it crash* is the main philosophy of the system. As processes don't share any state (to share state, they must send messages to each other), their state is isolated from other processes. As such, a single crashing process will never take down the system. When a process crashes, its supervisor process can decide to restart it.

Let it crash also allows you to program for the happy case. Using pattern matching and function guards to assure a sane state means less error handling code is needed, which usually results in clean, concise, and readable code.

9.3 Zotonic's Architecture

Before we discuss Zotonic's performance optimizations, let's have a look at its architecture. Figure 9.1 describes Zotonic's most important components.

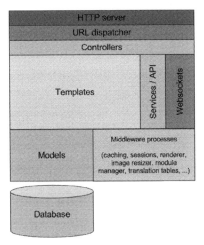

Figure 9.1: The architecture of Zotonic

The diagram shows the layers of Zotonic that an HTTP request goes through. For discussing performance issues we'll need to know what these layers are, and how they affect performance.

First, Zotonic comes with a built in web server, Mochiweb (another Erlang project). It does not require an external web server. This keeps the deployment dependencies to a minimum.[1]

Like many web frameworks, a URL routing system is used to match requests to controllers. Controllers handle each request in a RESTful way, thanks to the Webmachine library.

Controllers are "dumb" on purpose, without much application-specific logic. Zotonic provides a number of standard controllers which, for the development of basic web applications, are often good

---

[1] However, it is possible to put another web server in front, for example when other web systems are running on the same server. But for normal cases, this is not needed. It is interesting that a typical optimisation that other frameworks use is to put a caching web server such as Varnish in front of their application server for serving static files, but for Zotonic this does not speed up those requests significantly, as Zotonic also caches static files in memory.)

enough. For instance, there is a `controller_template`, whose sole purpose it is to reply to HTTP GET requests by rendering a given template.

The template language is an Erlang-implementation of the well-known Django Template Language, called ErlyDTL. The general principle in Zotonic is that the templates drive the data requests. The templates decide which data they need, and retrieve it from the models.

Models expose functions to retrieve data from various data sources, like a database. Models expose an API to the templates, dictating how they can be used. The models are also responsible for caching their results in memory; they decide when and what is cached and for how long. When templates need data, they call a model as if it were a globally available variable.

A model is an Erlang wrapper module which is responsible for certain data. It contains the necessary functions to retrieve and store data in the way that the application needs. For instance, the central model of Zotonic is called `m.rsc`, which provide access to the generic resource ("page") data model. Since resources use the database, `m_rsc.erl` uses a database connection to retrieve its data and pass it through to the template, caching it whenever it can.

This "templates drive the data" approach is different from other web frameworks like Rails and Django, which usually follow a more classical MVC approach where a controller assigns data to a template. Zotonic follows a less "controller-centric" approach, so that typical websites can be built by just writing templates.

Zotonic uses PostgreSQL for data persistence. Section 9.8 explains the rationale for this choice.

Additional Zotonic Concepts

While the main focus of this chapter are the performance characteristics of the web request stack, it is useful to know some of the other concepts that are at the heart of Zotonic.

Virtual hosting A single Zotonic instance typically serves more than one site. It is designed for virtual hosting, including domain aliases and SSL support. And due to Erlang's process-isolation, a crashing site does not affect any of the other sites running in the same VM.

Modules Modules are Zotonic's way of grouping functionality together. Each module is in its own directory containing Erlang files, templates, assets, etc. They can be enabled on a per-site basis. Modules can hook into the admin system: for instance, the `mod_backup` module adds version control to the page editor and also runs a daily full database backup. Another module, `mod_github`, exposes a webhook which pulls, rebuilds and reloads a Zotonic site from github, allowing for continuous deployment.

Notifications To enable the loose coupling and extensibility of code, communication between modules and core components is done by a notification mechanism which functions either as a map or fold over the observers of a certain named notification. By listening to notifications it becomes easy for a module to override or augment certain behaviour. The calling function decides whether a map or fold is used. For instance, the `admin_menu` notification is a fold over the modules which allow modules to add or remove menu items in the admin menu.

Data model The main data model that Zotonic uses can be compared to Drupal's Node module; "every thing is a thing". The data model consists of hierarchically categorized resources which connect to other resources using labelled edges. Like its source of inspiration, the Anymeta CMS, this data model is loosely based on the principles of the Semantic Web.

Zotonic is an extensible system, and all parts of the system add up when you consider performance. For instance, you might add a module that intercepts web requests, and does something on each request. Such a module might impact the performance of the entire system. In this chapter we'll leave this out of consideration, and instead focus on the core performance issues.

9.4 Problem Solving: Fighting the Slashdot Effect

Most web sites live an unexceptional life in a small place somewhere on the web. That is, until one of their pages hit the front page of a popular website like CNN, BBC or Yahoo. In that case, the traffic to the website will likely increase to tens, hundreds, or even thousands of page requests per second in no time.

Such a sudden surge overloads a traditional web server and makes it unreachable. The term "Slashdot Effect" was named after the web site that started this kind of overwhelming referrals. Even worse, an overloaded server is sometimes very hard to restart. As the newly started server has empty caches, no database connections, often un-compiled templates, etc.

Many anonymous visitors requesting exactly the same page around the same time shouldn't be able to overload a server. This problem is easily solved using a caching proxy like Varnish, which caches a static copy of the page and only checks for updates to the page once in a while.

A surge of traffic becomes more challenging when serving dynamic pages for every single visitor; these can't be cached. With Zotonic, we set out to solve this problem.

We realized that most web sites have

- only have a limited number of very popular pages,
- a long tail of far less popular pages, and
- many shared parts on all pages (menu, most read items, news, etc.).

and decided to

- cache hot data in memory so no communication needed to access it,
- share renderings of templates and sub-templates between requests and on pages on the web site, and
- explicitly design the system to prevent overload on server start and restart.

Cache Hot Data

Why fetch data from an external source (database, memcached) when another request fetched it already a couple of milliseconds ago? We always cache simple data requests. In the next section the caching mechanism is discussed in detail.

Share Rendered Templates and Sub-templates Between Pages

When rendering a page or included template, a developer can add optional caching directives. This caches the rendered result for a period of time.

Caching starts what we called the *memo* functionality: while the template is being rendered and one or more processes request the same rendering, the later processes will be suspended. When the rendering is done all waiting processes will be sent the rendering result

The memoization alone—without any further caching—gives a large performance boost by drastically reducing the amount of parallel template processing.

Prevent Overload on Server Start or Restart

Zotonic introduces several bottlenecks on purpose. These bottlenecks limit the access to processes that use limited resources or are expensive (in terms of CPU or memory) to perform. Bottlenecks are currently set up for the template compiler, the image resizing process, and the database connection pool.

The bottlenecks are implemented by having a limited worker pool for performing the requested action. For CPU or disk intensive work, like image resizing, there is only a single process handling the requests. Requesting processes post their request in the Erlang request queue for the process and wait until their request is handled. If a request times out it will just crash. Such a crashing request will return HTTP status 503 *Service not available*.

Waiting processes don't use many resources and the bottlenecks protect against overload if a template is changed or an image on a hot page is replaced and needs cropping or resizing.

In short: a busy server can still dynamically update its templates, content and images without getting overloaded. At the same time it allows single requests to crash while the system itself continues to operate.

The Database Connection Pool

One more word on database connections. In Zotonic a process fetches a database connection from a pool of connections for every single query or transaction. This enables many concurrent processes to share a very limited number of database connections. Compare this with most (PHP) systems where every request holds a connection to the database for the duration of the complete request.

Zotonic closes unused database connections after a time of inactivity. One connection is always left open so that the system can always handle an incoming request or background activity quickly. The dynamic connection pool drastically reduces the number of open database connections on most Zotonic web sites to one or two.

9.5 Caching Layers

The hardest part of caching is cache invalidation: keeping the cached data fresh and purging stale data. Zotonic uses a central caching mechanism with dependency checks to solve this problem.

This section describes Zotonic's caching mechanism in a top-down fashion: from the browser down through the stack to the database.

Client-Side Caching

The client-side caching is done by the browser. The browser caches images, CSS and JavaScript files. Zotonic does not allow client-side caching of HTML pages, it always dynamically generates all pages. Because it is very efficient in doing so (as described in the previous section) and not caching HTML pages prevents showing old pages after users log in, log out, or comments are placed.

Zotonic improves client-side performance in two ways:

1. It allows caching of static files (CSS, JavaScript, images etc.)
2. It includes multiple CSS or JavaScript files in a single response

The first is done by adding the appropriate HTTP headers to the request[2]:

```
Last-Modified: Tue, 18 Dec 2012 20:32:56 GMT
Expires: Sun, 01 Jan 2023 14:55:37 GMT
Date: Thu, 03 Jan 2013 14:55:37 GMT
Cache-Control: public, max-age=315360000
```

Multiple CSS or JavaScript files are concatenated into a single file, separating individual files by a tilde and only mentioning paths if they change between files:

```
http://example.org/lib/bootstrap/css/bootstrap
  ~bootstrap-responsive~bootstrap-base-site~
  /css/jquery.loadmask~z.growl~z.modal~site~63523081976.css
```

The number at the end is a timestamp of the newest file in the list. The necessary CSS link or JavaScript script tag is generated using the {% lib %} template tag.

Server-Side Caching

Zotonic is a large system, and many parts in it do caching in some way. The sections below explain some of the more interesting parts.

Static CSS, JS and Image Files

The controller handling the static files has some optimizations for handling these files. It can decompose combined file requests into a list of individual files.

The controller has checks for the If-Modified-Since header, serving the HTTP status 304 *Not Modified* when appropriate.

On the first request it will concatenate the contents of all the static files into one byte array (an Erlang *binary*).[3] This byte array is then cached in the central depcache (see Section 9.5) in two forms: compressed (with gzip) and uncompressed. Depending on the Accept-Encoding headers sent by the browser, Zotonic will serve either the compressed or uncompressed version.

This caching mechanism is efficient enough that its performance is similar to many caching proxies, while still fully controlled by the web server. With an earlier version of Zotonic and on simple hardware (quad core 2.4 GHz Xeon from 2008) we saw throughputs of around 6000 requests/second and were able to saturate a gigabit ethernet connection requesting a small (~20 KB) image file.

Rendered Templates

Templates are compiled into Erlang modules, after which the byte code is kept in memory. Compiled templates are called as regular Erlang functions.

The template system detects any changes to templates and will recompile the template during runtime. When compilation is finished Erlang's hot code upgrade mechanism is used to load the newly compiled Erlang module.

---

[2] Note that Zotonic does not set an ETag. Some browsers check the ETag for every use of the file by making a request to the server. Which defies the whole idea of caching and making fewer requests.

[3] A byte array, or binary, is a native Erlang data type. If it is smaller than 64 bytes it is copied between processes, larger ones are shared between processes. Erlang also shares parts of byte arrays between processes with references to those parts and not copying the data itself, thus making these byte arrays an efficient and easy to use data type.

The main page and template controllers have options to cache the template rendering result. Caching can also be enabled only for anonymous (not logged in) visitors. As for most websites, anonymous visitors generate the bulk of all requests and those pages will be not be personalized and (almost) be identical. Note that template rendering results is an intermediate result and not the final HTML. This intermediate result contains (among others) untranslated strings and JavaScript fragments. The final HTML is generated by parsing this intermediate structure, picking the correct translations and collecting all javascript.

The concatenated JavaScript, along with a unique page ID, is placed at the position of the `{% script %}` template tag. This should be just above the closing </body> body tag. The unique page ID is used to match this rendered page with the handling Erlang processes and for WebSocket/Comet interaction on the page.

Like with any template language, templates can include other templates. In Zotonic, included templates are usually compiled inline to eliminate any performance lost by using included files.

Special options can force runtime inclusion. One of those options is caching. Caching can be enabled for anonymous visitors only, a caching period can be set, and cache dependencies can be added. These cache dependencies are used to invalidate the cached rendering if any of the shown resources is changed.

Another method to cache parts of templates is to use the `{% cache %}` ... `{% endcache %}` block tag, which caches a part of a template for a given amount of time. This tag has the same caching options as the include tag, but has the advantage that it can easily be added in existing templates.

In-Memory Caching

All caching is done in memory, in the Erlang VM itself. No communication between computers or operating system processes is needed to access the cached data. This greatly simplifies and optimizes the use of the cached data.

As a comparison, accessing a memcache server typically takes 0.5 milliseconds. In contrast, accessing main memory within the same process takes 1 nanoseconds on a CPU cache hit and 100 nanoseconds on a CPU cache miss—not to mention the huge speed difference between memory and network.[4]

Zotonic has two in-memory caching mechanisms [5]:

1. Depcache, the central per-site cache
2. Process Dictionary Memo Cache

Depcache

The central caching mechanism in every Zotonic site is the *depcache*, which is short for *dep*endency *cache*. The depcache is an in-memory key-value store with a list of dependencies for every stored key.

For every key in the depcache we store:

- the key's value;
- a serial number, a global integer incremented with every update request;
- the key's expiration time (counted in seconds);

---

[4] See "Latency Numbers Every Programmer Should Know" at
http://www.eecs.berkeley.edu/~rcs/research/interactive_latency.html.

[5] In addition to these mechanisms, the database server performs some in-memory caching, but that is not within the scope of this chapter.

- a list of other keys that this key depends on (e.g., a resource ID displayed in a cached template); and
- if the key is still being calculated, a list of processes waiting for the key's value.

If a key is requested then the cache checks if the key is present, not expired, and if the serial numbers of all the dependency keys are lower than serial number of the cached key. If the key was still valid its value is returned, otherwise the key and its value is removed from the cache and undefined is returned.

Alternatively if the key was being calculated then the requesting process would be added to the waiting list of the key.

The implementation makes use of ETS, the Erlang Term Storage, a standard hash table implementation which is part of the Erlang OTP distribution. The following ETS tables are created by Zotonic for the depcache:

- Meta table: the ETS table holding all stored keys, the expiration and the depending keys. A record in this table is written as #meta{key, expire, serial, deps}.
- Deps table: the ETS table stores the serial for each key.
- Data table: the ETS table that stores each key's data.
- Waiting PIDs dictionary: the ETS table that stores the IDs of all processes waiting for the arrival of a key's value.

The ETS tables are optimized for parallel reads and usually directly accessed by the calling process. This prevents any communication between the calling process and the depcache process.

The depcache process is called for:

- memoization where processes wait for another process's value to be calculated;
- *put* (store) requests, serializing the serial number increments; and
- delete requests, also serializing the depcache access.

The depcache can get quite large. To prevent it from growing too large there is a garbage collector process. The garbage collector slowly iterates over the complete depcache, evicting expired or invalidated keys. If the depcache size is above a certain threshold (100 MiB by default) then the garbage collector speeds up and evicts 10% of all encountered items. It keeps evicting until the cache is below its threshold size.

100 MiB might sound small in this area of multi-TB databases. However, as the cache mostly contains textual data it will be big enough to contain the hot data for most web sites. Otherwise the size of the cache can be changed in configuration.

Process Dictionary Memo Cache

The other memory-caching paradigm in Zotonic is the process dictionary memo cache. As described earlier, the data access patterns are dictated by the templates. The caching system uses simple heuristics to optimize access to data.

Important in this optimization is data caching in the Erlang process dictionary of the process handling the request. The process dictionary is a simple key-value store in the same heap as the process. Basically, it adds state to the functional Erlang language. Use of the process dictionary is usually frowned upon for this reason, but for in-process caching it is useful.

When a resource is accessed (remember, a resource is the central data unit of Zotonic), it is copied into the process dictionary. The same is done for computational results—like access control checks—and other data like configuration values.

Every property of a resource—like its title, summary or body text—must, when shown on a page, perform an access control check and then fetch the requested property from the resource. Caching all the resource's properties and its access checks greatly speeds up resource data usage and removes many drawbacks of the hard-to-predict data access patterns by templates.

As a page or process can use a lot of data this memo cache has a couple of pressure valves:

1. When holding more than 10,000 keys the whole process dictionary is flushed. This prevents process dictionaries holding many unused items, like what happens when looping through long lists of resources. Special Erlang variables like $ancestors are kept.
2. The memo cache must be programmatically enabled. This is automatically done for every incoming HTTP or WebSocket request and template rendering.
3. Between HTTP/WebSocket requests the process dictionary is flushed, as multiple sequential HTTP/WebSocket requests share the same process.
4. The memo cache doesn't track dependencies. Any depcache deletion will also flush the complete process dictionary of the process performing the deletion.

When the memo cache is disabled then every lookup is handled by the depcache. This results in a call to the depcache process and data copying between the depcache and the requesting process.

9.6 The Erlang Virtual Machine

The Erlang Virtual Machine has a few properties that are important when looking at performance.

Processes are Cheap

The Erlang VM is specifically designed to do many things in parallel, and as such has its own implementation of multiprocessing within the VM. Erlang processes are scheduled on a reduction count basis, where one reduction is roughly equivalent to a function call. A process is allowed to run until it pauses to wait for input (a message from some other process) or until it has executed a fixed number of reductions. For each CPU core, a scheduler is started with its own run queue. It is not uncommon for Erlang applications to have thousands to millions of processes alive in the VM at any given point in time.

Processes are not only cheap to start but also cheap in memory at 327 words per process, which amounts to ~2.5 KiB on a 64 bit machine.[6] This compares to ~500 KiB for Java and a default of 2 MiB for pthreads.

Since processes are so cheap to use, any processing that is not needed for a request's result is spawned off into a separate process. Sending an email or logging are both examples of tasks that could be handled by separate processes.

Data Copying is Expensive

In the Erlang VM messages between processes are relatively expensive, as the message is copied in the process. This copying is needed due to Erlang's per-process garbage collector. Preventing data copying is important; which is why Zotonic's depcache uses ETS tables, which can be accessed from any process.

---

[6]See http://www.erlang.org/doc/efficiency_guide/advanced.html#id68921

Separate Heap for Bigger Byte Arrays

There is a big exception for copying data between processes. Byte arrays larger than 64 bytes are not copied between processes. They have their own heap and are separately garbage collected.

This makes it cheap to send a big byte array between processes, as only a reference to the byte array is copied. However, it does make garbage collection harder, as all references must be garbage collected before the byte array can be freed.

Sometimes, references to parts of a big byte array are passed: the bigger byte array can't be garbage collected until the reference to the smaller part is garbage collected. A consequence is that copying a byte array is an optimization if that frees up the bigger byte array.

String Processing is Expensive

String processing in any functional language can be expensive because strings are often represented as linked lists of integers, and, due to the functional nature of Erlang, data cannot be destructively updated.

If a string is represented as a list, then it is processed using tail recursive functions and pattern matching. This makes it a natural fit for functional languages. The problem is that the data representation of a linked list has a big overhead and that messaging a list to another process always involves copying the full data structure. This makes a list a non-optimal choice for strings.

Erlang has its own middle-of-the-road answer to strings: io-lists. Io-lists are nested lists containing lists, integers (single byte value), byte arrays and references to parts of other byte arrays. Io-lists are extremely easy to use and appending, prefixing or inserting data is inexpensive, as they only need changes to relatively short lists, without any data copying.[7]

An io-list can be sent as-is to a "port" (a file descriptor), which flattens the data structure to a byte stream and sends it to a socket.

Example of an io-list:

```
[ <<"Hello">>, 32, [ <<"Wo">>, [114, 108], <<"d">>]].
```

which flattens to the byte array:

```
<<"Hello World">>.
```

Interestingly, most string processing in a web application consists of:

1. Concatenating data (dynamic and static) into the resulting page.
2. HTML escaping and sanitizing content values.

Erlang's io-list is the perfect data structure for the first use case. And the second use case is resolved by an aggressive sanitization of all content *before* it is stored in the database.

These two combined means that for Zotonic a rendered page is just a big concatenation of byte arrays and pre-sanitized values in a single io-list.

---

[7] Erlang can also *share* parts of a byte array with references to those parts, thus circumventing the need to copy that data. An insert into a byte array can be represented by an io-list of three parts: a references to the unchanged head bytes, the inserted value, and a reference to the unchanged tail bytes.

Implications for Zotonic

Zotonic makes heavy use of a relatively big data structure, the *Context*. This is a record containing all data needed for a request evaluation. It contains:

- The request data: headers, request arguments, body data etc.
- Webmachine status
- User information (e.g., user ID, access control information)
- Language preference
- `User-Agent` class (e.g., text, phone, tablet, desktop)
- References to special site processes (e.g., notifier, depcache, etc.)
- Unique ID for the request being processed (this will become the page ID)
- Session and page process IDs
- Database connection process during a transaction
- Accumulators for reply data (e.g., data, actions to be rendered, JavaScript files)

All this data can make a large data structure. Sending this large Context to different processes working on the request would result in a substantial data copying overhead.

That is why we try to do most of the request processing in a single process: the Mochiweb process that accepted the request. Additional modules and extensions are called using function calls instead of using inter-process messages.

Sometimes an extension is implemented using a separate process. In that case the extension provides a function accepting the Context and the process ID of the extension process. This interface function is then responsible of efficiently messaging the extension process.

Zotonic also needs to send a message when rendering cacheable sub-templates. In this case the Context is pruned of all intermediate template results and some other unneeded data (like logging information) before the Context is messaged to the process rendering the sub-template.

We don't care too much about messaging byte arrays as they are, in most cases, larger than 64 bytes and as such will not be copied between processes.

For serving large static files, there is the option of using the Linux `sendfile()` system call to delegate sending the file to the operating system.

9.7 Changes to the Webmachine Library

Webmachine is a library implementing an abstraction of the HTTP protocol. It is implemented on top of the Mochiweb library which implements the lower level HTTP handling, like acceptor processes, header parsing, etc.

Controllers are made by creating Erlang modules implementing callback functions. Examples of callback functions are `resource_exists`, `previously_existed`, `authorized`, `allowed_methods`, `process_post`, etc. Webmachine also matches request paths against a list of dispatch rules; assigning request arguments and selecting the correct controller for handling the HTTP request.

With Webmachine, handling the HTTP protocol becomes easy. We decided early on to build Zotonic on top of Webmachine for this reason.

While building Zotonic a couple of problems with Webmachine were encountered.

1. When we started, it supported only a single list of dispatch rules; not a list of rules per host (i.e., site).
2. Dispatch rules are set in the application environment, and copied to the request process when dispatching.

3. Some callback functions (like `last_modified`) are called multiple times during request evaluation.
4. When Webmachine crashes during request evaluation no log entry is made by the request logger.
5. No support for HTTP Upgrade, making WebSockets support harder.

The first problem (no partitioning of dispatch rules) is only a nuisance. It makes the list of dispatch rules less intuitive and more difficult to interpret.

The second problem (copying the dispatch list for every request) turned out to be a show stopper for Zotonic. The lists could become so large that copying it could take the majority of time needed to handle a request.

The third problem (multiple calls to the same functions) forced controller writers to implement their own caching mechanisms, which is error prone.

The fourth problem (no log on crash) makes it harder to see problems when in production.

The fifth problem (no HTTP Upgrade) prevents us from using the nice abstractions available in Webmachine for WebSocket connections.

The above problems were so serious that we had to modify Webmachine for our own purposes.

First a new option was added: dispatcher. A dispatcher is a module implementing the `dispatch/3` function which matches a request to a dispatch list. The dispatcher also selects the correct site (virtual host) using the HTTP Host header. When testing a simple "hello world" controller, these changes gave a threefold increase of throughput. We also observed that the gain was much higher on systems with many virtual hosts and dispatch rules.

Webmachine maintains two data structures, one for the request data and one for the internal request processing state. These data structures were referring to each other and actually were almost always used in tandem, so we combined them in a single data structure. Which made it easier to remove the use of the process dictionary and add the new single data structure as an argument to all functions inside Webmachine. This resulted in 20% less processing time per request.

We optimized Webmachine in many other ways that we will not describe in detail here, but the most important points are:

- Return values of some controller callbacks are cached (`charsets_provided`, `content_types_provided`, `encodings_provided`, `last_modified`, and `generate_etag`).
- More process dictionary use was removed (less global state, clearer code, easier testing).
- Separate logger process per request; even when a request crashes we have a log up to the point of the crash.
- An HTTP Upgrade callback was added as a step after the *forbidden* access check to support WebSockets.
- Originally, a controller was called a "resource". We changed it to "controller" to make a clear distinction between the (data-)resources being served and the code serving those resources.
- Some instrumentation was added to measure request speed and size.

9.8 Data Model: a Document Database in SQL

From a data perspective it is worth mentioning that all properties of a "resource" (Zotonic's main data unit) are serialized into a binary blob; "real" database columns are only used for keys, querying and foreign key constraints.

Separate "pivot" fields and tables are added for properties, or combinations of properties that need indexing, like full text columns, date properties, etc.

When a resource is updated, a database trigger adds the resource's ID to the pivot queue. This pivot queue is consumed by a separate Erlang background process which indexes batches of resources at a time in a single transaction.

Choosing SQL made it possible for us to hit the ground running: PostgreSQL has a well known query language, great stability, known performance, excellent tools, and both commercial and non-commercial support.

Beyond that, the database is not the limiting performance factor in Zotonic. If a query becomes the bottleneck, then it is the task of the developer to optimize that particular query using the database's query analyzer.

Finally, the golden performance rule for working with any database is: Don't hit the database; don't hit the disk; don't hit the network; hit your cache.

9.9 Benchmarks, Statistics and Optimizations

We don't believe too much in benchmarks as they often test only minimal parts of a system and don't represent the performance of the whole system. Especially as a system has many moving parts and in Zotonic the caching system and handling common access patterns are an integral part of the design.

A Simplified Benchmark

What a benchmark *might do* is show where you could optimize the system first.

With this in mind we benchmarked Zotonic using the TechEmpower JSON benchmark, which is basically testing the request dispatcher, JSON encoder, HTTP request handling and the TCP/IP stack.

The benchmark was performed on a Intel i7 quad core M620 @ 2.67 GHz. The command was `wrk -c 3000 -t 3000 http://localhost:8080/json`. The results are shown in Table 9.1.

Platform	x1000 Requests/sec
Node.js	27
Cowboy (Erlang)	31
Elli (Erlang)	38
Zotonic	5.5
Zotonic w/o access log	7.5
Zotonic w/o access log, with dispatcher pool	8.5

Table 9.1: Benchmark Results

Zotonic's dynamic dispatcher and HTTP protocol abstraction gives lower scores in such a micro benchmark. Those are relatively easy to solve, and the solutions were already planned:

- Replace the standard webmachine logger with a more efficient one
- Compile the dispatch rules in an Erlang module (instead of a single process interpreting the dispatch rule list)
- Replace the MochiWeb HTTP handler with the Elli HTTP handler
- Use byte arrays in Webmachine instead of the current character lists

Real-Life Performance

For the 2013 abdication of the Dutch queen and subsequent inauguration of the new Dutch king a national voting site was built using Zotonic. The client requested 100% availability and high performance, being able to handle 100,000 votes per hour.

The solution was a system with four virtual servers, each with 2 GB RAM and running their own independent Zotonic system. Three nodes handled voting, one node was for administration. All nodes were independent but the voting nodes shared every vote with the at least two other nodes, so no vote would be lost if a node crashed.

A single vote gave ~30 HTTP requests for dynamic HTML (in multiple languages), Ajax, and static assets like css and javascript. Multiple requests were needed for selecting the three projects to vote on and filling in the details of the voter.

When tested we easily met the customer's requirements without pushing the system to the max. The voting simulation was stopped at 500,000 complete voting procedures per hour, using bandwidth of around 400 mbps, and 99% of request handling times were below 200 milliseconds.

From the above it is clear that Zotonic can handle popular dynamic web sites. On real hardware we have observed much higher performance, especially for the underlying I/O and database performance.

9.10 Conclusion

When building a content management system or framework it is important to take the full stack of your application into consideration, from the web server, the request handling system, the caching systems, down to the database system. All parts must work well together for good performance.

Much performance can be gained by preprocessing data. An example of preprocessing is pre-escaping and sanitizing data before storing it into the database.

Caching hot data is a good strategy for web sites with a clear set of popular pages followed by a long tail of less popular pages. Placing this cache in the same memory space as the request handling code gives a clear edge over using separate caching servers, both in speed and simplicity.

Another optimization for handling sudden bursts in popularity is to dynamically match similar requests and process them once for the same result. When this is well implemented, a proxy can be avoided and all HTML pages generated dynamically.

Erlang is a great match for building dynamic web based systems due to its lightweight multiprocessing, failure handling, and memory management.

Using Erlang, Zotonic makes it possible to build a very competent and well-performing content management system and framework without needing separate web servers, caching proxies, memcache servers, or e-mail handlers. This greatly simplifies system management tasks.

On current hardware a single Zotonic server can handle thousands of dynamic page requests per second, thus easily serving the fast majority of web sites on the world wide web.

Using Erlang, Zotonic is prepared for the future of multi-core systems with dozens of cores and many gigabytes of memory.

9.11 Acknowledgements

The authors would like to thank Michiel Kløhnhammer (Maximonster Interactive Things), Andreas Stenius, Maas-Maarten Zeeman and Atilla Erdődi.

[chapter 10]

Secrets of Mobile Network Performance
Bryce Howard

10.1   Introduction

The last few years have brought us significant progress in mobile cellular network performance. But many mobile applications cannot fully benefit from this advance due to inflated network latencies.

Latency has long been synomonous with mobile networking. Though progress has been made in recent years, the reductions to network latency have not kept pace with the increases in speed. As a consequence of this disparity, it is latency, not throughput, that is most often the factor limiting the performance of network transactions.

There are two logical sections to this chapter. The first portion will explore the particulars of mobile cellular networking that contribute to the latency problem. In the second portion software techniques to minimize the performance impact of elevated network latency will be introduced.

10.2   What Are You Waiting For?

Latency represents the time needed for a data packet to transit across a network or series of networks. Mobile networks inflate the latencies already present in most Internet-based communications by a number of factors, including network type (e.g., HSPA+ vs. LTE), carrier (e.g., AT&T vs. Verizon) or circumstance (e.g., standing vs. driving, geography, time of day, etc.). It's difficult to state exact values for mobile network latency, but it can be found to vary from tens to hundreds of milliseconds.

Round-trip time (RTT) is a measure of the latency encountered by a data packet as it travels from its source to its destination and back. Round-trip time has an overwhelming effect upon the performance of many network protocols. The reason for this can be illustrated by the venerable sport of Ping-Pong.

In a regular game of Ping-Pong, the time needed for the ball to travel between players is hardly noticable. However as the players stand further apart they begin to spend more time waiting for the ball than doing anything else. The same 5-minute game of Ping-Pong at regulation distance would last for hours if the players stood a thousand feet apart, however as ridiculous as this seems. Substitute client and server for the 2 players, and round-trip time for distance between players, and you begin to see the problem.

Most network protocols play a game of Ping-Pong as part of their normal operation. These volleys, if you will, are the round-trip message exchanges needed to establish and maintain a logical network session (e.g., TCP) or carry out a service request (e.g., HTTP). During the course of these message exchanges little or no data is transmitted and network bandwidth goes largely unused. Latency compounds the extent of this underutilization to a large degree; every message exchange causes a delay of, at minimum, the network's round-trip time. The cumulative performance impact of this is remarkable.

Consider an HTTP request to download a 10KiB object would involve 4 message exchanges. Now figure a round-trip time of 100ms (pretty reasonable for a mobile network). Taking both of these figures into account and we arrive at an effective throughput of 10KiB per 400ms, or 25KiB per second.

Notice that bandwidth was completely irrelevant in the preceding example—no matter how fast the network the result remains the same, 25KiB/s. The performance of the previous operation, or any like it, can be improved only with a single, clear-cut strategy: *avoid round-trip message exchanges between the network client and server*.

10.3 Mobile Cellular Networks

The following is a simplified introduction to the components and conventions of mobile cellular networks that factor into the latency puzzle.

A mobile cellular network is represented by a series of interconnected components having highly specialized functions. Each of these components is a contributor to network latency in some way, but to varying degrees. There exist conventions unique to cellular networks, such as radio resource management, that also factor into the mobile network latency equation.

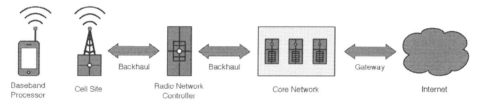

Figure 10.1: Components of a mobile cellular network

Baseband Processor

Inside most mobile devices are actually two very sophisticated computers. The application processor is responsible for hosting the operating system and applications, and is analogous to your computer or laptop. The *baseband processor* is responsible for all wireless network functions, and is analogous to a computer modem that uses radio waves instead of a phone line.[1]

The baseband processor is a consistent but usually neglible latency source. High-speed wireless networking is a frighteningly complicated affair. The sophisticated signal processing it requires contributes a fixed delay, in the range of microseconds to milliseconds, to most network communications.

---

[1] In fact many mobile phones manage the baseband processor with an AT-like command set. See http://www.3gpp.org/ftp/Specs/html-info/0707.htm

Cell Site

A *cell site*, synonymous with *transceiver base station* or *cell tower*, serves as the access point for the mobile network. It's the cell site's responsibility to provide network coverage within a region known as a *cell*.

Like the mobile devices it serves, a cell site is burdened by the sophisticated processing associated with high-speed wireless networking, and contributes the same mostly neglible latency. However, a cell site must simultaneously service hundreds to thousands of mobile devices. Variances in system load will produce changes in throughput and latency. The sluggish, unreliable network performance at crowded public events is often the result of the cell site's processing limits being reached.

The latest generation of mobile networks have expanded the role of the cell site to include direct management of its mobile devices. Many functions that were formerly responsibilities of the *radio network controller*, such as network registration or transmission scheduling are now handled by the cell site. For reasons explained later in this chapter, this role shift accounts for much of the latency reduction achieved by the latest generation of mobile cellular networks.

Backhaul Network

A *backhaul network* is the dedicated WAN connection between a cell site, its controller, and the core network. Backhaul networks have long been, and continue to be notorious contributors of latency.

Backhaul network latency classically arises from the circuit-switched, or frame-based transport protocols employed on older mobile networks (e.g., GSM, EV-DO). Such protocols exhibit latencies due to their synchronous nature, where logical connections are represented by a channel that may only receive or transmit data during a brief, pre-assigned time period. In contrast, the latest generation of mobile networks employ IP-based packet-switched backhaul networks that support asynchronous data transmission. This switchover has drastically reduced backhaul latency.

The bandwidth limitations of the physical infrastructure are a continuing bottleneck. Many backhauls were not designed to handle the peak traffic loads that modern high-speed mobile networks are capable of, and often demonstrate large variances in latency and throughput as they become congested. Carriers are making efforts to upgrade these networks as quickly as possible, but this component remains a weak point in many network infrastructures.

Radio Network Controller

Conventionally, the *radio network controller* manages the neighboring cell sites and the mobile devices they service.

The radio network controller directly coordinates the activities of mobile devices using a message-based management scheme known as signaling. As a consequence of topology all message traffic between the mobile devices and the controller must transit through a a high-latency backhaul network. This alone is not ideal, but is made worse by the fact many network operations, such as network registration and transmission scheduling, require multiple back-and-forth message exchanges. Classically, the radio network controller has been a primary contributor of latency for this reason.

As mentioned earlier, the controller is absolved of its device management duties in the latest generation of mobile networks, with much of these tasks now being handled directly by the cell sites themselves. This design decision has eliminated the factor of backhaul latency from many network functions.

Core Network

The *core network* serves as the gateway between the carrier's private network and the public Internet. It's here where carriers employ in-line networking equipment to enforce quality-of-service policies or bandwidth metering. As a rule any interception of network traffic will introduce latency. In practice this delay is generally neglible but its presence should be noted.

Power Conservation

One of the most significant sources of mobile network latency is directly related to the limited capacity of mobile phone batteries.

The network radio of a high-speed mobile device can consume over 3 Watts of power when in operation. This figure is large enough to drain the battery of an iPhone 5 in just over one hour. For this reason mobile devices remove or reduce power to the radio circuitry at every opportunity. This is ideal for extending battery life but also introduces a startup delay any time the radio circuitry is repowered to deliver or receive data.

All mobile cellular network standards formalize a *radio resource management* (RRM) scheme to conserver power. Most RRM conventions define three states—*active*, *idle* and *disconnected*—that each represent some compromise between startup latency and power consumption.

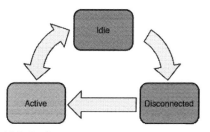

Figure 10.2: Radio resource management state transitions

Active

Active represents a state where data may be transmitted and received at high speed with minimal latency.

This state consumes large amounts of power even when idle. Small periods of network inactivity, often less than second, trigger transition to the lower power *idle* state. The performance implication of this is important to note: sufficiently long pauses during a network transaction can trigger additional delays as the device fluctuates between the active and idle states.

Idle

Idle is a compromise of lower power usage and moderate startup latency.

The device remains connected to the network, unable to transmit or receive data but capable of receiving network requests that require the active state to fulfill (e.g., incoming data). After a reasonable period of network inactivity, usually a minute or less, the device will transition to the *disconnected* state.

Idle contributes latency in two ways. First, it requires some time for the radio to repower and synchronize its analog circuitry. Second, in an attempt to conserve even more energy the radio listens only intermittently and slightly delays any response to network notifications.

Disconnected

Disconnected has the lowest power usage with the largest startup delays.

The device is disconnected from the mobile network and the radio deactivated. The radio is activated, however infrequently, to listen for network requests arriving over a special broadcast channel.

Disconnected shares the same latency sources as idle plus the additional delays of network reconnection. Connecting to a mobile network is a complicated process involving multiple rounds of message exchanges (i.e., signaling). At minimum, restoring a connection will take hundreds of milliseconds, and it's not unusual to see connection times in the seconds.

10.4 Network Protocol Performance

Now onto the things we actually have some control over.

The performance of network transactions are disproportionately affected by inflated round-trip times. This is due to the round-trip message exchanges intrinsic to the operation of most network protocols. The remainder of this chapter focuses on understanding why these messages exchanges are occurring and how their frequency can be reduced or even eliminated.

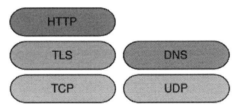

Figure 10.3: Network protocols

10.5 Transmission Control Protocol

The Transport Control Protocol (TCP) is a session-oriented network transport built atop the conventions of IP networking. TCP affects the error-free duplex communications channel essential to other protocols such as HTTP or TLS.

TCP demonstrates a lot of the round-trip messaging we are trying to avoid. Some can be eliminated with adoption of protocol extensions like *Fast Open*. Others can be minimized by tuning system parameters, such as the *initial congestion window*. In this section we'll explore both of these approaches while also providing some background on TCP internals.

TCP Fast Open

Initiating a TCP connection involves a 3-part message exchange convention known as the three-way handshake. TCP Fast Open (TFO) is an extension to TCP that eliminates the round-trip delay normally caused by the handshake process.

The TCP three-way handshake negotiates the operating parameters between client and server that make robust 2-way communication possible. The initial SYN (*synchronize*) message represents the client's connection request. Provided the server accepts the connection attempt it will reply with a SYN-ACK (*synchronize* and *acknowledge*) message. Finally, the client acknowledges the server with an ACK message. At this point a logical connection has been formed and the client may begin sending data. If you're keeping score you'll note that, at minimum, the three-way handshake introduces a delay equivalent to the current round-trip time.

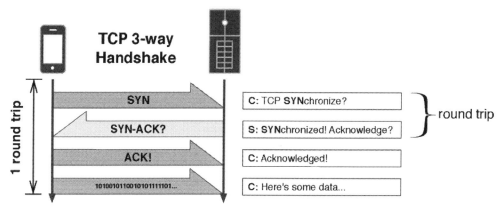

Figure 10.4: TCP 3-Way handshake

Conventionally, outside of connection recycling, there's been no way to avoid the delay of the TCP three-way handshake. However, this has changed recently with introduction of the TCP Fast Open IETF specification[2].

TCP Fast Open (TFO) allows the client to start sending data before the connection is logically established. This effectively negates any round-trip delay from the three-way handshake. The cumulative effect of this optimization is impressive. According to Google research[3] TFO can reduce page load times by as much as 40%. Although still only a draft specification, TFO is already supported by major browsers (Chrome 22+) and platforms (Linux 3.6+), with other vendors pledging to fully support it soon.

TCP Fast Open is a modification to the three-way handshake allowing a small data payload (e.g., HTTP request) to be placed within the SYN message. This payload is passed to the application server while the connection handshake is completed as it would otherwise.

Earlier extension proposals like TFO ultimately failed due to security concerns. TFO addresses this issue with the notion of a secure token, or *cookie*, assigned to the client during the course of a conventional TCP connection handshake, and expected to be included in the SYN message of a TFO-optimized request.

There are some minor caveats to the use of TFO. The most notable is lack of any idempotency guarantees for the request data supplied with the initiating SYN message. TCP ensures duplicate packets (duplication happens frequently) are ignored by the receiver, but this same assurance does not apply to the connection handhshake. There are on-going efforts to standardize a solution in the draft specification, but in the meantime TFO can still be safely deployed for idempotent transactions.

---

[2] http://datatracker.ietf.org/doc/draft-ietf-tcpm-fastopen
[3] http://research.google.com/pubs/pub36640.html

Initial Congestion Window

The *initial congestion window* (initcwnd) is a configurable TCP setting with large potential to accelerate smaller network transactions.

A recent IETF specification[4] promotes increasing the common initial congestion window setting of 3 segments (i.e., packets) to 10. This proposal is based upon extensive research[5] conducted by Google that demonstrates a 10% average performance boost. The purpose and potential impact of this setting can't be appreciated without an introduction TCP's *congestion window* (cwnd).

TCP guarantees reliability to client and server when operating over an otherwise unreliable network. This amounts to a promise that all data are received as they were sent, or at least appear to be. Packet loss is the largest obstacle to meeting the contract of reliablity; it requires detection, correction and prevention.

TCP employs a *positive acknowledgement* convention to detect missing packets in which every sent packet should be acknowledged by its intended receiver, the absence of which implies it was lost in transit. While awaiting acknowledgement, transmitted packets are preserved in a special buffer referred to as the congestion window. When this buffer becomes full, an event known as *cwnd exhaustion*, all transmission stops until receiver acknowledgements make room available to send more packets. These events play a significant role in TCP performance.

Apart from the limits of network bandwidth, TCP throughput is ultimately constrained by the frequency of cwnd exhaustion events, the likelihood of which relates to the size of the congestion window. Achieving peak TCP performance requires a congestion window complementing current network conditions: too large and it risks network congestion—an overcrowding condition marked by extensive packet loss; too small and precious bandwidth goes unused. Logically, the more known about network conditions the more likely an optimal congestion window will be chosen. Reality is that key network attributes, such as capacity and latency, are difficult to measure and constantly in flux. It complicates matters further that any Internet-based TCP connection will span across numerous networks.

Lacking means to accurately determine network capacity, TCP instead infers it from the conditon of *network congestion*. TCP will expand the congestion window just to the point it begins seeing packet loss, suggesting somewhere downstream there's a network unable to handle the current transmission rate. Employing this *congestion avoidance* scheme, TCP eventually minimizes cwnd exhaustion events to the extent it consumes all the connection capacity it has been allotted. And now, finally, we arrive at the purpose and importance of the TCP initial congestion window setting.

Network congestion can't be detected without signs of packet loss. A fresh, or idle connection lacks evidence of the packet losses needed to establish an optimal congestion window size. TCP adopts the tact it's better to start with a congestion window with the least likelihood of causing congestion; this originally implied a setting of 1 segment (~1480 bytes), and for some time this was recommended. Later experimentation demonstrated a setting as high as 4 could be effective. In practice you usually find the initial congestion window set to 3 segments (~4 KiB).

The initial congestion window is detrimental to the speed of small network transactions. The effect is easy to illustrate. At the standard setting of 3 segments, cwnd exhaustion would occur after only 3 packets, or 4 KiB, were sent. Assuming the packets were sent contiguously, the corresponding acknowledgements will not arrive any sooner than the connection's round-trip time allows. If the RTT were 100 ms, for instance, the effective transmission rate would be a pitiful 400 bytes/second.

---

[4] http://datatracker.ietf.org/doc/rfc6928
[5] http://research.google.com/pubs/pub36640.html

Although TCP will eventually expands its congestion window to fully consume available capacity, it gets off to a very slow start. As a matter of fact, this convention is known as *slow start*.

To the extent slow start impacts the performance of smaller downloads it begs reevaluating the risk-reward proposition of the initial congestion window. Google did just that[6] and discovered an initial congestion window of 10 segments (~14 KiB) generated the most throughput for the least congestion. Real world results demonstrate a 10% overall reduction in page load times. Connections with elevated round-trip latencies will experience even greater results.

Modifying the intial congestion window from its default is not straightforward. Under most server operating systems it's as a system-wide setting configurable only by a priviledged user. Rarely can this setting be configured on the client by a non-priviledged application, or even at all. It's important to note a larger initial congestion window on the server accelerates downloads, whereas on the client it accelerates uploads. The inability to change this setting on the client implies special efforts should be given to minimizing request payload sizes.

10.6 Hypertext Transport Protocol

This section dicusses techniques to mitigate the effects high round-trip latencies have upon Hypertext Transfer Protocol (HTTP) performance.

Keepalive

Keepalive is an HTTP convention enabling use of the same TCP connection across sequential requests. At minimum a single round-trip—required for TCP's three-way handshake—is avoided, saving tens or hundreds of milliseconds per request. Further, keepalive has the additional, and often unheralded, performance advantage of preserving the current TCP congestion window between requests, resulting in far fewer cwnd exhaustion events.

CWND Aware Messaging

When used as a message transport, HTTP may often encounter spurious and puzzling delays generated by TCP cwnd exhaustion events. Significant idle times between messages, typically anything greater than a second, forces TCP to reset its congestion window.

Holding message payloads beneath the initial congestion window setting —usually about 3 segments, or approximately 4KiB—can prevent cwnd exhaustion. We introduce 2 techniques—header reduction and delta encoding—that may prevent message payloads from exceeding this threshold.

Header Reduction

Perhaps surprising to some, many HTTP request types are not formally required to include any headers. This can save some serious space. It is good rule of thumb to begin with zero headers, and include only what's necessary. Be on the lookout for any headers automagically tacked on by the HTTP client or server. Some configuration may be necessary to disable this behavior.

---
[6]http://research.google.com/pubs/pub36640.html

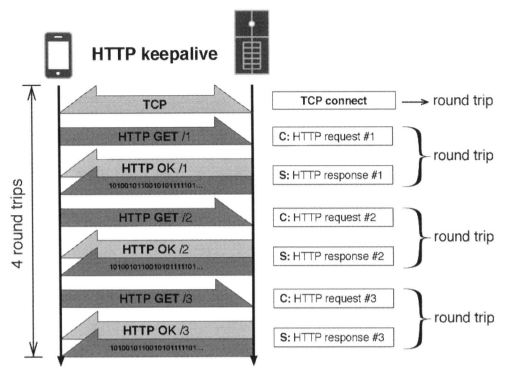

Figure 10.5: HTTP keepalive

Delta Encoding

Delta encoding is compression technique that leverages the similarities between consecutive messages. A delta-encoded message is represented only by its differences from the previous. JSON-formatted messages with consistent formatting are particularly well suited for this technique.

Pipelining

Pipelining is an HTTP convention for submitting multiple sequential requests in a single transaction. This has the performance advantages of HTTP keepalive, while also eliminating the round-trips typically needed for the additional HTTP requests.

Effectively, pipelining distributes the delay of a network round-trip amongst multiple HTTP transactions. For instance, 5 pipelined HTTP requests across a 100ms RTT connection will incur an average round-trip latency of 20ms. For the same conditions, 10 pipelined HTTP requests reduce the average latency to 10ms.

There are notable downsides to HTTP pipelining preventing its wider adoption, namely a history of spotty HTTP proxy support and suceptibility to denial-of-service attacks.

10.7 Transport Layer Security

Transport Layer Security (TLS) is a session-oriented network protocol allowing sensitive information to be securely exchanged over a public network. While TLS is highly effective at securing

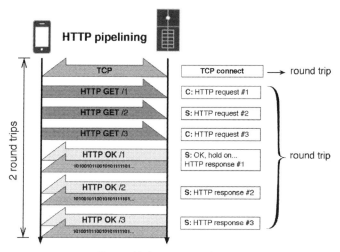

Figure 10.6: HTTP pipelining

communications its performance suffers when operating on high latency networks.

TLS employs a complicated handshake involving two exchanges of client-server messages. A TLS-secured HTTP transaction may appear noticeably slower for this reason. Often, observations that TLS is slow are in reality a complaint about the multiple round-trip delays introduced by its handshake protocol.

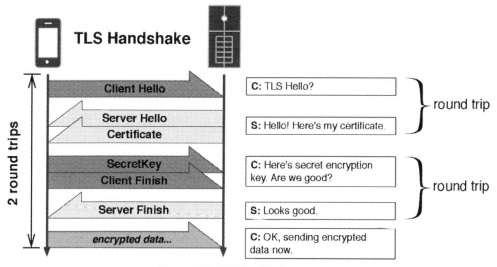

Figure 10.7: TLS handshake sequence

The good news: any technique that preserves the TCP connection between transactions, such as HTTP's keepalive convention, also preserves the TLS session. However, it's not always practical to maintain a long-lived secure TCP connection. Offered here are two methods that accelerate the TLS handshake itself.

Session Resumption

The TLS *session resumption* feature allows a secure session to be preserved between TCP connections. Session resumption eliminates the initial handshake message exchange reserved for the public key cryptography that validates the server's identity and establishes the symmetric encryption key. While there's some performance benefit to avoiding computationally expensive public crypto operations, the greater time savings belongs to eliminating the round-trip delay of a single message exchange.

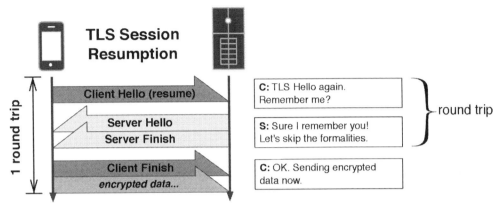

Figure 10.8: TLS session resumption

Earlier revisions of TLS (i.e., SSL) depended upon the server to preserve the session state, which presented a real challenge to highly distributed server architectures. TLS *session tickets* offer a much simpler solution. This extension allows the client to preserve session state in the form an encrypted payload (i.e., session ticket) granted by the server during the handshake process. Resuming a session requires that the client submit this ticket at the beginning of the handshake.

False Start

False start is a protocol modification originating from a clever observation of the TLS handshake: technically, the client may send encrypted data immediately after transmitting its final handshake message to the server. Acting on this insight, false start eliminates the round-trip delay normally occurring as the client awaited the final handshake message from the server.

False start exhibits the same performance benefit as session resumption with the added benefit of being stateless—client and server are relieved of the burden to manage session state. The majority of web clients support false start with just minor changes. And surprisingly, in about 99% of the cases, server support requires no changes at all, making this optimization immediately deployable in most infrastructures.

10.8 DNS

The Domain Name System (DNS) provides the name-to-address resolution needed for most IP-based network transactions. As a protocol, DNS is a fairly simple affair, typically operating without need for a reliable transport protocol (e.g., TCP). Regardless, DNS queries often exhibit large and wildly varying response times (for reasons too complicated and numerous to elaborate upon here).

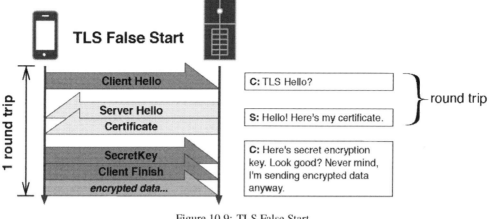

Figure 10.9: TLS False Start

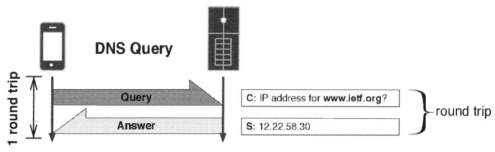

Figure 10.10: DNS query

Generally, the hosting platform provides a cache implementation to avoid frequent DNS queries. The semantics of DNS caching are simple. Each DNS response contains a time-to-live (TTL) attribute declaring how long the result may cached. TTLs can range from seconds to days but are typically on the order of several minutes. Very low TTL values, usually under a minute, are used to affect load-distribution or minimize downtime from server replacement or ISP failover.

The native DNS cache implementations of most platforms don't account for elevated round-trip times of mobile networks. Many mobile applications could benefit from a cache implementation that augments or replaces the stock solution. Suggested here are several cache strategies, that if deployed for application use, will eliminate any random and spurious delays caused by unnecessary DNS queries.

Refresh on Failure

Highly-available systems usually rely upon redundant infrastructures hosted within their IP address space. Low-TTL DNS entries have the benefit of reducing the time a network client may refer to the address of a failed host, but at the same time triggers a lot of extra DNS queries. The TTL is a compromise between minimizing downtime and maximizing client performance.

It makes no sense to generally degrade client performance when server failures are the exception to the rule. There is a simple solution to this dilemma, rather than strictly obeying the TTL a cached DNS entry is only refreshed when a non-recoverable error is detected by higher-level protocol such as TCP or HTTP. Under most scenarios this technique emulates the behavior of a TTL-conformant DNS cache while nearly eliminating the performance penalties normally associated with any DNS-based high-availability solution.

It should be noted this cache technique would likely be incompatible with any DNS-based load distribution scheme.

Asynchronous Refresh

Asynchronous refresh is an approach to DNS caching that (mostly) obeys posted TTLs while largely eliminating the latency of frequent DNS queries. An asynchronous DNS client library, such as c-ares[7], is needed to implement this technique.

The idea is straightforward, a request for an expired DNS cache entry returns the stale result while a non-blocking DNS query is scheduled in the background to refresh the cache. If implemented with a fallback to blocking (i.e., synchronous) queries for very stale entries, this technique is nearly immune to DNS delays while also remaining compatible with many DNS-based failover and load-distribution schemes.

10.9 Conclusion

Mitigating the impact of mobile networks' inflated latency requires reducing the network round-trips that exacerbate its effect. Employing software optimizations solely focused on minimizing or eliminating round-trip protocol messaging is critical to surmounting this daunting performance issue.

---

[7] http://c-ares.haxx.se/

[chapter 11]

Warp

Kazu Yamamoto, Michael Snoyman, and Andreas Voellmy

Warp is a high-performance HTTP server library written in Haskell, a purely functional programming language. Both Yesod, a web application framework, and `mighty`, an HTTP server, are implemented over Warp. According to our throughput benchmark, `mighty` provides performance on a par with `nginx`. This article will explain the architecture of Warp and how we achieved its performance. Warp can run on many platforms, including Linux, BSD variants, Mac OS, and Windows. To simplify our explanation, however, we will only talk about Linux for the remainder of this article.

11.1 Network Programming in Haskell

Some people believe that functional programming languages are slow or impractical. However, to the best of our knowledge, Haskell provides a nearly ideal approach for network programming. This is because the Glasgow Haskell Compiler (GHC), the flagship compiler for Haskell, provides lightweight and robust user threads (sometimes called green threads). In this section, we briefly review some well-known approaches to server-side network programming and compare them with network programming in Haskell. We demonstrate that Haskell offers a combination of programmability and performance not available in other approaches: Haskell's convenient abstractions allow programmers to write clear, simple code, while GHC's sophisticated compiler and multi-core run-time system produce multi-core programs that execute in a way very similar to the most advanced hand-crafted network programs.

Native Threads

Traditional servers use a technique called thread programming. In this architecture, each connection is handled by a single process or native thread (sometimes called an OS thread).

This architecture can be further segmented based on the mechanism used for creating the processes or native threads. When using a thread pool, multiple processes or native threads are created in advance. An example of this is the prefork mode in Apache. Otherwise, a process or native thread is spawned each time a connection is received. Figure 11.1 illustrates this.

The advantage of this architecture is that it enables developers to write clear code. In particular, the use of threads allows the code to follow a simple and familiar flow of control and to use simple procedure calls to fetch input or send output. Also, because the kernel assigns processes or native threads to available cores, we can balance utilization of cores. Its disadvantage is that a large number

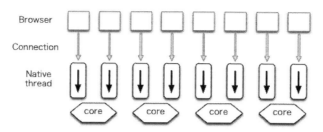

Figure 11.1: Native threads

of context switches between kernel and processes or native threads occur, resulting in performance degradation.

Event-Driven Architecture

In the world of high-performance servers, the recent trend has been to take advantage of event-driven programming. In this architecture multiple connections are handled by a single process (Figure 11.2). Lighttpd is an example of a web server using this architecture.

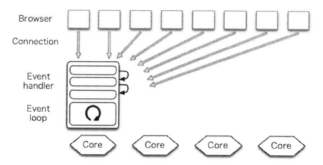

Figure 11.2: Event-driven architecture

Since there is no need to switch processes, fewer context switches occur, and performance is thereby improved. This is its chief advantage.

On the other hand, this architecture substantially complicates the network program. In particular, this architecture inverts the flow of control so that the event loop controls the overall execution of the program. Programmers must therefore restructure their program into event handlers, each of which execute only non-blocking code. This restriction prevents programmers from performing I/O using procedure calls; instead more complicated asynchronous methods must be used. Along the same lines, conventional exception handling methods are no longer applicable.

One Process Per Core

Many have hit upon the idea of creating n event-driven processes to utilize n cores (Figure 11.3). Each process is called a *worker*. A service port must be shared among workers. Using the prefork technique, port sharing can be achieved.

In traditional process programming, a process for a new connection is forked after the connection is accepted. In contrast, the prefork technique forks processes before new connections are accepted. Despite the shared name, this technique should not be confused with Apache's prefork mode.

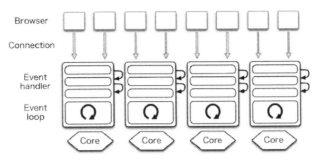

Figure 11.3: One process per core

One web server that uses this architecture is nginx. Node.js used the event-driven architecture in the past, but recently it also implemented the prefork technique. The advantage of this architecture is that it utilizes all cores and improves performance. However, it does not resolve the issue of programs having poor clarity, due to the reliance on handler and callback functions.

User Threads

GHC's user threads can be used to help solve the code clarity issue. In particular, we can handle each HTTP connection in a new user thread. This thread is programmed in a traditional style, using logically blocking I/O calls. This keeps the program clear and simple, while GHC handles the complexities of non-blocking I/O and multi-core work dispatching.

Under the hood, GHC multiplexes user threads over a small number of native threads. GHC's run-time system includes a multi-core thread scheduler that can switch between user threads cheaply, since it does so without involving any OS context switches.

GHC's user threads are lightweight; modern computers can run 100,000 user threads smoothly. They are robust; even asynchronous exceptions are caught (this feature is used by the timeout handler, described in Section 11.2 and in Section 11.7.) In addition, the scheduler includes a multi-core load balancing algorithm to help utilize capacity of all available cores.

When a user thread performs a logically blocking I/O operation, such as receiving or sending data on a socket, a non-blocking call is actually attempted. If it succeeds, the thread continues immediately without involving the I/O manager or the thread scheduler. If the call would block, the thread instead registers interest for the relevant event with the run-time system's I/O manager component and then indicates to the scheduler that it is waiting. Independently, an I/O manager thread monitors events and notifies threads when their events occur, causing them to be re-scheduled for execution. This all happens transparently to the user thread, with no effort on the Haskell programmer's part.

In Haskell, most computation is non-destructive. This means that almost all functions are thread-safe. GHC uses data allocation as a safe point to switch context of user threads. Because of functional programming style, new data are frequently created and it is known that such data allocation occurs regularly enough for context switching[1].

Though some languages provided user threads in the past, they are not commonly used now because they were not lightweight or were not robust. Note that some languages provide library-level coroutines but they are not preemptive threads. Note also that Erlang and Go provide lightweight processes and lightweight goroutines, respectively.

---

[1] http://www.aosabook.org/en/ghc.html

As of this writing, `mighty` uses the prefork technique to fork processes in order to use more cores. (Warp does not have this functionality.) Figure 11.4 illustrates this arrangement in the context of a web server with the prefork technique written in Haskell, where each browser connection is handled by a single user thread, and a single native thread in a process running on a CPU core handles work from several connections.

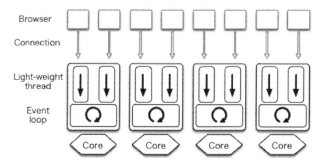

Figure 11.4: User threads with one process per core

We found that the I/O manager component of the GHC run-time system itself has performance bottlenecks. To solve this problem, we developed a *parallel I/O manager* that uses per-core event registration tables and event monitors to greatly improve multi-core scaling. A Haskell program with the parallel I/O manager is executed as a single process and multiple I/O managers run as native threads to use multiple cores (Figure 11.5). Each user thread is executed on any one of the cores.

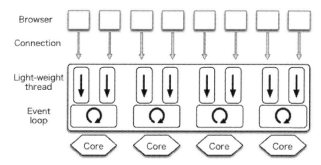

Figure 11.5: User threads in a single process

GHC version 7.8—which includes the parallel I/O manager—will be released in the autumn of 2013. With GHC version 7.8, Warp itself will be able to use this architecture without any modifications and `mighty` will not need to use the prefork technique.

11.2 Warp's Architecture

Warp is an HTTP engine for the Web Application Interface (WAI). It runs WAI applications over HTTP. As we described above, both Yesod and `mighty` are examples of WAI applications, as illustrated in Figure 11.6.

The type of a WAI application is as follows:

```
type Application = Request -> ResourceT IO Response
```

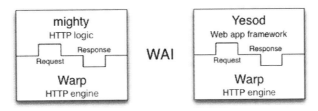

Figure 11.6: Web Application Interface (WAI)

In Haskell, argument types of functions are separated by right arrows and the rightmost one is the type of the return value. So, we can interpret the definition as: a WAI Application takes a Request and returns a Response, used in the context where I/O is possible and resources are well managed.

After accepting a new HTTP connection, a dedicated user thread is spawned for the connection. It first receives an HTTP request from a client and parses it to Request. Then, Warp gives the Request to the WAI application and receives a Response from it. Finally, Warp builds an HTTP response based on the Response value and sends it back to the client. This is illustrated in Figure 11.7.

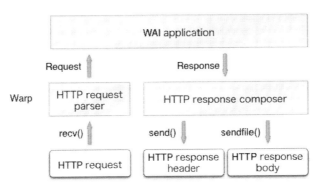

Figure 11.7: The architecture of Warp

The user thread repeats this procedure as necessary and terminates itself when the connection is closed by the peer or an invalid request is received. The thread also terminates if a significant amount of data is not received after a certain period of time (i.e., a timeout has occurred).

11.3 The Performance of Warp

Before we explain how to improve the performance of Warp, we would like to show the results of our benchmark. We measured throughput of mighty version 2.8.4 (with Warp version 1.3.8.1) and nginx version 1.4.0. Our benchmark environment is as follows:

- Two "12 core" machines (Intel Xeon E5645, two sockets, 6 cores per 1 CPU) connected with 1 gbps Ethernet.
- One machine directly runs Linux version 3.2.0 (Ubuntu 12.04 LTS).
- The other directly runs FreeBSD 9.1.

We tested several benchmark tools in the past and our favorite one was httperf. Since it uses select() and is just a single process program, it reaches its performance limits when we try to measure HTTP servers on multi-core machines. So, we switched to weighttp, which is based on libev (the epoll family) and can use multiple native threads. We used weighttp from FreeBSD as follows:

weighttp -n 100000 -c 1000 -t 10 -k http://<ip_address>:<port_number>/

This means that 1,000 HTTP connections are established, with each connection sending 100 requests. 10 native threads are spawned to carry out these jobs.

The target web servers were compiled on Linux. For all requests, the same index.html file is returned. We used nginx's index.html, whose size is 151 bytes.

Since Linux/FreeBSD have many control parameters, we need to configure the parameters carefully. You can find a good introduction to Linux parameter tuning in ApacheBench and HTTPerf.[2] We carefully configured both mighty and nginx as follows:

- enabled file descriptor cache
- disabled logging
- disabled rate limitation

Here is the result:

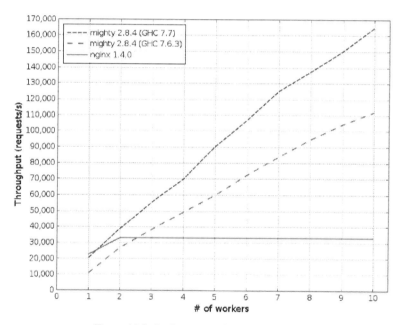

Figure 11.8: Performance of Warp and nginx

The x-axis is the number of workers and the y-axis gives throughput, measured in requests per second.

- mighty 2.8.4 (GHC 7.7): compiled with GHC version 7.7.20130504 (to be GHC version 7.8). It uses the parallel I/O manager with only one worker. GHC run-time option, +RTS -qa -A128m -N<x> is specified where <x> is the number of cores and 128m is the allocation area size used by the garbage collector.
- mighty 2.8.4 (GHC 7.6.3): compiled with GHC version 7.6.3 (which is the latest stable version).

---

[2]http://gwan.com/en_apachebench_httperf.html

11.4 Key Ideas

We kept four key ideas in mind when implementing our high-performance server in Haskell:

1. Issuing as few system calls as possible
2. Using specialized function implementations and avoiding recalculation
3. Avoiding locks
4. Using proper data structures

Issuing as Few System Calls as Possible

Although system calls are typically inexpensive on most modern operating systems, they can add a significant computational burden when called frequently. Indeed, Warp performs several system calls when serving each request, including `recv()`, `send()` and `sendfile()` (a system call that allows zero-copying a file). Other system calls, such as `open()`, `stat()` and `close()` can often be omitted when processing a single request, thanks to a cache mechanism described in Section 11.7.

We can use the `strace` command to see what system calls are actually used. When we observed the behavior of `nginx` with `strace`, we noticed that it used `accept4()`, which we did not know about at the time.

Using Haskell's standard network library, a listening socket is created with the non-blocking flag set. When a new connection is accepted from the listening socket, it is necessary to set the corresponding socket as non-blocking as well. The network library implements this by calling `fcntl()` twice: once to get the current flags and twice to set the flags with the non-blocking flag enabled.

On Linux, the non-blocking flag of a connected socket is always unset even if its listening socket is non-blocking. The system call `accept4()` is an extension version of `accept()` on Linux. It can set the non-blocking flag when accepting. So, if we use `accept4()`, we can avoid two unnecessary calls to `fcntl()`. Our patch to use `accept4()` on Linux has been already merged to the network library.

Specialized Functions and Avoiding Recalculation

GHC provides a profiling mechanism, but it has a limitation: correct profiling is only possible if a program runs in the foreground and does not spawn child processes. If we want to profile live activities of servers, we need to take special care.

`mighty` has this mechanism. Suppose that n is the number of workers in the configuration file of `mighty`. If n is greater than or equal to 2, `mighty` creates n child processes and the parent process just works to deliver signals. However, if n is 1, `mighty` does not create any child process. Instead, the executed process itself serves HTTP. Also, `mighty` stays in its terminal if debug mode is on.

When we profiled `mighty`, we were surprised that the standard function to format date strings consumed the majority of CPU time. As many know, an HTTP server should return GMT date strings in header fields such as `Date`, `Last-Modified`, etc.:

Date: Mon, 01 Oct 2012 07:38:50 GMT

So, we implemented a special formatter to generate GMT date strings. A comparison of our specialized function and the standard Haskell implementation using the `criterion` benchmark library showed that ours was much faster. But if an HTTP server accepts more than one request per second, the server repeats the same formatting again and again. So, we also implemented a cache mechanism for date strings.

We also explain specialization and avoiding recalculation in Section 11.5 and Section 11.6.

Avoiding Locks

Unnecessary locks are evil for programming. Our code sometimes uses unnecessary locks imperceptibly because, internally, the run-time systems or libraries use locks. To implement high-performance servers, we need to identify such locks and avoid them if possible. It is worth pointing out that locks will become much more critical under the parallel I/O manager. We will talk about how to identify and avoid locks in Section 11.7 and Section 11.8.

Using Proper Data Structures

Haskell's standard data structure for strings is `String`, which is a linked list of Unicode characters. Since list programming is the heart of functional programming, `String` is convenient for many purposes. But for high-performance servers, the list structure is too slow and Unicode is too complex since the HTTP protocol is based on *byte* streams. Instead, we use `ByteString` to express strings (or buffers). A `ByteString` is an array of bytes with metadata. Thanks to this metadata, splicing without copying is possible. This is described in detail in Section 11.5.

Other examples of proper data structures are `Builder` and double `IORef`. They are explained in Section 11.6 and Section 11.7, respectively.

11.5 HTTP Request Parser

Besides the many issues involved with efficient concurrency and I/O in a multi-core environment, Warp also needs to be certain that each core is performing its tasks efficiently. In that regard, the most relevant component is the HTTP request processor. Its purpose is to take a stream of bytes coming from the incoming socket, parse out the request line and individual headers, and leave the request body to be processed by the application. It must take this information and produce a data structure which the application (whether a Yesod application, `mighty`, or something else) will use to form its response.

The request body itself presents some interesting challenges. Warp provides full support for pipelining and chunked request bodies. As a result, Warp must "dechunk" any chunked request bodies before passing them to the application. With pipelining, multiple requests can be transferred on a single connection. Therefore, Warp must ensure that the application does not consume too many bytes, as that would remove vital information from the next request. It must also be sure to discard any data remaining from the request body; otherwise, the remainder will be parsed as the beginning of the next request, causing either an invalid request or a misunderstood request.

As an example, consider the following theoretical request from a client:

```
POST /some/path HTTP/1.1
Transfer-Encoding: chunked
Content-Type: application/x-www-form-urlencoded

0008
message=
```

```
000a
helloworld
0000

GET / HTTP/1.1
```

The HTTP parser must extract the `/some/path` pathname and the `Content-Type` header and pass these to the application. When the application begins reading the request body, it must strip off the chunk headers (e.g., `0008` and `000a`) and instead provide the actual content, i.e., `message=helloworld`. It must also ensure that no more bytes are consumed after the chunk terminator (`0000`) so as to not interfere with the next pipelined request.

Writing the Parser

Haskell is known for its powerful parsing capabilities. It has traditional parser generators as well as combinator libraries, such as Parsec and Attoparsec. Parsec and Attoparsec's textual modules work in a fully Unicode-aware manner. However, HTTP headers are guaranteed to be ASCII, so Unicode awareness is an overhead we need not incur.

Attoparsec also provides a binary interface for parsing, which would let us bypass the Unicode overhead. But as efficient as Attoparsec is, it still introduces an overhead relative to a hand-rolled parser. So for Warp, we have not used any parser libraries. Instead, we perform all parsing manually.

This gives rise to another question: how do we represent the actual binary data? The answer is a `ByteString`, which is essentially three pieces of data: a pointer to some piece of memory, the offset from the beginning of that memory to the data in question, and the size of our data.

The offset information may seem redundant. We could instead insist that our memory pointer point to the beginning of our data. However, by including the offset, we enable data sharing. Multiple `ByteString`s can all point to the same chunk of memory and use different parts of it (also known as *splicing*). There is no worry of data corruption, since `ByteString`s (like most Haskell data) are immutable. When the final pointer to a piece of memory is no longer used, then the memory buffer is deallocated.

This combination is perfect for our use case. When a client sends a request over a socket, Warp will read the data in relatively large chunks (currently 4096 bytes). In most cases, this is large enough to encompass the entire request line and all request headers. Warp will then use its hand-rolled parser to break this large chunk into lines. This can be done efficiently for the following reasons:

1. We need only scan the memory buffer for newline characters. The bytestring library provides such helper functions, which are implemented with lower-level C functions like `memchr`. (It's actually a little more complicated than that due to multiline headers, but the same basic approach still applies.)
2. There is no need to allocate extra memory buffers to hold the data. We just take splices from the original buffer. See Figure 11.9 for a demonstration of splicing individual components from a larger chunk of data. It's worth stressing this point: we actually end up with a situation which is more efficient than idiomatic C. In C, strings are null-terminated, so splicing requires allocating a new memory buffer, copying the data from the old buffer, and appending the null character.

Once the buffer has been broken into lines, we perform a similar maneuver to turn the header lines into key/value pairs. For the request line, we parse the requested path fairly deeply. Suppose we have a request for:

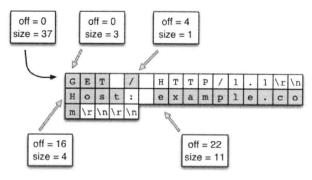

Figure 11.9: Splicing ByteStrings

```
GET /buenos/d%C3%ADas HTTP/1.1
```

In this case, we would need to perform the following steps:

1. Separate the request method, path, and version into individual pieces.
2. Tokenize the path along forward slashes, ending up with ["buenos", "d%C3%ADas"].
3. Percent-decode the individual pieces, ending up with ["buenos", "d\195\173as"].
4. UTF8-decode each piece, finally arriving at Unicode-aware text: ["buenos", "días"].

There are a few performance gains we achieve with this process:

1. As with newline checking, finding forward slashes is a very efficient operation.
2. We use an efficient lookup table for turning the Hex characters into numerical values. This code is a single memory lookup and involves no branching.
3. UTF8-decoding is a highly optimized operation in the text package. Likewise, the text package represents this data in an efficient, packed representation.
4. Due to Haskell's laziness, this calculation will be performed on demand. If the application in question does not need the textual version of the path, none of these steps will be performed.

The final piece of parsing we perform is dechunking. In many ways, dechunking is a simpler form of parsing. We parse a single Hex number, and then read the stated number of bytes. Those bytes are passed on verbatim (without any buffer copying) to the application.

Conduit

This article has mentioned a few times the concept of passing the request body to the application. It has also hinted at the issue of the application passing a response back to the server, and the server receiving data from and sending data to the socket. A final related point not yet discussed is *middleware*, which are components sitting between the server and application that modify the request or response. The definition of a middleware is:

```
type Middleware = Application -> Application
```

The intuition behind this is that a middleware will take some "internal" application, preprocess the request, pass it to the internal application to get a response, and then postprocess the response. For our purposes, a good example would be a gzip middleware, which automatically compresses response bodies.

A prerequisite for the creation of such middlewares is a means of modifying both incoming and outgoing data streams. A standard approach historically in the Haskell world has been *lazy I/O*. With lazy I/O, we represent a stream of values as a single, pure data structure. As more data is requested from this structure, I/O actions are performed to grab the data from its source. Lazy I/O provides a huge level of composability. However, for a high-throughput server, it presents a major obstacle: resource finalization in lazy I/O is non-deterministic. Using lazy I/O, it would be easy for a server under high load to quickly run out of file descriptors.

It would also be possible to use a lower-level abstraction, essentially dealing directly with read and write functions. However, one of the advantages of Haskell is its high-level approach, allowing us to reason about the behavior of our code. It's also not obvious how such a solution would deal with some of the common issues which arise when creating web applications. For example, it's often necessary to have a buffering solution, where we read a certain amount of data at one step (e.g., the request header processing), and read the remainder in a separate part of the code base (e.g., the web application).

To address this dilemma, the WAI protocol (and therefore Warp) is built on top of the conduit package. This package provides an abstraction for streams of data. It keeps much of the composability of lazy I/O, provides a buffering solution, and guarantees deterministic resource handling. Exceptions are also kept where they belong, in the parts of your code which deal with I/O, instead of hiding them in a data structure claiming to be pure.

Warp represents the incoming stream of bytes from the client as a Source, and writes data to be sent to the client to a Sink. The Application is provided a Source with the request body, and provides a response as a Source as well. Middlewares are able to intercept the Sources for the request and response bodies and apply transformations to them. Figure 11.10 demonstrates how a middleware fits between Warp and an application. The composability of the conduit package makes this an easy and efficient operation.

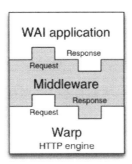

Figure 11.10: Middlewares

Elaborating on the gzip middleware example, conduit allows us to create a middleware which runs in a nearly optimal manner. The original Source provided by the application is connected to the gzip Conduit. As each new chunk of data is produced by the initial Source, it is fed into the zlib library, filling up a buffer with compressed bytes. When that buffer is filled, it is emitted, either to another middleware, or to Warp. Warp then takes this compressed buffer and sends it over the socket to the client. At this point, the buffer can either be reused, or its memory freed. In this way, we have optimal memory usage, do not produce any extra data in the case of network failure, and lessen the garbage collection burden for the run time system.

Conduit itself is a large topic, and therefore will not be covered in more depth. It would suffice to say for now that conduit's usage in Warp is a contributing factor to its high performance.

Slowloris Protection

We have one final concern: the Slowloris attack. This is a form of Denial of Service (DoS) attack wherein each client sends very small amounts of information. By doing so, the client is able to maintain a higher number of connections on the same hardware/bandwidth. Since the web server has a constant overhead for each open connection regardless of bytes being transferred, this can be an effective attack. Therefore, Warp must detect when a connection is not sending enough data over the network and kill it.

We discuss the timeout manager in more detail below, which is the true heart of Slowloris protection. When it comes to request processing, our only requirement is to tease the timeout handler to let it know more data has been received from the client. In Warp, this is all done at the conduit level. As mentioned, the incoming data is represented as a Source. As part of that Source, every time a new chunk of data is received, the timeout handler is teased. Since teasing the handler is such a cheap operation (essentially just a memory write), Slowloris protection does not hinder the performance of individual connection handlers in a significant way.

11.6 HTTP Response Composer

This section describes the HTTP response composer of Warp. A WAI Response has three constructors:

```
ResponseFile Status ResponseHeaders FilePath (Maybe FilePart)
ResponseBuilder Status ResponseHeaders Builder
ResponseSource Status ResponseHeaders (Source (ResourceT IO) (Flush Builder))
```

ResponseFile is used to send a static file while ResponseBuilder and ResponseSource are for sending dynamic contents created in memory. Each constructor includes both Status and ResponseHeaders. ResponseHeaders is defined as a list of key/value header pairs.

Composer for HTTP Response Header

The old composer built HTTP response header with a Builder, a rope-like data structure. First, it converted Status and each element of ResponseHeaders into a Builder. Each conversion runs in O(1). Then, it concatenates them by repeatedly appending one Builder to another. Thanks to the properties of Builder, each append operation also runs in O(1). Lastly, it packs an HTTP response header by copying data from Builder to a buffer in O(N).

In many cases, the performance of Builder is sufficient. But we experienced that it is not fast enough for high-performance servers. To eliminate the overhead of Builder, we implemented a special composer for HTTP response headers by directly using memcpy(), a highly tuned byte copy function in C.

Composer for HTTP Response Body

For ResponseBuilder and ResponseSource, the Builder values provided by the application are packed into a list of ByteString. A composed header is prepended to the list and send() is used to send the list in a fixed buffer.

For ResponseFile, Warp uses send() and sendfile() to send an HTTP response header and body, respectively. Figure 11.7 illustrates this case. Again, open(), stat(), close() and other system calls can be omitted thanks to the cache mechanism described in Section 11.7. The following subsection describes another performance tuning in the case of `ResponseFile`.

Sending the Header and Body Together

When we measured the performance of Warp to send static files, we always did it with high concurrency (multiple connections at the same time) and achieved good results. However, when we set the concurrency value to 1, we found Warp to be really slow.

Observing the results of the `tcpdump` command, we realized that this is because originally Warp used the combination of `writev()` for header and `sendfile()` for body. In this case, an HTTP header and body are sent in separate TCP packets (Figure 11.11).

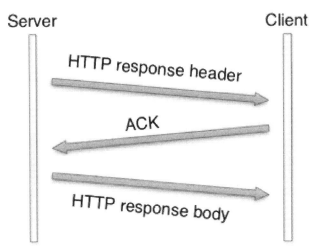

Figure 11.11: Packet sequence of old Warp

To send them in a single TCP packet (when possible), new Warp switched from `writev()` to `send()`. It uses `send()` with the `MSG_MORE` flag to store a header and `sendfile()` to send both the stored header and a file. This made the throughput at least 100 times faster according to our throughput benchmark.

11.7 Clean-up with Timers

This section explain how to implement connection timeout and how to cache file descriptors.

Timers for Connections

To prevent Slowloris attacks, communication with a client should be canceled if the client does not send a significant amount of data for a certain period. Haskell provides a standard function called `timeout` whose type is as follows:

```
Int -> IO a -> IO (Maybe a)
```

The first argument is the duration of the timeout, in microseconds. The second argument is an action which handles input/output (IO). This function returns a value of Maybe a in the IO context. Maybe is defined as follows:

```
data Maybe a = Nothing | Just a
```

Nothing indicates an error (with no reason specified) and Just encloses a successful value a. So, timeout returns Nothing if an action is not completed in a specified time. Otherwise, a successful value is returned wrapped with Just. The timeout function eloquently shows how great Haskell's composability is.

timeout is useful for many purposes, but its performance is inadequate for implementing high-performance servers. The problem is that for each timeout created, this function will spawn a new user thread. While user threads are cheaper than system threads, they still involve an overhead which can add up. We need to avoid the creation of a user thread for each connection's timeout handling. So, we implemented a timeout system which uses only one user thread, called the timeout manager, to handle the timeouts of all connections. At its core are the following two ideas:

- double IORefs
- safe swap and merge algorithm

Suppose that status of connections is described as Active and Inactive. To clean up inactive connections, the timeout manager repeatedly inspects the status of each connection. If status is Active, the timeout manager turns it to Inactive. If Inactive, the timeout manager kills its associated user thread.

Each status is referred to by an IORef. IORef is a reference whose value can be destructively updated. In addition to the timeout manager, each user thread repeatedly turns its status to Active through its own IORef as its connection actively continues.

The timeout manager uses a list of the IORef to these statuses. A user thread spawned for a new connection tries to prepend its new IORef for an Active status to the list. So, the list is a critical section and we need atomicity to keep the list consistent.

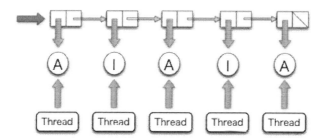

Figure 11.12: A list of status values. A and I indicates Active and Inactive, respectively

A standard way to keep consistency in Haskell is MVar. But MVar is slow, since each MVar is protected with a home-brewed lock. Instead, we used another IORef to refer to the list and atomicModifyIORef to manipulate it. atomicModifyIORef is a function for atomically updating an IORef's values. It is implemented via CAS (Compare-and-Swap), which is much faster than locks.

The following is the outline of the safe swap and merge algorithm:

```
do xs <- atomicModifyIORef ref (\ys -> ([], ys)) -- swap with an empty list, []
   xs' <- manipulates_status xs
   atomicModifyIORef ref (\ys -> (merge xs' ys, ()))
```

The timeout manager atomically swaps the list with an empty list. Then it manipulates the list by toggling thread status or removing unnecessary status for killed user threads. During this process, new connections may be created and their status values are inserted via `atomicModifyIORef` by their corresponding user threads. Then, the timeout manager atomically merges the pruned list and the new list. Thanks to the lazy evaluation of Haskell, the application of the merge function is done in O(1) and the merge operation, which is in O(N), is postponed until its values are actually consumed.

Timers for File Descriptors

Let's consider the case where Warp sends the entire file by `sendfile()`. Unfortunately, we need to call `stat()` to know the size of the file because `sendfile()` on Linux requires the caller to specify how many bytes to be sent (`sendfile()` on FreeBSD/MacOS has a magic number *0* which indicates the end of file).

If WAI applications know the file size, Warp can avoid `stat()`. It is easy for WAI applications to cache file information such as size and modification time. If the cache timeout is fast enough (say 10 seconds), the risk of cache inconsistency is not serious. Because we can safely clean up the cache, we don't have to worry about leakage.

Since `sendfile()` requires a file descriptor, the naive sequence to send a file is `open()`, `sendfile()` repeatedly if necessary, and `close()`. In this subsection, we consider how to cache file descriptors to avoid calling `open()` and `close()` more than is necessary. Caching file descriptors should work as follows: if a client requests that a file be sent, a file descriptor is opened by `open()`. And if another client requests the same file shortly thereafter, the previously opened file descriptor is reused. At a later time, the file descriptor is closed by `close()` if no user thread uses it.

A typical tactic for this case is reference counting. We were not sure that we could implement a robust reference counter. What happens if a user thread is killed for unexpected reasons? If we fail to decrement its reference counter, the file descriptor leaks. We noticed that the connection timeout scheme is safe to reuse as a cache mechanism for file descriptors because it does not use reference counters. However, we cannot simply reuse the timeout manager for several reasons.

Each user thread has its own status—status is not shared. But we would like to cache file descriptors to avoid `open()` and `close()` by sharing. So, we need to search for the file descriptor for a requested file in a collection of cached file descriptors. Since this search should be fast, we should not use a list. Because requests are received concurrently, two or more file descriptors for the same file may be opened. Thus, we need to store multiple file descriptors for a single file name. The data structure we are describing is called a *multimap*.

We implemented a multimap whose look-up is $O(logN)$ and pruning is $O(N)$ with red-black trees whose nodes contain non-empty lists. Since a red-black tree is a binary search tree, look-up is $O(log(N))$ where n is the number of nodes. We can also translate it into an ordered list in $O(N)$. In our implementation, pruning nodes which contain a file descriptor to be closed is also done during this step. We adopted an algorithm to convert an ordered list to a red-black tree in $O(N)$.

11.8 Future Work

We have several ideas for improvement of Warp in the future, but we will only explain two here.

Memory Allocation

When receiving and sending packets, buffers are allocated. These buffers are allocated as "pinned" byte arrays, so that they can be passed to C procedures like `recv()` and `send()`. Since it is best to receive or send as much data as possible in each system call, these buffers are moderately sized. Unfortunately, GHC's method for allocating large (larger than 409 bytes in 64 bit machines) pinned byte arrays takes a global lock in the run-time system. This lock may become a bottleneck when scaling beyond 16 cores, if each core user thread frequently allocates such buffers.

We performed an initial investigation of the performance impact of large pinned array allocation for HTTP response header generation. For this purpose, GHC provides `eventlog` which can record timestamps of each event. We surrounded a memory allocation function with the function to record a user event. Then we compiled `mighty` with it and recorded the eventlog. The resulting eventlog is illustrated in Figure 11.13.

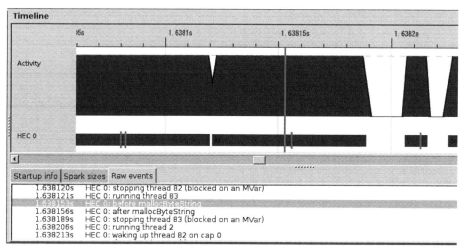

Figure 11.13: Eventlog

The small vertical bars in the row labelled "HEC 0" indicate the event created by us. So, the area surrounded by two bars is the time consumed by memory allocation. It is about 1/10 of an HTTP session. We are discussing how to implement memory allocation without locks.

New Thundering Herd

The thundering herd problem is an "old-but-new" problem. Suppose that processes or native threads are pre-forked to share a listening socket. They call `accept()` on the socket. When a connection is created, old Linux and FreeBSD implementations wake up all of the processes or threads. Only one of them can accept it and the others sleep again. Since this causes many context switches, we face a performance problem. This is called the *thundering herd*. Recent Linux and FreeBSD implementations wake up only one process or native thread, making this problem a thing of the past.

Recent network servers tend to use the epoll family. If workers share a listening socket and they manipulate connections through the epoll family, thundering herd appears again. This is because the convention of the epoll family is to notify all processes or native threads. nginx and mighty are victims of this new thundering herd.

The parallel I/O manager is free from the new thundering herd problem. In this architecture, only one I/O manager accepts new connections through the epoll family. And other I/O managers handle established connections.

11.9 Conclusion

Warp is a versatile web server library, providing efficient HTTP communication for a wide range of use cases. In order to achieve its high performance, optimizations have been performed at many levels, including network communications, thread management, and request parsing.

Haskell has proven to be an amazing language for writing such a code base. Features like immutability by default make it easier to write thread-safe code and avoid extra buffer copying. The multi-threaded run time drastically simplifies the process of writing event-driven code. And GHC's powerful optimizations mean that in many cases, we can write high-level code and still reap the benefits of high performance. Yet with all of this performance, our code base is still relatively tiny (under 1300 SLOC at time of writing). If you are looking to write maintainable, efficient, concurrent code, Haskell should be a strong consideration.

[chapter 12]

Working with Big Data in Bioinformatics
Eric McDonald and C. Titus Brown

12.1 Introduction

Bioinformatics and Big Data

The field of bioinformatics seeks to provide tools and analyses that facilitate understanding of the molecular mechanisms of life on Earth, largely by analyzing and correlating genomic and proteomic information. As increasingly large amounts of genomic information, including both genome sequences and expressed gene sequences, becomes available, more efficient, sensitive, and specific analyses become critical.

In DNA sequencing, a chemical and mechanical process essentially "digitizes" the information present in DNA and RNA. These sequences are recorded using an *alphabet* of one letter per nucleotide. Various analyses are performed on this sequence data to determine how it is structured into larger building blocks and how it relates to other sequence data. This serves as the basis for the study of biological evolution and development, genetics, and, increasingly, medicine.

Data on nucleotide chains comes from the sequencing process in strings of letters known as *reads*. (The use of the term *read* in the bioinformatics sense is an unfortunate collision with the use of the term in the computer science and software engineering sense. This is especially true as the performance of reading reads can be tuned, as we will discuss. To disambiguate this unfortunate collision we refer to sequences from genomes as *genomic reads*.) To analyze larger scale structures and processes, multiple genomic reads must be fit together. This fitting is different than a jigsaw puzzle in that the picture is often not known *a priori* and that the pieces may (and often do) overlap. A further complication is introduced in that not all genomic reads are of perfect fidelity and may contain a variety of errors, such as insertions or deletions of letters or substitutions of the wrong letters for nucleotides. While having redundant reads can help in the assembly or fitting of the puzzle pieces, it is also a hindrance because of this imperfect fidelity in all of the existing sequencing technologies. The appearance of erroneous genomic reads scales with the volume of data and this complicates assembly of the data.

As sequencing technology has improved, the volume of sequence data being produced has begun to exceed the capabilities of computer hardware employing conventional methods for analyzing such data. (Much of the state-of-the-art in sequencing technology produces vast quantities of genomic reads, typically tens of millions to billions, each having a sequence of 50 to 100 nucleotides.) This trend is expected to continue and is part of what is known as the *Big Data* [Varc] problem in the high performance computing (HPC), analytics, and information science communities. With hardware becoming a limiting factor, increasing attention has turned to ways to mitigate the problem with software solutions. In this chapter, we present one such software solution and how we tuned and scaled it to handle terabytes of data.

Our research focus has been on efficient *pre-processing*, in which various filters and binning approaches trim, discard, and bin the genomic reads, in order to improve downstream analyses. This approach has the benefit of limiting the changes that need to be made to downstream analyses, which generally consume genomic reads directly.

In this chapter, we present our software solution and describe how we tuned and scaled it to efficient handle increasingly large amounts of data.

What is the khmer Software?

Khmer is our suite of software tools for pre-processing large amounts of genomic sequence data prior to analysis with conventional bioinformatics tools[eab]—no relation to the ethnic group indigenous to Southeast Asia. This name comes by free association with the term *k-mer*: as part of the pre-processing, genetic sequences are decomposed into overlapping substrings of a given length, k. As chains of many molecules are often called *polymers*, chains of a specific number of molecules are called *k-mers*, each substring representing one such chain. Note that, for each genomic read, the number of k-mers will be the number of nucleotides in the sequence minus k plus one. So, nearly every genomic read will be decomposed into many overlapping k-mers.

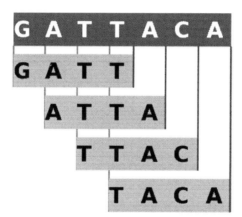

Figure 12.1: Decomposition of a genomic sequence into 4-mers. In khmer, the forward sequence and reverse complement of each k-mer are hashed to the same value, in recognition that DNA is double-stranded. See Future Directions.

Since we want to tell you about how we measured and tuned this piece of open source software, we'll skip over much of the theory behind it. Suffice it to say that k-mer counting is central to much of its operation. To compactly count a large number of k-mers, a data structure known as a *Bloom filter* [Vard] is used (Figure 12.2). Armed with k-mer counts, we can then exclude highly redundant data from further processing, a process known as "digital normalization". We can also treat low abundance sequence data as probable errors and exclude it from further processing, in an approach to error trimming. These normalization and trimming processes greatly reduce the amount of raw sequence data needed for further analysis, while mostly preserving information of interest.

Khmer is designed to operate on large data sets of millions to billions of genomic reads, containing tends of billions of unique k-mers. Some of our existing data sets require up to a terabyte of system

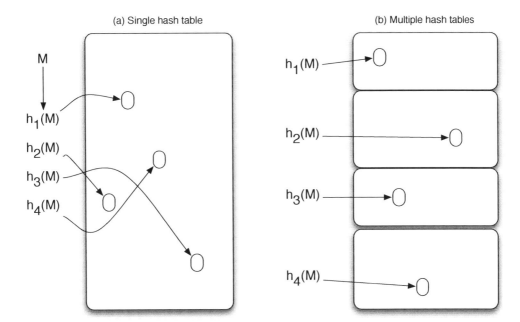

Figure 12.2: A Bloom filter is essentially a large, fixed-size hash table, into which elements are inserted or queried using multiple orthogonal hash functions, with no attempt at collision tracking; they are therefore *probabilistic* data structures. Our implementation uses multiple distinct hash tables each with its own hash function, but the properties are identical. We typically recommend that khmer's Bloom filters be configured to use as much main memory as is available, as this reduces collisions maximally.

memory simply to hold the k-mer counts in memory, but this is not due to inefficient programming: in [PHCK+12] we show that khmer is considerably more memory efficient than any exact set membership scheme for a wide regime of interesting k-mer problems. It is unlikely that significant improvements in memory usage can be obtained easily.

Our goal, then, is simple: in the face of these large data sets, we would like to optimize khmer for processing time, including most especially the time required to load data from disk and count k-mers.

For the curious, the khmer sources and documentation can be cloned from GitHub at http://github.com/ged-lab/khmer.git. Khmer has been available for about four years, but only with the posting of several preprint papers have others started to use it; we estimate the user population at around 100 groups based on e-mail interactions in 2012, although it seems to be growing rapidly as it becomes clear that a large class of assembly problems is more readily tractable with khmer [BHZ+12].

12.2 Architecture and Performance Considerations

Khmer started as an exploratory programming exercise and is evolving into more mature research code over time. From its inception, the focus has been on solving particular scientific problems with as much as accuracy or "correctness" as possible. Over time, as the software has come into greater use around the world, issues such as packaging, performance, and scalability have become more prominent. These issues were not necessarily neglected in earlier times, but they now have a higher profile than they once did. Our discussion will center around how we have analyzed and solved particular performance and scaling challenges. Beacuse khmer is research code still under development, it routinely receiving new features and has a growing collection of impermanent scripts built up around it. We must be careful to ensure that changes made to improve performance or scalability do not break existing interfaces or to cause the software not decrease in accuracy or correctness. For this reason, we have proceeded along a strategy that combines automated testing with careful, incremental optimization and parallelization. In conjunction with other activities pertaining to the software, we expect this process to be essentially perpetual.

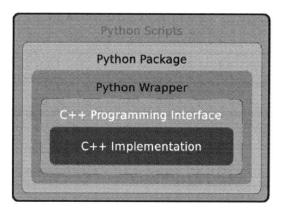

Figure 12.3: A layered view of the khmer software

The core of the software is written in C++. This core consists of a data pump (the component which moves data from online storage into physical RAM), parsers for genomic reads in several common formats, and several k-mer counters. An *application programming interface* (API) is built around the core. This API can, of course, be used from C++ programs, as we do with some of our test drivers, but also serves as the foundation for a Python wrapper. A Python package is built upon the Python wrapper. Numerous Python scripts are distributed along with the package. Thus, the khmer software, in its totality, is the combination of core components, written in C++ for speed, higher-level interfaces, exposed via Python for ease of manipulation, and an assortment of tool scripts, which provide convenient ways to perform various bioinformatics tasks.

The khmer software supports batch operation in multiple phases, each with separate data inputs and outputs. For example, it can take a set of genomic reads, count k-mers in these, and then, optionally, save the Bloom filter hash tables for later use. Later, it can use saved hash tables to perform k-mer abundance filtering on a new set of genomic reads, saving the filtered data. This flexibility to reuse earlier outputs and to decide what to keep allows a user to tailor a procedure specific to his/her needs and storage constraints.

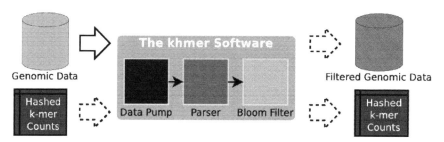

Figure 12.4: Data flow through the khmer software

Lots and lots of data (potentially terabytes) must be moved from disk to memory by the software. Having an efficient data pump is crucial, as the input throughput from storage to CPU may be three or even four orders of magnitude less than the throughput for data transfer from physical RAM to CPU. For some kinds of data files, a decompressor must be used. In either case, a parser must work efficiently with the resultant data. The parsing task revolves around variable-length lines, but also must account for invalid genomic reads and preserving certain pieces of biological information, which may be exploited during later assembly, such as pairings of the ends of sequence fragments. Each genomic read is broken up into a set of overlapping k-mers and each k-mer is registered with or compared against the Bloom filter. If a previously stored Bloom filter is being updated or used for comparison, then it must be loaded from storage. If a Bloom filter is being created for later use or updated, then it must be saved to storage.

The data pump always performs sequential access on files and can potentially be asked to read large chunks of data at one time. With this in mind, the following are some of the questions which come to mind:

- Are we fully exploiting the fact that the data is accessed sequentially?
- Are enough pages of data being prefetched into memory to minimize access latency?
- Can asynchronous input be used instead of synchronous input?
- Can we efficiently bypass system caches to reduce buffer-to-buffer copies in memory?
- Does the data pump expose data to the parser in a manner that does not create any unnecessary accessor or decision logic overhead?

Parser efficiency is essential, as data enters in a fairly liberal string format and must be converted into an internal representation before any further processing is done. Since each individual data record is relatively small (100–200 bytes), but there are millions to billions of records, we have focused quite a bit of effort on optimizing the record parser. The parser, at its core, is a loop which breaks up the data stream into genomic reads and stores them in records, performing some initial validation along the way.

Some considerations regarding parser efficiency are:

- Have we minimized the number of times that the parser is touching the data in memory?
- Have we minimized the number of buffer-to-buffer copies while parsing genomic reads from the data stream?
- Have we minimized function call overhead inside the parsing loop?
- The parser must deal with messy data, including ambiguous bases, too-short genomic reads, and character case. Is this DNA sequence validation being done as efficiently as possible?

For iterating over the k-mers in a genomic read and hashing them, we could ask:

- Can the k-mer iteration mechanism be optimized for both memory and speed?
- Can the Bloom filter hash functions be optimized in any way?
- Have we minimized the number of times that the hasher is touching the data in memory?
- Can we increment hash counts in batches to exploit a warm cache?

12.3 Profiling and Measurement

Simply reading the source code with an eye on performance revealed a number of areas for improvement. However, we wanted to systematically quantify the amount of time spent in various sections of the code. To do this, we used several profilers: the GNU Profiler (gprof) and the Tuning and Analysis Utilities (TAU). We also created instruments within the source code itself, allowing a fine granularity view of key performance metrics.

Code Review

Blindly applying tools to measure a system (software or otherwise) is rarely a good idea. Rather, it is generally a good idea to gain some understanding of the system before measuring it. To this end, we reviewed the code by eye first.

Manually tracing the execution paths of an unfamiliar code is a good idea. (One of the authors, Eric McDonald, was new to the khmer software at the time he joined the project and he did this.) While it is true that profilers (and other tools) can generate call graphs, those graphs are only abstract summaries. Actually walking the code paths and seeing the function calls is a much more immersive and enlightening experience. Debuggers can be used for such walks, but do not readily lend themselves to the exploration of code paths less travelled. Also, moving through an execution path step-by-step can be quite tedious. Breakpoints can be used for testing whether certain points in the code are hit during normal execution, but setting them requires some *a priori* knowledge of the code. As an alternative, the use of an editor with multiple panes works quite well. Four display panes can often simultaneously capture all of the information a person needs to know—and is mentally capable of handling—at any given point.

The code review showed a number of things, some, but not all, of which were later corroborated by profiling tools. Some of the things we noticed were:

- We expected the highest traffic to be in the k-mer counting logic.
- Redundant calls to the `toupper` function were present in the highest traffic regions of the code.
- Input of genomic reads was performed line-by-line and on demand and without any readahead tuning.
- A copy-by-value of the genomic read struct performed for every parsed and valid genomic read.

Although the preceding may seem like fairly strong self-criticism, we would like to stress that a greater emphasis had been placed on utility and correctness of khmer up to this point. Our goal was to optimize existing and mostly correct software, not to redevelop it from scratch.

Tools

Profiling tools primarily concern themselves with the amount of time spent in any particular section of code. To measure this quantity, they inject instrumentation into the code at compile time. This instrumentation does change the size of functions, which may affect inlining during optimization. The instrumentation also directly introduces some overhead on the total execution time; in particular, the profiling of high traffic areas of code may result in a fairly significant overhead. So, if you are also measuring the total elapsed time of execution for your code, you need to be mindful of how profiling itself affects this. To gauge this, a simple external data collection mechanism, such as /usr/bin/time, can be used to compare non-profiling and profiling execution times for an identical set of optimization flags and operating parameters.

We gauged the effect of profiling by measuring the difference between profiled and non-profiled code across a range of k sizes—smaller k values lead to more k-mers per genomic read, increasing profiler-specific effects. For $k = 20$, we found that non-profiled code ran about 19% faster than profiled code, and, for $k = 30$, that non-profiled code ran about 14% faster than profiled code.

Prior to any performance tuning, our profiling data showed that the k-mer counting logic was the highest traffic portion of the code, as we had predicted by eye. What was a little surprising was how significant of a fraction it was (around 83% of the total time), contrasted to I/O operations against storage (around 5% of the total time, for one particular medium and low bandwidth contention).

Given that our trial data sets were about 500 MB and 5 GB, we did not anticipate seeing much in the way of cache effects.[1] Indeed, when we controlled for cache effects, we found that they did not amount to more than a couple of seconds at most and were thus not much larger than the error bars on our total execution times. This left us with the realization that I/O was not our primary bottleneck at that juncture in the code optimization process.

Once we began parallelizing the khmer software, we wrote some driver programs, which used OpenMP[mem], to test our parallelization of various components. While gprof is good at profiling single-threaded execution, it lacks the ability to trace per-thread execution when multiple threads are in use and it does not understand parallelization machinery, such as OpenMP. For C/C++ codes, OpenMP parallelization is determined by compiler pragmas. GNU C/C++ compilers, in the version 4.x series, honor these pragmas if supplied with the -fopenmp switch. When OpenMP pragmas are being honored, the compilers inject thread-handling instrumentation at the locations of the pragmas and around the basic blocks or other groupings with which they are associated.

As gprof could not readily give us the per-thread reporting and the OpenMP support that we desired, we turned to another tool. This was the Tuning and Analysis Utilities (TAU) [eaa] from a collaboration led by the University of Oregon. There are a number of parallel profiling tools out there—many of them focus on programs using MPI (Message Passing Interface) libraries, which are popular for some kinds of scientific computing tasks. TAU supports MPI profiling as well, but as MPI is not really an option for the khmer software in its current manifestation, we ignored this aspect of TAU. Likewise, TAU is not the only tool available for per-thread profiling. The combination of per-thread profiling and the ability to integrate closely with OpenMP is one of the reasons that it was appealing to us. TAU is also entirely open source and not tied to any one vendor.

Whereas gprof relies solely upon instrumentation injected into source code at compile time (with some additional bits linked in), TAU provides this and other instrumentation options as well. These options are library interposition (primarily used for MPI profiling) and dynamic instrumentation of binaries. To support these other options, TAU provides an execution wrapper, called `tau_exec`. Compile-time instrumentation of source code is supported via a wrapper script, called `tau_cxx.sh`.

TAU needs additional configuration to support some profiling activities. To get tight OpenMP integration, for example, TAU needs to be configured and built with support for OPARI. Similarly, to use the performance counters exposed by newer Linux kernels, it needs to be configured and built with support for PAPI. Also, once TAU is built, you will likely want to integrate it into your build system for convenience. For example, we setup our build system to allow the `tau_cxx.sh` wrapper script to be used as the C++ compiler when TAU profiling is desired. If you attempt to build and use TAU, you will definitely want to read the documentation. While much more powerful than gprof, it is not nearly as facile or intuitive.

Manual Instrumentation

Examining the performance of a piece of software with independent, external profilers is a quick and convenient way to learn something about the execution times of various parts of software at a first glance. However, profilers are generally not so good at reporting how much time code spends in a particular spinlock within a particular function or what the input rate of your data is. To augment or complement external profiling capabilities, manual instrumentation may needed. Also, manual

---

[1] If the size of a data cache is larger than the data being used in I/O performance benchmarks, then retrieval directly from the cache rather than the original data source may skew the measurements from successive runs of the benchmarks. Having a data source larger than the data cache helps guarantee data cycling in the cache, thereby giving the appearance of a continuous stream of non-repeating data.

instrumentation can be less intrusive than automatic instrumentation, since you directly control what gets observed. To this end, we created an extensible framework to internally measure things such as throughputs, iteration counts, and timings around atomic or fine-grained operations within the software itself. As a means of keeping ourselves honest, we internally collected some numbers that could be compared with measurements from the external profilers.

For different parts of the code, we needed to have different sets of metrics. However, all of the different sets of metrics have certain things in common. One thing is that they are mostly timing data and that you generally want to accumulate timings over the duration of execution. Another thing is that a consistent reporting mechanism is desirable. Given these considerations, we provided an abstract base class, `IPerformanceMetrics`, for all of our different sets of metrics. The `IPerformanceMetrics` class provides some convenience methods: `start_timers`, `stop_timers`, and `timespec_diff_in_nsecs`. The methods for starting and stopping timers measure both elapsed real time and elapsed per-thread CPU time. The third method calculates the difference between two standard C library `timespec` objects in nanoseconds, which is of quite sufficient resolution for our purposes.

To ensure that the overhead of the manually-inserted internal instrumentation is not present in production code, we carefully wrapped it in conditional compilation directives so that a build can specify to exclude it.

12.4 Tuning

Making software work more efficiently is quite a gratifying experience, especially in the face of trillions of bytes passing through it. Our narrative will now turn to the various measures we took to improve efficiency. We divide these into two parts: optimization of the reading and parsing of input data and optimization of the manipulation and writing of the Bloom filter contents.

12.5 General Tuning

Before diving into some of the specifics of how we tuned the khmer software, we would like to briefly mention some options for general performance tuning. Production code is often built with a set of safe and simple optimizations enabled; these optimizations can be generally proven not to change the semantics of the code (i.e., introduce bugs) and only require a single compilation pass. Compilers do provide additional optimization options, however. These additional options can be broadly categorized as *aggressive optimizations*, which is a fairly standard term in compiler literature, and *profile-guided optimizations* (PGO)[Varf]. (The two categories are not mutually-exclusive, strictly speaking, but typically involve different approaches.)

Aggressive optimizations may be unsafe (i.e., introduce bugs) in some cases or actually decrease performance in other cases. Aggressive optimizations may be unsafe for a variety of reasons, including sloppiness in floating-point accuracy or assumptions about different operands being associated with different memory addresses. Aggressive optimizations may also be specific to a particular CPU family. Profile-guided optimizations rely on profiling information to make more educated guesses on how to optimize a program during compilation and linking. One frequently-seen profile-guided optimization is the optimization of locality—attempting to place highly-correlated functions as neighbors inside the text segment of the executable image so that they will be loaded into the same memory pages together at runtime.

At this stage in our project, we have avoided both categories of additional optimizations in favor of targeted algorithmic improvements—improvements that provide benefits across many different CPU architectures. Also, from the standpoint of build system complexity, aggressive optimizations can create portability issues and profile-guided optimizations add to the total number of moving parts which may fail. Given that we do not distribute pre-compiled executables for various architectures and that our target audience is usually not too savvy about the intricacies of software development or build systems, it is likely that we will continue avoiding these optimizations until we feel that the benefits outweigh the drawbacks. In light of these considerations, our main focus has been on improving the efficiency of our algorithms rather than other kinds of tuning.

Data Pump and Parser Operations

Our measurements showed that the time spent counting k-mers dominated the time performing input from storage. Given that interesting fact, it may seem like we should have devoted all of our efforts to improving the Bloom filter's performance. But, taking a look at the data pump and parser was worthwhile for several reasons. One reason was that we needed to alter the design of the existing data pump and parser to accommodate their use by multiple threads to achieve scalability. Another reason was that we were interested in reducing memory-to-memory copies, which could impact the efficiency of the Bloom filter at its interface with the parser. A third reason is that we wanted to position ourselves to provide an aggressive readahead or prefetch of data, in case we were able to improve the efficiency of the k-mer counting logic to the point that input time became competitive with counting time. Unrelated to performance tuning, there were also issues with maintainability and extensibility.

As it turns out, all of the above reasons converged on a new design. We will discuss the thread-safety aspects of this design in more detail later. For now, we will focus upon the reduction of memory-to-memory copies and the ability to perform fairly aggressive prefetching of data.

Typically, when a program retrieves data from a block storage device (e.g., a hard disk), a certain number of the blocks are cached by the operating system, in case the blocks are needed again. There is some time overhead associated with this caching activity; also, the amount of data to prefetch into the cache cannot be finely tuned. Furthermore, the cache cannot be accessed directly by a user process and so must be copied from the cache into the address space of the user process. This is a memory-to-memory copy.

Some operating systems, such as Linux, allow for their readahead windows to be tuned some. One can make calls to `posix_fadvise(2)` and `readahead(2)` for a particular file descriptor, for example. However, these allow rather limited control and do not bypass caching. We are interested in bypassing the cache maintained by the OS. This cache actually can be bypassed if a file is opened with the `O_DIRECT` flag and the file system supports it. Using direct input is not entirely straightforward, as the reads from storage must be multiples of the storage medium's block size and must be placed into an area of memory, which has a base address that is a multiple of the same block size. This requires a program to perform housekeeping which a file system would normally do. We implemented direct input, including the necessary housekeeping. There are, however, some cases where direct input will not work or is otherwise undesirable. For those cases, we still attempt to tune the readahead window. Our access of storage is sequential and we can tell the operating system to read further ahead than it normally would by using `posix_fadvise(2)` to provide a hint.

Minimizing buffer-to-buffer copies is a challenge shared between the data pump and the parser. In the ideal scenario, we would read once from storage into our own buffer and then scan our buffer once per genomic read to demarcate a sequence with an offset and length within the buffer. However, the logic for managing the buffer is complex enough and the logic for parsing (accounting for our particular nuances) is complex enough that maintaining an intermediary line buffer is quite useful for programmer comprehension. To reduce the impact of this intermediary buffer, we encourage the compiler to rather aggressively inline this portion of the code. We may ultimately eliminate the intermediary buffer if performance of this particular region of the code becomes a big enough issue, but that may come at the expense of an understandable software design.

Bloom Filter Operations

Recalling that we are working with sequences composed of an alphabet of four letters: A, C, G, and T, you might ask whether these are uppercase or lowercase letters. Since our software operates directly on user-provided data, we cannot rely on the data to be consistently upper- or lower-case, since both sequencing platforms and other software packages may alter the case. While this is easy to fix for individual genomic reads, we need to repeat this for each base in millions or billions of read!

Prior to performance tuning the code was insensitive to case right up to the points where it validated the DNA string and where it generated the hash codes. At these points, it would make redundant calls to the C library's toupper function to normalize the sequences to uppercase, using macros such as the following:

```
#define is_valid_dna(ch) \
    ((toupper(ch)) == 'A' || (toupper(ch)) == 'C' || \
     (toupper(ch)) == 'G' || (toupper(ch)) == 'T')
```

and:

```
#define twobit_repr(ch) \
    ((toupper(ch)) == 'A' ? 0LL : \
     (toupper(ch)) == 'T' ? 1LL : \
     (toupper(ch)) == 'C' ? 2LL : 3LL)
```

If you read the manual page for the toupper function or inspect the headers for the GNU C library, you might find that it is actually a locale-aware function and not simply a macro. So, this means that there is the overhead of calling a potentially non-trivial function involved—at least when the GNU C library is being used. But, we are working with an alphabet of four ASCII characters. A locale-aware function is overkill for our purposes. So, not only do we want to eliminate the redundancy but we want to use something more efficient.

We decided to normalize the sequences to uppercase letters prior to validating them. (And, of course, validation happens before attempting to convert them into hash codes.) While it might be ideal to perform this normalization in the parser, it turns out that sequences can be introduced to the Bloom filter via other routes. So, for the time being, we chose to normalize the sequences immediately prior to validating them. This allows us to drop all calls to toupper in both the sequence validator and in the hash encoders.

Considering that terabytes of genomic data may be passing through the sequence normalizer, it is in our interests to optimize it as much as we can. One approach is:

```
#define quick_toupper( c ) (0x60 < (c) ? (c) - 0x20 : (c))
```

For each and every byte, the above should execute one compare, one branch, and possibly one addition. Can we do better than this? As it turns out, yes. Note that every lowercase letter has an

ASCII code which is 32 (hexadecimal 20) greater than its uppercase counterpart and that 32 is a power of 2. This means that the ASCII uppercase and lowercase characters differ by a single bit only. This observation screams "bitmask!"

```
c &= 0xdf; // quicker toupper
```

The above has one bitwise operation, no compares, and no branches. Uppercase letters pass through unmolested; lowercase letters become uppercase. Perfect, just we wanted. For our trouble, we gained about a 13% speedup in the runtime of the entire process (!)

Our Bloom filter's hash tables are... "expansive". To increment the counts for the hash code of a particular k-mer means hitting almost N different memory pages, where N is the number of hash tables allocated to the filter. In many cases, the memory pages which need to be updated for the next k-mer are entirely different than those for the current one. This can lead the much cycling of memory pages from main memory without being able to utilize the benefits of caching. If we have a genomic read with a 79-character long sequence and are scanning k-mers of length 20, and if we have 4 hash tables, then up to 236 (59 * 4) different memory pages are potentially being touched. If we are processing 50 million reads, then it is easy to see how costly this is. What to do about it?

One solution is to batch the hash table updates. By accumulating a number of hash codes for various k-mers and then periodically using them to increment counts on a table-by-table basis, we can greatly improve cache utilization. Initial work on this front looks quite promising and, hopefully, by the time you are reading this, we will have fully integrated this modification into our code. Although we did not mention it earlier in our discussion of measurement and profiling, `cachegrind`, a program which is part of the open-source Valgrind [eac] distribution, is a very useful tool for gauging the effectiveness of this kind of work.

12.6 Parallelization

With the proliferation of multi-core architectures in today's world, it is tempting to try taking advantage of them. However, unlike many other problem domains, such as computational fluid dynamics or molecular dynamics, our Big Data problem relies on high throughput processing of data—it must become essentially I/O-bound beyond a certain point of parallelization. Beyond this point, throwing additional threads at it does not help as the bandwidth to the storage media is saturated and the threads simply end up with increased blocking or I/O wait times. That said, utilizing some threads can be useful, particularly if the data to be processed is held in physical RAM, which generally has a much higher bandwidth than online storage. As discussed previously, we have implemented a prefetch buffer in conjunction with direct input. Multiple threads can use this buffer; more will be said about this below. I/O bandwidth is not the only finite resource which multiple threads must share. The hash tables used for k-mer counting are another one. Shared access to these will also be discussed below.

Thread-Safety and Threading

Before proceeding into details, it may be useful to clear up a couple items about terminology. People often confuse the notion of something being thread-safe with that of something being threaded. If something is thread-safe, then it can be simultaneously accessed by multiple threads without fear of corrupted fetches or stores. If something is multi-threaded, then it is simultaneously operated by multiple threads of execution.

As part of our parallelization work, we remodeled portions of the C++ core implementation to be thread-safe without making any assumptions about a particular threading scheme or library. Therefore, the Python `threading` module can be used in the scripts which use the Python wrapper around the core implementation, or a C++ driver around the core could use a higher-level abstraction, like OpenMP as we mentioned earlier, or explicitly implement threading with pthreads, for example. Achieving this kind of independence from threading scheme and guaranteeing thread-safety, while not breaking existing interfaces to the C++ library, was an interesting software engineering challenge. We solved this by having portions of the API, which were exposed as thread-safe, maintain their own per-thread state objects. These state objects are looked up in a C++ Standard Template Library (STL) map, where thread identification numbers are the keys. The identification number for a particular thread is found by having that thread itself query the OS kernel via a system call. This solution does introduce a small amount of overhead from having a thread inquire about its identification number on every entry to a function exposed via the API, but it neatly avoids the problem of breaking existing interfaces, which were written with a single thread of execution in mind.

Data Pump and Parser Operations

The multi-core machines one encounters in the HPC world may have multiple memory controllers, where one controller is closer (in terms of signal travel distance) to one CPU than another CPU. These are *Non-Uniform Memory Access* (NUMA) architectures. A ramification of working with machines of this architecture is that memory fetch times may vary significantly depending on physical address. As bioinformatics software often requires a large memory footprint to run, it is often found running on these machines. Therefore, if one is using multiple threads, which may be pinned to various *NUMA nodes*, the locality of the physical RAM must be taken into consideration. To this end, we divide our prefetch buffer into a number of segments equal to the number of threads of execution. Each thread of execution is responsible for allocating its particular segment of the buffer. The buffer segment is administered via a state object, maintained on a per-thread basis.

Bloom Filter Operations

The Bloom filter hash tables consume the majority of main memory (see Figure 12.1) and therefore cannot usefully be split into separate copies among threads. Rather, a single set of tables must be shared by all of the threads. This implies that there will be contention among the threads for these resources. Memory barriers [Vare] or some form of locking are needed to prevent two or more threads from attempting to access the same memory location at the same time. We use atomic addition operations to increment the counters in the hash tables. These atomic operations [Varb] are supported on a number of platforms by several compiler suites, the GNU compilers among those, and are not beholden to any particular threading scheme or library. They establish memory barriers around the operands which they are to update, thus adding thread-safety to a particular operation.

A performance bottleneck, which we did not address, is the time to write the hash tables out to storage after k-mer counting is complete. We did not feel that this was such a high priority because the write-out time is constant for a given Bloom filter size and is not dependent upon the amount of input data. For a particular 5 GB data set, which we used for benchmarking, we saw that k-mer counting took over six times as long as hash table write-out. For even larger data sets, the ratio becomes more pronounced. That said, we are ultimately interested in improving performance here too. One possibility is to amortize the cost of the write-out over the duration of the k-mer counting phase of operation. The URL-shortener site, bit.ly, has a counting Bloom filter implementation, called `dablooms` [bsd], which achieves this by memory-mapping its output file to the hash table memory. Adopting their idea, in conjunction with batch updates of the hash tables, would effectively give us asynchronous output in bursts over a process' lifetime and chop off the entire write-out time from the end of execution. Our output is not simply tables of counts, however, but also includes a header with some metadata; implementing memory-mapping in light of this fact is an endeavor that needs to be approached thoughtfully and carefully.

Scaling

Was making the khmer software scalable worth our effort? Yes. Of course, we did not achieve perfectly linear speedup. But, for every doubling of the number of cores, we presently get about a factor of 1.9 speedup.

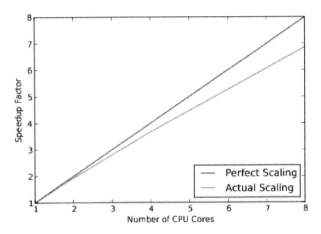

Figure 12.5: Speedup factor from 1 to 8 CPU cores

In parallel computing, one must be mindful of Amdahl's Law [Vara] and the Law of Diminishing Returns. The common formulation of Amdahl's Law, in the context of parallel computing, is $S(N) = \frac{1}{(1-P)+\frac{P}{N}}$, where S is the speedup achieved given N CPU cores and, P, the proportion of the code which is parallelized. For $\lim_{N \to \infty} S = \frac{1}{(1-P)}$, a constant. The I/O bandwidth of the storage system, which the software utilizes, is finite and non-scalable; this contributes to a non-zero $(1-P)$. Moreover, contention for shared resources in the parallelized portion means that $\frac{P}{N}$ is, in reality, $\frac{P}{Nl}$, where $l < 1$ versus the ideal case of $l = 1$. Therefore, returns will diminish over a finite number of cores even more rapidly.

Using faster storage systems, such as solid-state drives (SSDs) as opposed to hard-disk drives (HDDs), increases I/O bandwidth (and thus reduces $(1-P)$), but that is beyond the purview of software. While we cannot do much about hardware, we can still try to improve l. We think that we can further improve our access patterns around shared resources, such as the hash table memory, and that we can better streamline the use of per-thread state objects. Doing these two things will likely grant us an improvement to l.

12.7 Conclusion

The khmer software is a moving target. New features are being added to it regularly, and we are working on incorporating it into various software stacks in use by the bioinformatics community. Like many pieces of software in academia, it started life as an exploratory programming exercise and evolved into research code. Correctness was and is a primary goal of the project. While performance and scalability cannot truly be regarded as afterthoughts, they yield precedence to correctness and utility. That said, our efforts regarding scalability and performance have produced good results, including speedups in single-threaded execution and the ability to significantly reduce total execution time by employing multiple threads. Thinking about performance and scalability issues led to the redesign of the data pump and parser components. Going forward, these components should be able to benefit not only from scalability but improved maintainability and extensibility.

12.8 Future Directions

Looking forward, once we have addressed the basic performance issues, we are primarily interested in growing the programmer's API, providing well tested use cases and documentation, and providing well-characterized components for integration into larger pipelines. More broadly, we would like to take advantage of advances in the theory of low-memory data structures to simplify certain use cases, and we are also interested in investigating distributed algorithms for some of the more intractable data set challenges facing us in the near future.

Some additional concerns facing khmer development include an expansion of the hashing options to allow the use of different hash functions for single-stranded DNA and the addition of a rolling hash function to permit $k > 32$.

We look forward to continuing the development of this software and hope to have an impact on the Big Data problem facing molecular biologists and bioinformaticians. We hope that you enjoyed reading about some high performance, open source software being employed in the sciences.

12.9 Acknowledgements

We thank Alexis Black-Pyrkosz and Rosangela Canino-Koning for comments and discussion.

Bibliography

[ABB+86]   Mike Accetta, Robert Baron, William Bolosky, David Golub, Richard Rashid, Avadis Tavanian, and Michael Young. Mach: A New Kernel Foundation for UNIX Development. In *Proceedings of the Summer 1986 USENIX Technical Conference and Exhibition*, pages 93–112, June 1986.

[AOS+00]   Alexander B. Arulanthu, Carlos O'Ryan, Douglas C. Schmidt, Michael Kircher, and Jeff Parsons. The Design and Performance of a Scalable ORB Architecture for CORBA Asynchronous Messaging. In *Proceedings of the Middleware 2000 Conference*. ACM/IFIP, April 2000.

[ATK05]   Anatoly Akkerman, Alexander Totok, and Vijay Karamcheti. Infrastructure for Automatic Dynamic Deployment of J2EE Applications in Distributed Environments. In *3rd International Working Conference on Component Deployment (CD 2005)*, pages 17–32, Grenoble, France, November 2005.

[BHZ+12]   CT Brown, A Howe, Q Zhang, A Pyrkosz, and TH Brom. A reference-free algorithm for computational normalization of shotgun sequencing data. In review at PLoS One, July 2012; Preprint at http://arxiv.org/abs/1203.4802, 2012.

[bsd]   bit.ly software developers. dablooms: a scalable, counting Bloom filter. `http://github.com/bitly/dablooms`.

[BW11]   Amy Brown and Greg Wilson. *The Architecture Of Open Source Applications*. lulu.com, June 2011.

[CJRS89]   David D. Clark, Van Jacobson, John Romkey, and Howard Salwen. An Analysis of TCP Processing Overhead. *IEEE Communications Magazine*, 27(6):23–29, June 1989.

[CT90]   David D. Clark and David L. Tennenhouse. Architectural Considerations for a New Generation of Protocols. In *Proceedings of the Symposium on Communications Architectures and Protocols (SIGCOMM)*, pages 200–208. ACM, September 1990.

[DBCP97]   Mikael Degermark, Andrej Brodnik, Svante Carlsson, and Stephen Pink. Small Forwarding Tables for Fast Routing Lookups. In *Proceedings of the ACM SIGCOMM '97 Conference on Applications, Technologies, Architectures, and Protocols for Computer Communication*, pages 3–14. ACM Press, 1997.

[DBO+05]   Gan Deng, Jaiganesh Balasubramanian, William Otte, Douglas C. Schmidt, and Aniruddha Gokhale. DAnCE: A QoS-enabled Component Deployment and Configuration

	Engine. In *Proceedings of the 3rd Working Conference on Component Deployment (CD 2005)*, pages 67–82, November 2005.
[DEG+12]	Abhishek Dubey, William Emfinger, Aniruddha Gokhale, Gabor Karsai, William Otte, Jeffrey Parsons, Csanad Czabo, Alessandro Coglio, Eric Smith, and Prasanta Bose. A Software Platform for Fractionated Spacecraft. In *Proceedings of the IEEE Aerospace Conference, 2012*, pages 1–20. IEEE, March 2012.
[DP93]	Peter Druschel and Larry L. Peterson. Fbufs: A High-Bandwidth Cross-Domain Transfer Facility. In *Proceedings of the 14th Symposium on Operating System Principles (SOSP)*, December 1993.
[eaa]	A. D. Malony et al. TAU: Tuning and Analysis Utilities. http://www.cs.uoregon.edu/Research/tau/home.php.
[eab]	C. Titus Brown et al. khmer: genomic data filtering and partitioning software. http://github.com/ged-lab/khmer.
[eac]	Julian Seward et al. Valgrind. http://valgrind.org/.
[EK96]	Dawson R. Engler and M. Frans Kaashoek. DPF: Fast, Flexible Message Demultiplexing using Dynamic Code Generation. In *Proceedings of ACM SIGCOMM '96 Conference in Computer Communication Review*, pages 53–59. ACM Press, August 1996.
[FHHC07]	D. R. Fatland, M. J. Heavner, E. Hood, and C. Connor. The SEAMONSTER Sensor Web: Lessons and Opportunities after One Year. *AGU Fall Meeting Abstracts*, December 2007.
[GHJV95]	Erich Gamma, Richard Helm, Ralph Johnson, and John Vlissides. *Design Patterns: Elements of Reusable Object-Oriented Software*. Addison-Wesley, 1995.
[GNS+02]	Aniruddha Gokhale, Balachandran Natarajan, Douglas C. Schmidt, Andrey Nechypurenko, Jeff Gray, Nanbor Wang, Sandeep Neema, Ted Bapty, and Jeff Parsons. CoSMIC: An MDA Generative Tool for Distributed Real-time and Embedded Component Middleware and Applications. In *Proceedings of the OOPSLA 2002 Workshop on Generative Techniques in the Context of Model Driven Architecture*. ACM, November 2002.
[HC01]	George T. Heineman and Bill T. Councill. *Component-Based Software Engineering: Putting the Pieces Together*. Addison-Wesley, 2001.
[HP88]	Norman C. Hutchinson and Larry L. Peterson. Design of the *x*-Kernel. In *Proceedings of the SIGCOMM '88 Symposium*, pages 65–75, August 1988.
[HV05]	Jahangir Hasan and T. N. Vijaykumar. Dynamic pipelining: Making IP-lookup Truly Scalable. In *SIGCOMM '05: Proceedings of the 2005 Conference on Applications, technologies, architectures, and protocols for computer communications*, pages 205–216. ACM Press, 2005.
[Insty]	Institute for Software Integrated Systems. Component-Integrated ACE ORB (CIAO). www.dre.vanderbilt.edu/CIAO, Vanderbilt University.

[KOS+08] John S. Kinnebrew, William R. Otte, Nishanth Shankaran, Gautam Biswas, and Douglas C. Schmidt. Intelligent Resource Management and Dynamic Adaptation in a Distributed Real-time and Embedded Sensor Web System. Technical Report ISIS-08-906, Vanderbilt University, 2008.

[mem] OpenMP members. OpenMP. http://openmp.org.

[MJ93] Steven McCanne and Van Jacobson. The BSD Packet Filter: A New Architecture for User-level Packet Capture. In *Proceedings of the Winter USENIX Conference*, pages 259–270, January 1993.

[MRA87] Jeffrey C. Mogul, Richard F. Rashid, and Michal J. Accetta. The Packet Filter: an Efficient Mechanism for User-level Network Code. In *Proceedings of the 11th Symposium on Operating System Principles (SOSP)*, November 1987.

[NO88] M. Nelson and J. Ousterhout. Copy-on-Write For Sprite. In *USENIX Summer Conference*, pages 187–201. USENIX Association, June 1988.

[Obj06] ObjectWeb Consortium. CARDAMOM - An Enterprise Middleware for Building Mission and Safety Critical Applications. cardamom.objectweb.org, 2006.

[OGS11] William R. Otte, Aniruddha Gokhale, and Douglas C. Schmidt. Predictable Deployment in Component-based Enterprise Distributed Real-time and Embedded Systems. In *Proceedings of the 14th international ACM Sigsoft Symposium on Component Based Software Engineering*, CBSE '11, pages 21–30. ACM, 2011.

[OGST13] William Otte, Aniruddha Gokhale, Douglas Schmidt, and Alan Tackett. Efficient and Deterministic Application Deployment in Component-based, Enterprise Distributed, Real-time, and Embedded Systems. *Elsevier Journal of Information and Software Technology (IST)*, 55(2):475–488, February 2013.

[OMG04] Object Management Group. *Lightweight CCM FTF Convenience Document*, ptc/04-06-10 edition, June 2004.

[OMG06] OMG. *Deployment and Configuration of Component-based Distributed Applications, v4.0*, Document formal/2006-04-02 edition, April 2006.

[OMG08] Object Management Group. *The Common Object Request Broker: Architecture and Specification Version 3.1, Part 2: CORBA Interoperability*, OMG Document formal/2008-01-07 edition, January 2008.

[PDZ00] Vivek S. Pai, Peter Druschel, and Willy Zwaenepoel. IO-Lite: A Unified I/O Buffering and Caching System. *ACM Transactions of Computer Systems*, 18(1):37–66, 2000.

[PHCK+12] J Pell, A Hintze, R Canino-Koning, A Howe, JM Tiedje, and CT Brown. Scaling metagenome sequence assembly with probabilistic de bruijn graphs. Accepted at PNAS, July 2012; Preprint at http://arxiv.org/abs/1112.4193, 2012.

[RDR+97] Y. Rekhter, B. Davie, E. Rosen, G. Swallow, D. Farinacci, and D. Katz. Tag Switching Architecture Overview. *Proceedings of the IEEE*, 85(12):1973–1983, December 1997.

[SHS+06]   Dipa Suri, Adam Howell, Nishanth Shankaran, John Kinnebrew, Will Otte, Douglas C. Schmidt, and Gautam Biswas. Onboard Processing using the Adaptive Network Architecture. In *Proceedings of the Sixth Annual NASA Earth Science Technology Conference*, June 2006.

[SK03]   Sartaj Sahni and Kun Suk Kim. Efficient Construction of Multibit Tries for IP Lookup. *IEEE/ACM Trans. Netw.*, 11(4):650–662, 2003.

[SNG+02]   Douglas C. Schmidt, Bala Natarajan, Aniruddha Gokhale, Nanbor Wang, and Christopher Gill. TAO: A Pattern-Oriented Object Request Broker for Distributed Real-time and Embedded Systems. *IEEE Distributed Systems Online*, 3(2), February 2002.

[SSRB00]   Douglas C. Schmidt, Michael Stal, Hans Rohnert, and Frank Buschmann. *Pattern-Oriented Software Architecture: Patterns for Concurrent and Networked Objects, Volume 2*. Wiley & Sons, New York, 2000.

[SV95]   M. Shreedhar and George Varghese. Efficient Fair Queueing using Deficit Round Robin. In *SIGCOMM '95: Proceedings of the conference on Applications, technologies, architectures, and protocols for computer communication*, pages 231–242. ACM Press, 1995.

[Vara]   Various. Amdahl's Law. http://en.wikipedia.org/w/index.php?title=Amdahl%27s_law&oldid=515929929.

[Varb]   Various. atomic operations. http://en.wikipedia.org/w/index.php?title=Linearizability&oldid=511650567.

[Varc]   Various. big data. http://en.wikipedia.org/w/index.php?title=Big_data&oldid=521018481.

[Vard]   Various. Bloom filter. http://en.wikipedia.org/w/index.php?title=Bloom_filter&oldid=520253067.

[Vare]   Various. memory barrier. http://en.wikipedia.org/w/index.php?title=Memory_barrier&oldid=517642176.

[Varf]   Various. profile-guided optimization. http://en.wikipedia.org/w/index.php?title=Profile-guided_optimization&oldid=509056192.

[Var05]   George Varghese. *Network Algorithmics: An Interdisciplinary Approach to Designing Fast Networked Devices*. Morgan Kaufmann Publishers (Elsevier), San Francisco, CA, 2005.

[VL97]   George Varghese and Tony Lauck. Hashed and Hierarchical Timing Wheels: Data Structures for the Efficient Implementation of a Timer Facility. *IEEE Transactions on Networking*, December 1997.

[WDS+11]   Jules White, Brian Dougherty, Richard Schantz, Douglas C. Schmidt, Adam Porter, and Angelo Corsaro. R&D Challenges and Solutions for Highly Complex Distributed Systems: a Middleware Perspective. *the Springer Journal of Internet Services and Applications special issue on the Future of Middleware*, 2(3), December 2011.

[WKNS05] Jules White, Boris Kolpackov, Balachandran Natarajan, and Douglas C. Schmidt. Reducing Application Code Complexity with Vocabulary-specific XML language Bindings. In *ACM-SE 43: Proceedings of the 43rd annual Southeast regional conference*, 2005.

Colophon

The cover font is Museo from the exljibris foundry, by Jos Buivenga. The text font is TeXGyre Termes and the heading font is TeXGyre Heros, both by Bogusław Jackowski and Janusz M. Nowacki. The code font is Inconsolata by Raph Levien.

The front cover photo is of the former workings of the turret clock of St. Stephen's Cathedral in Vienna. The workings can now be seen in the Vienna Clock Museum. The picture was taken by Michelle Enemark. (`http://www.mjenemark.com/`)

This book was built with open source software (with the exception of the cover). Programs like LaTeX, Pandoc, Python, and Calibre (`ebook-convert`) were especially helpful.

Made in the USA
Middletown, DE
17 December 2014